Learning
Together and Alone

Learning Together and Alone

Cooperative, Competitive, and Individualistic Learning

third edition

David W. Johnson / **Roger T. Johnson**
University of Minnesota

PRENTICE HALL, Englewood Cliffs, New Jersey 07632

Library of Congress Cataloging-in-Publication Data

Johnson, David W.
    Learning together and alone : cooperative, competitive, and
individualistic learning / David W. Johnson, Roger T. Johnson. —
3rd ed.
      p. cm.
    Includes bibliographical references (p.) and index.
    ISBN 0-13-528654-9
    1. Group work in eduction. 2. Individualized instruction.
3. Interaction analysis in education. 4. Lesson planning.
I. Johnson, Roger T. II. Title.
LB1032.J595 1991
371.1′02—dc20
                                         90-45532
                                         CIP

Editorial/production supervision: E. A. Pauw
Cover design: Mike Fender
Manufacturing buyer: Debbie Kesar
Prepress buyer: Mary Anne Gloriande

 © 1991, 1987, 1975 by Prentice-Hall, Inc.
A Division of Simon & Schuster
Englewood Cliffs, New Jersey 07632

Printed in the United States of America
10 9 8 7 6 5 4 3 2 1

ISBN   0-13-528654-9 NB2I

Prentice-Hall International (UK) Limited, *London*
Prentice-Hall of Australia Pty. Limited, *Sydney*
Prentice-Hall Canada Inc., *Toronto*
Prentice-Hall Hispanoamericana, S.A., *Mexico*
Prentice-Hall of India Private Limited, *New Delhi*
Prentice-Hall of Japan, Inc., *Tokyo*
Simon & Schuster Asia Pte. Ltd., *Singapore*
Editora Prentice-Hall do Brasil, Ltda., *Rio de Janeiro*

Contents

Preface

As you may have surmised, we are brothers, and as such we are very familiar with competition. For some years as we were growing up, we raced to see who would get through a door first, measured to see who got more cake (or more of anything), and argued to see who would sit by the window in the car. One incident we both remember vividly is the corncob fight. For a few years while we were growing up in Indiana, we lived (and worked!) on our grandfather's farm. We regularly practiced our accuracy with corncobs, and more than occasionally we practiced on each other. In one of these desperate battles, we had each gathered a large feed sack full of corncobs and were flinging and dodging through the barn. When the older one of us gained the upper hand, as he usually did, the younger brother scampered up the ladder into the hayloft, taking a well-placed cob in the seat of his pants. The hayloft advantage provided a problem for the older brother as he was nipped a couple of times without even coming close to his opponent. So taking a corncob between his teeth, he started up the ladder (the only way to the loft). As he got about halfway up, he realized he was getting pelted with more cobs than can be thrown at one time and looked up to see the younger brother standing at the top of the ladder shaking out his bag of corncobs and enjoying himself immensely. The tables turned, however, when the older brother reached the top of the ladder and the younger brother discovered he was out of corncobs. Then it was the younger brother's turn to be pelted as he crouched in the hay while the older brother let him have it—one by one. We still argue about who got the most out of the battle, the brother shooting the waterfall of corncobs down the ladder or the brother delivering the one-by-one pelting in the hayloft.

We are sure that people who knew us then are genuinely surprised to see us cooperating on this book and in the related workshops for teachers that we conduct. It should not be a surprise. The ideas presented here on how to recognize inappropriate competition and facilitate productive cooperation are important enough even for two brothers to cooperate in presenting them. We are also accidentally, but admirably, suited to work together on this topic. David struggled through graduate school at Columbia University, gaining the skills of an academic social psychologist, and Roger, after teaching several years at the elementary school level, took the easy route through the University of California at Berkeley as a part-time staff member in teacher education. With the years of classroom teaching experience and the research and writing in social psychology represented by our combined backgrounds and brought together at the University of Minnesota, we readily recognized the potential of this conceptual scheme—structuring learning in ways consistent with instructional aims.

We aren't against competition (although the literature and research on competition are damaging to its reputation). We are against *inappropriate* competition; and most of the competition in classrooms is inappropriate. We are for cooperation, not only because its sharing, helping, communicating, and mutual-concern aspects are consonant with our values but also because the research supports its use in a large number of situations. All the research we have reviewed, the research we have conducted, and our own instincts indicate that cooperation is the appropriate goal structure for most instructional situations. It also seems to be the least talked about, if not the least used, goal structure in schools. Individualization is in some places touted as a replacement for competition as the appropriate way to learn in schools. The idea of students working on individually assigned tasks at their own pace, toward a set goal, instead of competing against each other, is attractive to teachers, but the overuse of the individualistic goal structure is hard on teachers, requires a mountain of materials, and is described by many students as the "lonely" curriculum. The basic social competencies needed to interact effectively with other persons, furthermore, are completely ignored under an individualistic goal structure. We believe that all three goal structures should be used and that students need to learn how to function in all three. Students should master the skills to compete with enjoyment, to work individually on a task until it's completed, and to cooperate effectively with others to solve problems. Perhaps just as important, students should know *when* to compete, *when* to work on their own, and *when* to cooperate. The greatest need in classrooms is the carefully planned cooperative goal structure, which becomes the framework within which competition and individualization take place. We cover a lot of pages on cooperation.

In our work with teachers in goal structuring workshops and in our own classes at the University of Minnesota, we have found a few obstacles that hinder implementation. First, teachers often do not realize the enormous potential that facilitating appropriate goal structures has for their classroom. The research is clear (see Chapter 2). Achievement will go up, attitudes will become more positive, and missing skills will be mastered when goal structures are used appropriately. After all, goal structures concentrate on what is the most powerful variable in the learning situation: the interaction patterns and interdependencies of the students as they work toward a goal. The second obstacle to recognizing the importance of using cooperative as well as competitive and individualized activities is the powerful mythology that surrounds competition. How many times have you heard a version of social Darwinism that suggests "it's a dog-eat-dog world" or "a survival of the fittest society" or that "students need to learn how to compete so they can survive in the business world." Even the business world does not believe that the world is savagely competitive. As a social psychologist with management training, David could spend much of his time teaching people in business and industry how to reduce inappropriate competition and increase cooperation in their companies. Society cannot be described as competitive; it is by definition cooperative, a point that will be examined in detail in Chapter 3. Within the cooperative framework of society, however, there is competition, sometimes too much.

Another obstacle we have observed is the "I'm already doing that" feeling that many teachers have when we describe cooperation. If you really are doing it as well as it can be done, much of this book will not be useful. Yet frequently we find that teachers who say (or think) they are using goal structures appropriately are surprised by certain aspects of each when these goal structures are carefully described from a social psychological point of view and when the steps for implementing and monitoring them are explained (see Chapters 3, 4, and 5). Finally, the educational history of many students and teachers is such that they find cooperating within the school rather strange and difficult. Our own students seem relieved when they find that they are not going to have to compete against each other, and a sigh of relief seems to go through the classroom when the cooperative approach is announced. Students, however, are usually somewhat reluctant at first to cooperate with each other and tend to work individualistically when they should be cooperating. It takes some relationship building and trust development before they are able to share ideas and help each other effectively to produce a true group effort. Your students may have some of the same attitudes (so may the teachers in your school), and, if they do, you may need to teach and encourage the skills needed to work together (see Chapter 7).

We wish we could be with you as you implement appropriate goal structures in your instructional program. We would like to help. For most of you, this book and the ideas shared here are the best we can do. We assume your classes will blossom as our own have and as those of teachers near us have. One thing is for sure: for those of you who want to match the appropriate student interaction patterns with instructional goals and want to move to a predominantly cooperative classroom, the rationale for doing so is here, and you will be able to discuss goal structuring fluently with anyone. We hope that enough of the strategies are here also, but implementing ideas is your profession and if something is left out, we trust you to find and include it. Above all, enjoy the process. Practice your own skills as you encourage them in your students. You may even try a little cooperating with fellow teachers! In fact, we suggest that the best way to work with the ideas in this book is to approach the task cooperatively with a friend and fellow teacher to share thoughts and successes with. Enjoy yourself, persevere, and accept any resulting success with some modesty.

Thanks are due to many people for their help in writing this book and preparing the manuscript. Credit must be given to Edythe Johnson Holubec, our sister, who's always there to lend a hand cheerfully when it's needed; and Judy

Bartlett, our secretary, who is so often called on to assemble the whole from bits and pieces. We also owe much to many social psychologists who have conducted research and formulated theory in this area. We owe much to the teachers who have listened to our "bridge building" and given us help in "reconstructing" when we needed it. We owe much to our students, who have been patient with our enthusiasm and helpful in challenging and implementing our ideas. Finally, we owe much to our wives and children for making our lives truly cooperative.

Roger T. Johnson
David W. Johnson

*Learning
Together and Alone*

1

Cooperative, Competitive, and Individualistic Instruction

THE FISH'S PERSPECTIVE ON WATER

The scenes are familiar:

1. Three students sit around a table. "What are the mechanical, mathematical, and scientific analogies John Donne used in the poem 'A Valediction Forbidding Mourning'?" they are asked. They begin to discuss alternative answers. After prolonged consideration, one set of answers is tentatively adopted.
2. The official shouts, "Ready, set, go!" and the runners explode out of the blocks, race down the track, and lean forward into the tape in an attempt to win over their opponents.
3. A student sits alone at the computer. For the eighteenth time he begins a math drill-review program. "I am going to do this program over and over again until I get it 100 percent right!" he says to himself.

When individuals take action there are three ways what they do may be related to the actions of others. One's actions may promote the success of others, obstruct the success of others, or not have any effect at all on the success or failure of others. Whenever people strive to achieve a goal, they may engage in cooperative, competitive, or individualistic efforts. Such social interdependence exists continually. It is one of the most fundamental and ubiquitous aspects of being human, and it affects all aspects of our lives including our productivity, the quality of relationships, and our psychological health. Because we are immersed in it, social interdependence can escape our notice. Whether it is quite personal or so impersonal that we are barely aware of it, we regularly underestimate the role that social interdependence plays in human life. Since we can barely imagine its absence, we do not often consider its presence. Nothing is more basic to humans than being "for" or "against" other people.

In every classroom, no matter what the subject area or age of students, teachers may structure lessons so that students

1. Work collaboratively in small groups ensuring that all members master the assigned material.
2. Engage in a win-lose struggle to see who is best.
3. Work independently on their own learning goals at their own pace and in their own space to achieve a preset criterion of excellence.

Knowing how and when to structure students' learning goals cooperatively, competitively, or individualistically is an essential instructional skill all teachers need. Each way of structuring interdependence among students' learning goals has its place. An effective teacher will use all three appropriately. It may not be easy to do so because teacher training has by and large neglected preparation in the appropriate utilization of student-student interaction.

In this chapter the basic nature of cooperative, competitive, and individualistic goal structures is defined. The importance of using each goal structure appropriately is emphasized. The basic elements of cooperation and how it differs from traditional classroom grouping are discussed. Finally, the issue of how to use all three goal structures in an integrated way is presented.

SOCIAL INTERDEPENDENCE AND INSTRUCTION

Beliefs about the impact of teacher-student and student-materials interaction are as prevalent in our education system as concerns about reading, writing, and arithmetic. Some of the truisms heard are these:

If the teacher loves the student, the student will learn.

If the teacher does not smile at students until Christmas, students will toe the line all year long.

If the materials are well organized, student achievement will increase.

If you want to raise students' performance on standardized math tests, use _____ math series.

Sound familiar? These beliefs reflect the concern about teacher-student and student-materials interaction in instructional situations and they have received extensive attention in teacher preservice and in-service training. Teacher-student and student-materials interaction, however, are not the only forms of interaction within instructional situations. The interaction that most influences students' performance in instructional situations is student-student interaction.

How students interact with each other depends primarily on the type of interdependence the teacher structures among students' learning goals. In every classroom, instructional activities are aimed at accomplishing goals and are conducted under a goal structure. A *learning goal* is a desired future state of demonstrating competence or mastery in the subject area being studied, such as conceptual understanding of math processes, facility in the proper use of a language, or mastering the procedures of inquiry. A *goal structure* specifies the type of social interdependence among students as they strive to accomplish their learning goals. It specifies the ways in which students will interact with each other and the teacher during the instructional session.

Our horse, Maud, could give a fantastic ride! She did not like leaving the barn, and we would have to fight her all the time to get her any distance away from it. In her attempts to return to the barn, Maud would try to scrape us off on fences as we rode away from the barn. Once we did turn back toward the barn, however, we got the ride of our lives (the younger author never seemed to remember to duck as Maud flew through the barn door)! The point is that Maud was not committed to leaving the barn, but she had a strong commitment to return to it. All teachers have seen the difference between students who are committed to learning goals and those who are not. If students are not committed to instructional goals, they are like Maud going away from the barn. If students are committed to instructional goals, they are like Maud returning to the barn. Take the advice of the younger author and duck the barn door when you successfully "turn on" your students.

Social interdependence exists when each individual's outcomes are affected by the actions of others. Within any social situation, individuals may join together to achieve mutual goals, compete to see who is best, or act individualistically on their own. There are two types of social interdependence: competitive and cooperative. Interdependence may be differentiated from dependence and independence. *Social dependence* exists when the outcomes of Person A are affected by Person B's actions, but the reverse is not true. Peer tutoring, when the tutee's outcomes are affected by the tutor's actions but not vice versa, is an example. *Social independence* exists when individuals' outcomes are unaffected by each other's actions. The absence of social interdependence and dependence results in individualistic efforts. The nature and importance of each type of social interdependence is described below.

The way in which teachers structure interdependence among students' learning goals determines how students interact with each other, which, in turn, largely determines the cognitive and affective outcomes of instruction. An essential instructional skill that all teachers need is knowing how and when to structure students' learning goals cooperatively, competitively, and individualistically.

Each time teachers prepare for a lesson, they must make decisions about the teaching strategies they will use. Teachers may structure academic lessons so that sudents are (a) in a win-lose struggle to see who is best, (b) learning individually on their own without interacting with classmates, or (c) learning in pairs or small groups helping each other master the assigned material. Each goal structure has its place. In the ideal classroom all three goal structures would be appropriately used. All students would learn how to work collaboratively with others, compete for fun and enjoyment, and work autonomously on their own. Students would work on instructional tasks within the goal structure that is most productive for the type of task and instructional objectives. It is the teacher who decides which goal structure to implement within each instructional activity. No aspect of teaching is more important than the appropriate use of goal structures to determine social interdependence among students.

When students commit themselves psychologically to achievement in school, important factors are how likely they are to be successful in achieving academic goals and how challenging academic goals are to them. When teachers "grade on a curve" and receiving an A is defined as being successful—i.e., the goal—the vast majority of students will not expect to achieve the goal, whereas the high-ability students may see the goal as being too easy to be challenging. Thus a teacher may lose most students because of a low likelihood of success and the superior students, whose resources make achievement too easy, all in one swoop!

Commitment to academic goals also requires that students perceive the goals as being desirable and that they feel some satisfaction when the goals are achieved. There is consistent evidence that when classrooms are structured competitively or individualistically, success at academic tasks has little value for many students (Coleman, 1959; Bronfrenbrenner, 1970; Spilerman, 1971; DeVries, Muse, and Wells, 1971). Receiving recognition from one's peers is a source of satisfaction, yet there is recent evidence (as well as ancient folklore) that success on academic tasks in a competitively structured classroom has a negative effect on a student's sociometric status in the classroom (Slavin, 1974). Doing well frequently on quizzes resulted in losing friends!

The teacher's primary hope of inducing student commitment to academic goals is in structuring cooperative learning situations in the classroom. If you do not believe it now, keep reading, and by the time you finish this book you will!

Pervasiveness and Ubiquity of Cooperation

Pull together. In the mountains you must depend on each other for survival.

Willi Unsoeld

Within Yosemite National Park lies the famous Half Dome Mountain. The Half Dome is famous for its 2,000 feet of soaring, sheer cliff wall. Unusually beautiful

to the observer, and considered unclimbable for years, the Half Dome's northwest face was first scaled in 1957 by Royal Robbins and two companions. This incredibly dangerous climb took five days, with Robbins and his companions spending four nights on the cliff, sleeping in ropes with nothing below their bodies but air. Even today, the northwest face is a death trap to all but the finest and most skilled rock climbers. And far above the ground, moving slowly up the rock face, are two climbers.

The two climbers are motivated by a shared vision of successfully climbing the northwest face. As they move up the cliff, they are attached to each other by a rope ("the lifeline"). As one member climbs (the lead climber), the other (the belayer) ensures that the two have a safe anchor and that he or she can catch the climber if the climber falls. The lead climber does not begin climbing until the belayer says "go." Then the lead climber advances, puts in a piton, slips in the rope, and continues to advance. The pitons help the belayer catch the climber if the climber falls, and they mark the path up the cliff. The lifeline (i.e., rope) goes from the belayer through the pitons up to the climber. When the lead climber has completed the first leg of the climb, he or she becomes the belayer and the other member of the team begins to climb. The pitons placed by the lead climber serve to support the second member of the team and guide him or her up the rock face. The second member advances up the route marked out by the first member until the first leg is completed and then leapfrogs and becomes the lead climber for the second leg of the climb. The roles of lead climber and belayer are alternated until the summit is reached.

All human life is like mountain climbing. The human species seems to have a *cooperation imperative:* We desire and seek out opportunities to operate jointly with others to achieve mutual goals. We are attached to others through a variety of "lifelines," and we alternate supporting and leading others to ensure a better life for ourselves, our colleagues and neighbors, our children, and all generations to follow. Cooperation is an inescapable fact of life. From cradle to grave we cooperate with others. Each day, from our first waking moment until sleep overtakes us again, we cooperate within family, work, leisure, and community by working jointly to achieve mutual goals. Throughout history, people have come together to (1) accomplish feats that any one of them could not achieve alone and (2) share their joys and sorrows. From conceiving a child to sending a rocket to the moon, our successes require cooperation among individuals. The cooperation may be less clear than it is in climbing up a cliff, but it exists nonetheless. *Cooperation* is working together to accomplish shared goals. It is the use of small groups so that individuals work together to maximize their own and each other's productivity and achievement. Thus an individual seeks an outcome that is beneficial to him- or herself *and* beneficial to all other group members. In cooperative situations, individuals perceive that they can reach their goals only if the other group members also do so (Deutsch, 1962). Their goal attainments are positively correlated; consequently, individuals discuss their work, help and assist each other, and encourage each other to work hard.

Teachers can structure lessons cooperatively so that students work together to accomplish shared goals. Students are assigned to small groups and instructed to learn the assigned material and to make sure that the other members of the group also master the assignment. Individual performance is checked regularly to ensure all students are learning. A criteria-referenced evaluation system is used. Students discuss material with each other, help one another understand it, and encourage each other to work hard. In a cooperatively structured class, heterogeneous small groups made up of one high-, one medium-, and one low-ability student would be formed. The students are given three tasks: to learn the assigned material, to make sure that the other members of their group have learned the assigned material, and to make sure that everyone in the class has learned the assigned material. While the students work on assignments, they discuss the material with the other members of their group, explaining how to complete the work, listening to each other's explanations, encouraging each other to try to understand the solutions, and providing academic help and assistance.

When everyone in the group has mastered the material, they go look for another group to help until everyone in the class understands how to complete the assignments.

Cooperation pervades human nature and human life. Cooperation is built into our biology. Each person's body is made up of several systems (such as the muscular, digestive, and nervous systems) all cooperating together to keep the person alive and healthy. Members of our species, furthermore, are divided into males and females, both of which are necessary to conceive a child. Biologically, we are cooperative beings.

Cooperation is the heart of family life. Frank and Jane Johnson, for example, are husband and wife, parents, and lovers. Each day they leave for work to provide their family with shelter, food, clothing, and other necessities for survival (as well as a number of luxuries). In the late afternoon they come home to play with their children, prepare dinner, help their children with their homework, read them a bedtime story, put the children to bed, chat with each other, make a number of decisions about who will do what tomorrow, make love, and then go to sleep. Family members work together to achieve mutual goals.

Cooperation is the heart of all economic systems. Helen Misener, for example, is a manager for the Lion Corporation. Today she meets with a group of managers to plan how to market a new product, meets with a subordinate who is dissatisfied with his job and not performing well, and ensures that a rush order from a valued customer is sent on time. All members of the same company work together to achieve mutual goals. Different companies work together to move products from conception to manufacture to market to achieve mutual goals. Although it is not a personal relationship, cooperation exists among those who make cars and those who buy and use them, among those who farm and those who manufacture, and among all participants within an economic system.

Cooperation is the heart of all legal systems. Laws specify how we are to cooperate with each other as we travel to and from work (e.g., drive on the right side of the street, stop at red lights, drive under certain specified speeds), how to transfer property and goods (e.g., deeds and contracts), how to determine responsibility for one's actions, and so forth. Keith Clement, for example, is a lawyer who today meets with a client to plan how best to present his case, meets with the judge and prosecutor and attempts to plea bargain for a lesser charge in exchange for a guilty plea, and then meets again with his client to discuss what the client's options are. Cooperation exists between those who make, enforce, and follow laws. Legal systems exist to define cooperative interactions among members of a society, ensure that cooperation runs smoothly, punish those who violate the norms for appropriate cooperative behavior, and reestablish cooperation among societal members who have conflicts.

Cooperation is the key to our evolution as a species. Humans by their nature cooperate with each other. Just as the cheetah survives by speed and hawks survive by their eyesight, humans survive by their ability to "work together to get the job done." Among the hominids, the almost modern *Homo sapiens* appeared at least 300,000 years ago, and the anatomically modern *Homo sapiens sapiens,* 40,000 years ago (Rensberger, 1984). As anatomically modern people appeared in Europe, suddenly so did sculpture, musical instruments, lamps, trade, and innovation. Insofar as there was any single moment when we could be said to have become human, it was at the time of this Great Leap Forward in complexity of cooperation (Diamond, 1989). Only a few dozen millennia—a trivial fraction of our 6- to 10-million-year history—were needed for us to domesticate animals, develop agriculture and metallurgy, and invent writing. It was then only a short further step to the *Mona Lisa,* Beethoven's Ninth Symphony, the industrial revolution, and the computer.

Cooperation is the heart of the worldwide community of humans. From small tribes, to small communities, to small states and countries, to large countries, to a worldwide community, there has been an unmistakable increase in the size of the "we-group" (Bigelow, 1972). We now live in a world increasingly characterized by interdependence, pluralism, conflict, and rapid change. Instead of being a member of a discrete society, we live in a multiboundary world characterized by a diversity of worldwide systems in which all people affect and are affected by others across the globe. Today there is no nation independent from the rest of the world. Raw materials, manufactured goods, consumers and markets, monetary systems, and preservation of the environment all cross national borders. The major problems faced by individuals (e.g., contamination of the environment, warming of the atmosphere, world hunger, international terrorism, nuclear war) are increasingly ones that cannot be solved by actions taken only at the national level.

The magnitude and scope of world interdependence have greatly increased the past forty years. Global interdependence is reflected in technological, economic, ecological, and political systems. Technologically, jet engines and rocketry, transistors and microchips, nuclear fission and fusion, and many other technological advances are rapidly changing life on earth. Technologies know no boundaries. When scientists make a new discovery in one country, it is quickly picked up and utilized in other countries. The earth has shrunk as a result of advances in transportation technologies that reduce the time it takes to travel great distances. The increased ability to transport people and goods throughout the world has fundamentally changed the world's economy. Through advances in communication technologies the earth has expanded in terms of the number of people, places, events, and bits of information that are available to any one person.

Economically, we depend on other areas of the world to supply many of the raw materials used by our industries and the goods we consume daily. We also depend on other countries to buy our goods and services. Multinational assemblage of goods is common. Foreign investment by multinational corporations, international lending of money, and the buying and selling of foreign currencies have become the rule rather than the exception. When companies close plants in one part of the world, new jobs are created in other parts of the world. Rises or declines in interest rates have dramatic implications for debtor countries. Crop failures in one part of the world affect profits of farmers in another part of the world. Every country in the world is interdependent with other countries because of the distribution and exchange of raw materials and manufactured goods, because of the potential consumers and markets outside of national boundaries, and because of the worldwide monetary system. Such economic interdependence will continue to increase.

Ecologically, the pollution of one country often affects the well-being of other countries, deforestation in one country affects the weather of many other countries, and what affects the environment in one part of the world affects the environment in other parts of the world. Politically, an election in one country often has important implications for the balance of power among the world's superpowers. By politically deciding to change economic policy, countries can affect the stability of the governments of other countries. Technologically, economically, ecologically, and politically, we are all bound together on "spaceship earth."

Humans do not have a choice. We have to cooperate. Cooperation is an inescapable part of our lives. It is built into our biology and is the hallmark of our species. Cooperation is the cornerstone of human evolution and progress. It is the heart of interpersonal relationships, families, economic systems, and legal systems. World interdependence is now a reality based on technology, economics, ecology, and politics that go beyond national boundaries and tie all countries in the world together. The management of human interdependence on a global, national, regional, organizational, community, family, and interpersonal level is one of the most pressing issues of our time. Understanding the nature of interdependent systems and how to operate effectively within them is an essential quality of future citizens. The question is not whether we will cooperate. The question is, how well will we do it?

Competition

Winning isn't everything. It's the only thing!

Vince Lombardi

We do it on the tennis courts and putting greens, in the boardroom and the playing field, at the chalkboard and on the dance floor. It is eulogized at business club luncheons and exalted at Junior Achievement pep rallies. It is ballyhooed by economists and politicians as the cure for our financial ills, and it is glorified in locker room sermons as preparation for life in the real world. Some of us do it in three-piece suits and turbocharged automobiles, others in wet T-shirts and souped-up muscle cars. It even happens in classrooms! An example of one of the most common kinds of classroom competition is reported by Jules Henry (1963):

The teacher turns to the class and says, "Well, who can tell Boris what the number is?" There is a forest of hands and the teacher calls on Peggy, who says that 4 should be divided into both the numerator and denominator. It is obvious that Boris' failure made it possible for Peggy to succeed, and, since the excited handwaving of the children indicates that they wanted to exploit Boris' predicament to succeed where he was failing, it appears that at least some of the children were learning to hope (covertly) for the failure of fellow students.

Competing with and defeating an opponent is one of the most widely recognized aspects of interpersonal interaction in American society. The language of business, politics, and even education is filled with "win-lose" terms. You "win" a promotion or raise, "beat" the opposition, "outsmart" a teacher, become a "superstar," and put competitors "in their place." The creed of competition as a virtue is woven deeply into our social fabric. Applause for it in sports dates back at least as far as the Greeks. Praise for it as an economic regulator of price and production reaches back to at least 1776 with the publication of Adam Smith's *The Wealth of Nations.* And Herbert Spencer's thoughts centered on it in the 1860s when he argued that Darwin's survival-of-the-fittest concept of evolution could be transposed to human society. In a society that stresses winning, it is no wonder that competition often gets out of hand and barriers arise to competing appropriately.

Do we need to educate students to be winners? Is this a dog-eat-dog competitive world in which only the fittest survive and therefore students need to be tough competitors?

_____ Yes   _____ No

Do we need to educate students to be rugged individualists? Does everyone need to be able to survive on his own, to live without bending to the roar of the crowd?

_____ Yes   _____ No

Do we need to educate students to work with others under the discipline imposed by a common task and purpose? Is striving toward common goals the most important and pervasive activity of educated persons? Is it true that civilization exists only while humans strive to achieve common goals?

_____ Yes   _____ No

Competition is often sought out as a "change of pace" or "interlude" from the ongoing cooperation of human interaction. Competitive contests such as sports, games, and recreational activities are commonly enjoyed. In a competitive situation, individuals work against each other to achieve a goal that only one or a few can attain. Individuals are expected to work faster and more accurately than their peers. A competitive social situation is one in which the goals of the separate participants are so linked that there is a negative correlation among their goal attainments; when one student achieves a goal, all others with whom that student is competitively linked fail to achieve their goals (Deutsch, 1962). An individual can attain his or her goal only if the other participants cannot attain theirs. When lessons are structured competitively, students work against each other to achieve a goal that only one or a few can attain. Students are graded on a curve, which requires them to be more competitive. Thus individuals seek an outcome that is personally beneficial but detrimental to all others in the situation. They either study hard to do better than their classmates, or they take it easy because they do not believe they have a chance to win. In a competitively structured class, students would be given the task of completing the assignments faster and more accurately than the other students in the class. They would be warned to work by themselves, without discussing the assignments with other students, and to seek help from the teacher if they need it.

For competition to exist, there must be perceived scarcity. If I must defeat you in order to get what I want, then what I want is by definition scarce. Rewards are restricted so that only the few who are the best or highest performers are acknowledged as being successful or are rewarded in some way. Sometimes the scarcity is based on reality. Two hungry people may compete over one loaf of bread. Sometimes the scarcity is artificially created. Students may compete for a limited number of A's, but how many A's there are is an arbitrary decision made by the teacher and school. Schools create artificial shortages of A's in an attempt to motivate students through competition. Many competitions are based on such artificial shortages created for the contest.

Competitions vary as to how many winners there will be. Only one baseball team can be "world champions." Not everyone who applies to a college may be admitted, but how many applicants "win" by being accepted varies from college to college. Competitions also vary as to the criteria for selecting a winner. In many cases, such as art contests, winning is based on subjective judgment. In other cases, such as track races, winning is based on objective criteria. In either case, the criteria for success are uncertain in that what is needed for a win depends on the relative performance of the particular contestants. Competitions vary as to the interaction that takes place among participants. In a boxing match there is direct interaction between the two participants throughout the competition. In a track meet there is parallel interaction. Within college admissions, participants may never see each other. Whereas two javelin throwers take turns doing the same thing and do not interfere with each other, two chess players actively try to defeat each other. Finally, competitions require social comparisons. Competitive situations contain forced social comparisons in which participants are faced with information about their peers' performances, and this comparative information is both salient and obtrusive (Levine, 1983). Competitors get the information on how they performed relative to others whether they want it or not.*

Competition has been popular ever since Adam Smith, Herbert Spencer, and others proposed the social Darwinist premise of survival of the fittest in human society. Four of the myths that supported its popularity were that competition is unavoidable because it is human nature, competition motivates people to do their best, competition is enjoyable, and competition builds character. Although very few people would accept these myths today, only a few years ago these myths supported the popularity of competition. There are, in addition, individuals who believe competition is inherently destructive (Kohn, 1986).

> Competing with and defeating an opponent is one of the most widely recognized aspects of interpersonal interaction in our society. The language of business, politics, and even education is filled with "win-lose" terms. One "wins" a promotion or a raise, "beats" the opposition, "outsmarts" a teacher, puts competitors "in their place." In an environment that stresses winning, it is no wonder that competitive behavior persists where it is not appropriate. —*D. W. Johnson and F. P. Johnson (1987)*

Individualistic Efforts

Humans do not always interact with others. At times solitude is desired. A long hike to a mountain lake, a walk along a deserted seashore, recording thoughts in a journal, and even writing books are often done alone. There are times when individuals act independently from each other without any interdependence existing among them. In an *individualistic* situation, individuals work by themselves to accomplish goals unrelated to and independent from the goals of others. Individual goals are assigned, individuals' efforts are evaluated on a fixed set of standards, and individuals are rewarded on the basis of how their efforts compare to the preset criterion of excellence. Whether an individual accomplishes his or her goal has no influence on whether other individuals achieve their goals. Thus a person seeks an outcome that is personally beneficial, ignoring as irrelevant the goal achievement efforts of other participants in the situation. Teachers can structure lessons individualistically so that students work by themselves to accomplish learning goals unrelated to those of their classmates. In a class structured individualistically, students would be given the task of completing the assignments correctly to reach a preset criterion of excellence. Students would be told to work by themselves, without disturbing their neighbors, and to seek help and assistance from the teacher.

---

*For a heart-rending but true-life story of the misery of having to live with rabid competition among children, readers may write to our mother, Mrs. Frances W. Johnson.

Individualistic efforts have also been supported by myths. The most notable is the myth that frontiersmen conquered the wilderness through isolated, individual, unrelated actions.

Summary

Within any social situation, individuals may work together to achieve shared goals, compete to see who is best, or act independently without interacting with others. There may be nothing more basic in human life than working with, working against, and working separately from other people. Cooperation is by far the most pervasive and important type of social interdependence. We do not have a choice. We have to cooperate. Working together to accomplish shared goals pervades our biology as well as all interpersonal relationships and social systems. It is the brick and mortar of human evolution and progress. We have developed from small hunting-and-gathering societies into a world in which we are technologically, economically, ecologically, and politically interdependent. Cooperation, furthermore, provides the foundation on which competitive and individualistic efforts are based. Competing for fun and enjoyment is frequently sought out as a "change of pace" from the pervasiveness of cooperation. Cooperation and competition are relationship concepts. Like hugging, it takes two (or more). You cannot cooperate or compete with yourself. Cooperation and competition take place between people. They are both opposites of individualistic efforts—the solitary striving for goals independent from all other humans.

For the past 45 years competitive and individualistic goal structures have dominated American education. Students usually come to school with competitive expectations and pressures from their parents. Many teachers have tried to reduce classroom competition by switching from a norm-referenced to a criterion-referenced evaluation system. In both competitive and individualistic learning situations teachers try to keep students away from each other. "Do not copy!" "Move your desks apart!" "I want to see how well you can do, not your neighbor!" are all phrases that teachers commonly use in their classrooms. Students are repeatedly told, "Do not care about the other students in this class. Take care of yourself!" When a classroom is dominated by competition, students often experience classroom life as a "rat race" with the psychology of the 100-yard dash. When a classroom is dominated by individualistic efforts, students will concentrate on isolating themselves from each other, ignoring others, and focusing only on their own work. Many students begin to compete within individualistic situations, even though the structure does not require it.

There is a third option. Cooperative learning is the most important of the three ways of structuring learning situations, yet it is currently the least used. In most schools, class sessions are structured cooperatively only for 7 to 20 percent of the time (Johnson & Johnson, 1983a). The research indicates, however, that cooperative learning should be used whenever teachers want students to learn more, like school better, like each other better, have higher self-esteem, and learn more effective social skills.

TO CHOOSE OR NOT TO CHOOSE

Teachers have to choose a structure for each lesson they teach. If no overt choice is made, students will choose the goal structure they believe is most appropriate. When students are familiar with and have had experience learning within each type of goal structure, students will probably be very good judges as to which goal structure is most desirable for accomplishing specified learning goals. When students do not have past experience in each type of instructional situation, an informed and free choice cannot take place. Students' conceptions of the alternatives in a situation depend on their past experiences and their perceptions of the situational constraints. If students have rarely experienced a goal structure

TABLE 1.1 Goal Structures

	APPROPRIATE COOPERATION	APPROPRIATE COMPETITION	APPROPRIATE INDIVIDUALIZATION
Interdependence	Positive	Negative	None
Type of Instructional Activity	Any instructional task. The more conceptual and complex the task, the greater the cooperation.	Skill practice, knowledge recall and review, assignment is clear with rules for competing specified.	Simple skill or knowledge acquisition; assignment is clear and behavior specified to avoid confusion and need for extra help.
Perception of Goal Importance	Goal is perceived to be important.	Goal is not perceived to be of large importance to the students, and they can accept either winning or losing.	Goal is perceived as important for each student; students see tasks as worthwhile and relevant, and each student expects eventually to achieve his or her goal.
Teacher-Student Interaction	Teacher monitors and intervenes in learning groups to teach collaborative skills.	Teacher is perceived to be the major source of assistance, feedback, reinforcement, and support. Teacher available for questions and clarification of the rules; teacher referees disputes and judges correctness of answers; rewards the winners.	Teacher is perceived to be the major source of assistance, feedback, reinforcement, and support.

(continued)

TABLE 1.1 (*continued*)

	APPROPRIATE COOPERATION	APPROPRIATE COMPETITION	APPROPRIATE INDIVIDUALIZATION
Teacher Statements	"David, can you explain the group's answer to #3?" "Be sure to ask me for help only when you've consulted all group members for help."	"Who has the most so far?" "What do you need to do to win next time?"	"Do not bother David while he is working." "Raise your hand if you need help." "Let me know when you are finished."
Student-Materials Interaction	Materials are arranged according to purpose of lesson.	Set of materials for each triad or for each student.	Complete set of materials and instructions for each student. Rules, procedures, answers are clear. Adequate space for each student.
Student-Student Interaction	Prolonged and intense interaction among students, helping and sharing, oral rehearsal of material being studied, peer tutoring, and general support and encouragement.	Observing other students in one's triad. Some talking among students. Students grouped in homogeneous triads to ensure equal chance of winning.	None; students work on their own with little or no interaction with classmates.
Student Expectations	Group to be successful. All members to contribute to success. Positive interaction among group members. All members master the assigned material.	Review previously learned material. Have an equal chance of winning. Enjoy the activity, win or lose. Monitor the progress of competitors. Follow the rules. Be a good winner and loser.	Each student expects to be left alone by other students; to work at one's own pace; to take a major part of the responsibility for completing the task; to take a major part in evaluating own progress and quality of efforts toward learning.
Room Arrangement	Small groups.	Students placed in triads or small clusters.	Separate desks or carrels with as much space between students as can be provided.
Evaluation Procedures	Criterion-referenced.	Norm-referenced.	Criterion-referenced.

other than interpersonal competition in school, they will tend to compete when left to their own devices. If all the organizational pressures within the school are based on the traditional interpersonal competitive goal structure, students will tend to behave competitively whenever they are left "free" to choose. Under such conditions implementing no goal structure at all or giving students a superficial choice among the three goal structures is to ask students subtly (or not so subtly) to place the traditional interpersonal goal structure on themselves.

IMPORTANCE OF INSTRUCTIONAL USE OF INTERDEPENDENCE

There is a great deal of research indicating that, if student-student interdependence is structured carefully and appropriately, students will achieve at a higher level, use higher level reasoning strategies more frequently, have higher levels of achievement motivation, be more intrinsically motivated, develop more positive interpersonal relationships with each other, value the subject area being studied more, have higher self-esteem, and be more skilled interpersonally (see Chapter 2). This research covers the full range of subject areas and age levels and has been available for some time. Why is it then, that appropriately structuring learning goals to affect student-student interaction is not an established part of a teacher's training? Why has this powerful classroom strategy been neglected, while student-materials and teacher-student interactions have been emphasized? There is no clear answer to these questions, but the discrepancy between what we know and what we do can be corrected. It is not difficult to prepare educators to select the appropriate goal structure for an instructional activity, implement it so that a certain student-student interaction pattern is achieved, and then instruct students in the social skills they need to interact appropriately and effectively with each other. It is time we did so.

So wherever I am, there's always Pooh, there's always Pooh and me. "What would I do," I said to Pooh, "if it wasn't for you?" and Pooh said, "True! It isn't much fun for one, but two can stick together," says Pooh, says he. "That's how it is," says Pooh. —*A. A. Milne*

HISTORY OF INTERDEPENDENCE IN THE CLASSROOM

Throughout history combinations of cooperative, competitive, and individualistic instruction have been used. Recent educational history in the United States has seen an emphasis placed on competitive and individualistic learning. In the 1930s an organized advocacy of interpersonal competition in the schools was launched by a combination of various business interests. During the depression a political groundswell in the business sector led in 1934 to the formation of the Liberty League, which united with other organizations, such as the National Association of Manufacturers, to sell interpersonal competition to educators. Their efforts were so successful that by the 1960s interpersonal competition was considered to be the "traditional" way of structuring student-student interaction. In the late 1960s, however, individualistic learning gained a strong foothold within written curricula and teacher-training programs. The combination of interpersonal competition and individualistic learning has been so strong that numerous observational studies have found them to be used from 85 to 95 percent of the time in American schools.

At this time in our educational history the most underutilized goal structure (and the most powerful instructionally) is cooperation. Cooperative learning is not a new idea. It is as old as humankind. The capacity to work cooperatively has been a major contributor to the survival of our species. Throughout human history, it has been those individuals who could organize and coordinate their efforts to achieve a common purpose that have been most successful in virtually any human endeavor. This is as true of joining with one's partners to hunt or to raise a barn as it is of space exploration.

Cooperative learning is an old idea. The Talmud clearly states that in order to learn the Talmud one must have three things: a copy of the Talmud (a curriculum), a teacher, and *a learning partner* (because the Talmud is far too complex to understand by oneself). As early as the first century, Quintilian argued that students could benefit from teaching one another. Johann Amos Comenius (1592–1670) believed that students would benefit by both teaching and being taught by other students. In the late 1700s, Joseph Lancaster and Andrew Bell made extensive use of cooperative learning groups in England, and the idea was brought to America when a Lancastrian school was opened in New York City in 1806. Within the Common School Movement in the United States in the early 1800s there was a strong emphasis on cooperative learning to ensure that the diverse students attending school were socialized into "being an American." The "one-room schoolhouse" where one teacher taught students from many different grade levels required cooperative learning in order to function. Certainly, the use of cooperative learning is not new to American education. There have been periods in which cooperative learning had strong advocates and was widely used to promote the educational goals of that time.

One of the most successful advocates of cooperative learning was Colonel Francis Parker. In the last three decades of the nineteenth century, Parker brought to his advocacy of cooperative learning enthusiasm, idealism, practicality, and an intense devotion to freedom, democracy, and individuality in the public schools. He viewed mutual responsibility as the great, central principle of democracy. To Parker, democracy frees the development of individuality, which increases individuals' abilities to contribute to society through joint efforts. Parker emphasized that children are natural collaborators. He believed that the highest joy, after that of discovering the "truth," was sharing the truth with classmates, and that the proper motive for learning and work is helping others. If conditions were arranged in the classroom so that learning was shared by a group and carried on with both love and intelligence, then learning would never become drudgery.

Parker believed that students would fully develop their capacities only if shared learning was encouraged and competition was eliminated as the main motive in school tasks. He viewed competition, with its premium on rewards for effort and accomplishment, as killing intrinsic motivation to learn. He believed that (1) if children were motivated by hope of reward and by fear of punishment, they would only develop into selfish people, never satisfied and bent on using others for their own advancement; (2) children with inborn limitations, who failed under competition to equal their more gifted rivals, would feel inferior and despair; and (3) with competition as the chief incentive for work, the gulf between achievement and aspiration, instead of motivating, would only bring frustration and unhappiness, and work would tend to become mere drudgery.

Parker's fame and success rested on the vivid and regenerating spirit he brought into the schoolroom and on his power to create a classroom atmosphere that was truly cooperative and democratic. When he was superintendent of the public schools in Quincy, Massachusetts (1875–1880), more than 30,000 visitors a year came to examine his cooperative learning procedures (Campbell, 1965). As Bishop Spalding put it, when Parker took charge of the Quincy schools, they were quickly transformed, "as the spring rain and the sunshine transform the naked earth." Parker's instructional methods of promoting cooperation among students dominated American education through the turn of the century.

Following Parker's lead, John Dewey promoted the use of cooperative learning groups as part of his famous project method in instruction. Dewey, his colleagues, and members of the child development movement advocated the instructional use of cooperation in the nation's schools. They emphasized the social aspects of learning and the role of the school in educating students in democratic living. Dewey argued that if humans are to learn to live cooperatively, they must experience the living process of cooperation in schools. Life in the classroom should represent the democratic process in microcosm, and the heart of democratic living is cooperation in groups. Dewey argued that classroom life should embody democracy, not only in how students learn to make choices and carry out academic projects together, but also in how they learn to relate to one another. They should be taught, therefore, to empathize with others, to respect the rights of others, and to work together on rational problem solving.

In the 1930s an organized advocacy of interpersonal competition in the schools was launched by a combination of various business sectors (Pepitone, 1980). Issues of individual freedom to compete and simultaneous fears of collectivist domination were major concerns in the social climate of the 1930s. The emphasis on competition came despite the publication of two companion volumes (May and Doob's *Competition and Cooperation*, 1937, and Margaret Mead's *Cooperation and Competition Among Primitive Peoples*, 1936) that concluded that cooperative efforts were in a variety of ways superior to competitive efforts. In the midst of depression America, the Liberty League, formed in 1934 as a result of a political groundswell in the business sector, united with other organizations like the National Association of Manufacturers to "sell free enterprise to people . . . to force the minds of public opinion back into the mold of Americanism" (Rippa, 1976).

In the 1940s, Morton Deutsch, building on the theorizing of Kurt Lewin, proposed a theory of cooperative and competitive situations that has served as the primary foundation on which subsequent research on and discussion of cooperative learning have been based. Our own research is directly based on Deutsch's work. Research and theorizing on cooperation and competition continued throughout the 1950s and 1960s. Muzafer Sherif (Sherif & Hovland, 1961) conducted his famous studies on three summer camps within which he engineered intense intergroup competition and studied its resolution. Stuart Cook (1969), in collaboration with Shirley and Lawrence Wrightsman, conducted a study on the impact of cooperative interaction on relationships between black and white college students. James Coleman (1961) published an observational study of American high schools in which a pervasive competitiveness was documented. From an anthropological perspective, Millard C. Madsen (1967) and his associates developed a series of dyadic games that allowed comparison of children's preferences for competitive and cooperative interaction, across ages and various cultures. One of Madsen's students, Spencer Kagan, began a series of studies on cooperation and competition in children. Their research presents a consistent picture of rural children collaborating more than urban children, and middle-class urban American children being most strongly motivated to compete.

Beginning with the publication of *The Social Psychology of Education* (Johnson, 1970) and the first edition of *Learning Together and Alone* (Johnson & Johnson, 1975), a number of researchers began to develop cooperative learning procedures to be used in the classroom. They are too numerous to mention here, except for a few historical figures. David DeVries (who received his Ph.D. under the direction of James Coleman) and Keith Edwards at the Center for Social Organization of Schools combined cooperative learning, intergroup competition, and instructional games into a classroom procedure (DeVries, Slavin, Fennessey, Edwards & Lombardo, 1980). Their work has been continued and extended by one of DeVries' doctoral students, Robert Slavin. Shlomo Sharan and Rachel Hertz-Lazarowitz (1980) in Israel have continued and extended Dewey's project method, followed by a similar development by Spencer Kagan (1985). Elliot Aronson and his associates (Aronson, Blaney, Stephan, Sikes, & Snapp, 1978) developed the jigsaw procedure for using cooperative learning. Elizabeth Cohen (1986) developed a method of cooperative learning based on expectation-states theory. William Glasser (1986) promoted the use of cooperative relationships among students. Dean Tjosvold (1986) took cooperative learning and applied it to the business setting. These and many other committed social scientists and educators in the United States, Canada, and several other countries have done pioneering work in the study and implementation of cooperative learning lessons, curricula, strategies, and procedures.

The most underutilized goal structure (and the most powerful instructionally) is cooperation. Despite the considerable research validation of its effectiveness, and although noted authorities such as Coleman (1972) and Glasser (1969) have stated that a major goal of school is to educate students to work cooperatively with others, the procedures for implementing cooperation have only recently been clearly specified. In this book we present the conditions under which cooperative learning should be used and the specific procedures for doing so. After mastering this material, you will never again wonder how to reduce inappropriate competition and increase collaboration among students.

APPROPRIATELY USING INTERDEPENDENCE

The three goal structures are not in competition with each other. Survival of the fittest does not apply when it comes to structuring learning situations appropriately. Each goal structure has its place. In the ideal classroom all three are used. However, they will not all be used equally. The basic foundation of instruction, the underlying context on which all instruction rests, is cooperation. Unless they are used within a context of cooperation, competitive and individualistic instruction lose much of their effectiveness.

Cooperation exists within the classroom on both a macro and a micro level. On a macro level, cooperation pervades instruction on the social system level. Within instructional situations there are two complementary roles, teacher and student, who engage in specified role-related behaviors and conform to organizational norms and values concerning appropriate behavior. The teacher is a person who teaches students; students are persons who learn with the aid of a teacher. The roles are interrelated, reinforce each other, and are interdependent. Neither role can function or exist without the other. The individuals in the roles of both teacher and student must learn the role expectations of other members of the organization, accept them, and reliably fulfill them. Examples of teacher role requirements are putting students into contact with the subject matter, specifying learning goals, creating specific instructional conditions, disciplining students, and evaluating students. Examples of student role requirements are to be attentive, follow directions, exert effort to achieve assigned learning goals, arrive on time, and complete assignments. An example of a norm is that no physical violence takes place within the classroom, and an example of a value is that education is beneficial and worthwhile. Successful completion of the school's objectives depends on the fulfillment of the organizational role requirements and adherence to the norms and values of the school.

When cooperation on this macro level breaks down, competitive and individualistic learning activities become completely ineffectual. If students refuse to be "role-responsible," for example, no effective instruction can take place regardless of how interdependence among students is structured. It should be noted, furthermore, that in order for competition to take place there must be cooperation on rules, procedures, time, place, and criteria for determining the winner. Without this underlying collaborative system, no competition can take place. Skills and information learned individualistically, furthermore, must at some time be contributed to a collaborative effort. No skill is learned without its being enacted within a social system such as a family or business. Nothing is produced without its being part of a larger economic system. What is learned alone today is enacted in collaborative relationships tomorrow, or else it has no meaning or purpose.

On the micro level, cooperation is one of the three goal structures used to structure interdependence among students. Cooperative learning provides a context for the other two goal structures. Competition cannot exist if there is no underlying cooperation concerning rules and procedures. Most competitions have referees, umpires, judges, and teachers present to ensure that the basic cooperation over rules and procedures does not break down. Individualistic activities can be effectively used as part of a division of labor in which students master certain knowledge and skills that will later be used in cooperative activities. Within instructional situations cooperative learning must dominate. It has the most widespread and powerful effects on instructional outcomes; it is the most complex of the three goal structures to implement effectively; and it should be the one most frequently used. Competitive and individualistic learning should be used to supplement and enrich the basic cooperation taking place among students. Finally, it is apparent that when the three goal structures are used appropriately and in an integrated way, their sum is far more powerful than each one separately.

The appropriate use of all three goal structures will improve your teaching effectiveness and make your life as a teacher considerably more productive, satisfying, and enjoyable. It is the inappropriate use of a goal structure that causes problems for students (and subsequently the teacher). But when should you use each goal structure?

DECIDING ON A GOAL STRUCTURE

A teacher may wish to teach certain lessons or units cooperatively and others competitively or individualistically. Matching the goal structure and the learning activity is one of the most important steps in structuring your classroom. It needs to be done carefully. When instruction is not going well, the first issue to address is whether the goal structure is appropriate. The following questions may help in determining the appropriateness of the goal structure you are using:

1. What do I want students to obtain from the lesson? What are the cognitive and affective objectives?

2. What is the nature of the instructional task? Is it conceptual learning, drill-review, or mastery of simple information or skills?

3. How much assistance and guidance do students need to complete the task? Will instructions need to be repeated several times, or is the task simple and straightforward?

4. What materials and equipment are required by the lesson, and how available are they?

5. What types of instructional climate and interaction among students are necessary to facilitate the accomplishment of the learning objectives?

In deciding which goal structure to use, it is surprising that cooperative learning has been ignored for the past fifty years. One explanation is that more than 90 percent of all human interaction is cooperative, and therefore, we are blind to its importance! Cooperation to a human is like water to a fish; it is so pervasive that it remains unnoticed. Cooperation is a persuasive but *nonconscious* goal of education. Within most situations no alternative to cooperation seems possible to humans. All competitive and individualistic efforts take place within a broader cooperative framework. Cooperation is the forest, competitive and individualistic efforts are but trees.

FREQUENCY OF USE OF EACH METHOD OF STRUCTURING INTERDEPENDENCE

As a teacher, you will use all three goal structures over a period of time. What types of learning goals and what type of classroom climate you prefer will determine the frequency with which you use each one. Most teachers spend a large proportion of their time in promoting higher-level conceptual reasoning and problem-solving skills that give maximal thinking experience to the students, tasks that are best served by a cooperative goal structure. To a lesser extent, there are important and specific skills and knowledge that may be mastered by studying under an individualistic goal structure. Tasks calling for drill or review of facts may be learned under a competitive goal structure. Ideally, a cooperative goal structure may be used 60 to 70 percent of the time, an individualistic goal structure 20 percent of the time, and a competitive goal structure 10 to 20 percent of the time. With students now perceiving school as predominantly competitive, and with cooperation being used systematically in very few classrooms, your task in training students to function primarily within a cooperative goal structure and to shift quickly from one goal structure to another will not at first be an easy one.

Certainly, aggressiveness exists in nature, but there is also a healthy nonruthless competition, and there exist very strong drives toward social and cooperative behavior. These forces do not operate independently but together, as a whole, and the evidence strongly indicates that, in the social and biological development of all living creatures, of all these drives, the drive to cooperation is the most dominant, and biologically the most important. . . . It is probable that man owes more to the operation of this principle than to any other in his own biological and social evolution. —*Ashley Montagu (1966)*

BASIC PARTNERSHIP BETWEEN COOPERATIVE AND INDIVIDUALISTIC LEARNING

Probably the most frequent combination of goal structures used in classrooms is the combination of cooperative and individualistic learning situations. There are three major ways in which individualistic and cooperative goal structures may be combined. The first one is through task interdependence in which a division of labor is created. While working on a cooperative task, a group may arrive at a division of labor in which it is necessary for different students to master different skills or different information in order to provide the resources the group needs to achieve its goal successfully. An ideal teaching situation is to assign a cooperative project and provide individual tasks for various aspects of the problem so that different group members can master different skills and information for later integration into the group's product. An example of this approach is to assign the individual tasks of learning how to make a microscope slide, how to gather pond water, and how to use a microscope and then assign the cooperative task of writing a group report on the microscopic life in swamp water.

A second possible combination is through resource interdependence. This procedure is commonly referred to as a "jigsaw." A list of vocabulary words may be given to a cooperative learning group and then subdivided so that each member is responsible for (1) learning a subset of words and (2) teaching the words to the other group members.

Finally, individualistic and cooperative goal structures may be combined through reward interdependence. Students can study material within a cooperative learning group, take an achievement test individually, and then be rewarded on the basis of a performance ratio, such as the following:

1. Students receive 67 percent credit for every problem they solve correctly and 33 percent of the average performance of group members.
2. Students receive their individual score and then are given bonus points if all members of the group achieve a preset criterion for excellence.

Conversely, students could be assigned to a cooperative group and then study material individualistically, be tested individualistically, receive their own score, and receive bonus points based on the scores of the members of their group compared to a preset criterion for excellence. Since such a procedure does not include the interaction among group members that contributes to learning, this procedure should be used infrequently.

INTEGRATED USE OF ALL THREE GOAL STRUCTURES

All three methods of structuring interdependence among students may be used in an integrated way within classrooms. A typical schedule for doing so is as follows:

1. Assign students to heterogeneous cooperative learning groups.
2. Give each member an individualistic assignment of learning a subsection of the material the group needs to complete its assignment.
3. Give each group a cooperative assignment of learning all of the material with each member presenting his or her subsection to the entire group.
4. Conduct a competitive tournament to drill students on the material they have just learned.
5. Give a cooperative assignment to use the material learned to complete a group project.
6. Give an achievement test that each student takes individually and determine a group score on the basis of the performance of all group members.

An example of such an integrated unit is as follows:

1. Students are assigned to four-person heterogeneous cooperative learning groups.
2. Each group is given the cooperative assignment of ensuring that all group members learn a set of vocabulary words.
3. A list of 32 vocabulary words are given to each group. Each group member is given the individualistic assignment of mastering 8 of the vocabulary words and planning how to teach the 8 words to the other group members.
4. The group then meets with the cooperative goal of ensuring that all four members master all 32 vocabulary words. Each group member teaches his or her subset of 8 words to the other members.
5. A competitive class tournament is conducted to drill students on the 32 words and to see which group has been most successful in mastering the vocabulary words.
6. Each group is given the cooperative assignment of writing a story in which 95 percent of the assigned vocabulary words are used appropriately and correctly. The group is to produce one story that contains contributions from all group members.
7. A test on the 32 vocabulary words is given to students individually. All members of groups in which each member scored 95 percent or above receive an A on the unit.

When conducting an integrated unit, the following important issues should be kept in mind:

1. Emphasize the underlying cooperation. The individualistic and competitive aspects of the unit are supplements to the overall cooperation among students. Individualistic and competitive learning activities should enhance but not detract from cooperative learning.

2. Begin and end with a group meeting. At the initial group meeting the division of labor or jigsaw may be agreed on, and the goal of individualistically learning material to contribute to the overall success of the group is emphasized. During the final meeting students should discuss how well the group functioned.

3. Remember that students will bring more to the competition than you want them to. They will want to make more of winning the competition than is appropriate. Remember to keep the reward for winning minor. In the students' past, winning has too often been a "life or death" matter. You will have to teach students to compete appropriately for fun. You may wish to have a class discussion about how enjoyable the competition was.

4. Vary the number of instructional periods according to the unit. The individualistic assignments could be done as homework. Cooperative tasks could take more than one instructional period.

SUMMARY

Social interdependence to humans is like water to fish. Because we are immersed in it, it can escape our notice. There are two types of social interdependence: cooperative and competitive. The absence of interdependence results in individualistic efforts. For every learning task, teachers have a choice of structuring it competitively, individualistically, or cooperatively. Which structure is chosen determines how students interact with each other, which in turn determines the outcomes achieved. For the past fifty years competitive and individualistic efforts have dominated classrooms. Cooperative learning has been relatively ignored and underutilized by teachers even though it is by far the most important and powerful way to structure learning situations. Chapter 2, which reviews the basic research that has been conducted on the three goal structures, makes this point clearly. This does not mean, however, that competitive and individualistic learning should be abandoned. Each goal structure has its place, and when they are used appropriately, they form an integrated whole. In Chapters 3, 4, and 5, therefore, the appropriate use of each goal structure is discussed in depth.

Cooperation is by far the most pervasive and important type of social interdependence. We do not have a choice. We have to cooperate. Working together to accomplish shared goals pervades our biology and is the brick and mortar of human evolution and progress. Cooperation provides the foundation on which competitive and individualistic efforts are based. It is discussed thoroughly in Chapters 3, 6, 7, 8, and 9. Competing for fun and enjoyment is frequently sought out as a "change of pace" from the pervasiveness of cooperation. It is discussed in Chapter 5. Cooperation and competition involve relationships with other people. Like hugging, it takes two or more. You cannot cooperate or compete by yourself. Both are opposites of individualistic efforts—the solitary striving for goals independent from those of others. Individualistic learning is discussed in Chapter 4.

Cooperation is the most powerful of the three ways to structure learning situations (see Chapter 2). It is also the most complex to implement. Besides knowing what cooperative learning is, teachers have to understand the various types of cooperative learning (see Chapter 8) and the essential elements (see Chapter 5) that make cooperation work. Thus positive interdependence is discussed in Chapter 6, and the small group and interpersonal skills required to work cooperatively with others are discussed in Chapter 7. Finally, the questions most frequently asked about the use of cooperative learning are discussed in Chapter 10.

2

Goal Structures, Learning Processes, and Instructional Outcomes

INTRODUCTION

Linda Scott, in her Moundsview, Minnesota, fifth-grade classroom, assigns her students a set of math story problems to solve. She assigns her students to groups of three, ensuring that each group has high-, medium-, and low-performing math students and both male and female students. The instructional task is to solve each story problem correctly and to understand the correct process for doing so. Each group is given a set of story problems (one copy for each student) and a set of three "role" cards. Each group member is assigned one of the roles. The *reader* reads the problem aloud to the group. The *checker* makes sure that all members can explain how to solve each problem correctly. The *encourager* in a friendly way encourages all members of the group to participate in the discussion, sharing their ideas and feelings.

Within this lesson *positive interdependence* is structured by the group agreeing on (1) the answer and (2) the process for solving each problem. Since the group certifies that each member (1) has written the correct answer on his or her answer sheet and (2) can correctly explain how to solve each problem, *individual accountability* is structured by having the teacher pick one answer sheet at random to score for the group and choose one group member at random to explain how to solve a problem. The *cooperative skills* emphasized in the lesson are checking and encouraging. Finally, at the end of the period the groups *process* their functioning by answering two questions: (1) What is something each member did that was helpful for the group? (2) What is something each member could do to make the group even better tomorrow?

As a result of structuring this math lesson cooperatively, what instructional outcomes can the teacher expect?

Working together to get the job done can have profound effects on students and staff members. A great deal of research has been conducted on the relationship among cooperative, competitive, and individualistic efforts and instructional outcomes (Johnson & Johnson, 1974, 1978, 1983a, 1989a; Johnson, Johnson, & Maruyama, 1983; Johnson, Maruyama, Johnson, Nelson, & Skon, 1981; Pepitone, 1980; Sharan, 1989; Slavin, 1983). These research studies began in the late 1890s when Triplett (1898) in the United States and Mayer (1903) in Germany conducted a series of studies on the factors associated with competitive performance. The amount of research that has been conducted since is staggering. During the past ninety years more than 525 experimental and 100 correlational studies have been conducted by a wide variety of researchers in different decades, with subjects of different ages, in different academic areas, and in different settings. These studies have all been summarized and analyzed using meta-analysis procedures in a recent book (Johnson & Johnson, 1989a). We know far more about the efficacy of cooperative learning than we know about lecturing, age grouping, beginning reading instruction at age six, departmentalization, or almost any other facet of education. While there is not enough space in this chapter to review all of the research, a comprehensive review of all studies may be found in Johnson and Johnson (1989a). In most cases, references to individual studies are not included in this chapter. Rather, the reader is referred to reviews that contain the references to the specific studies that corroborate the point being made.

Building on the theorizing of Kurt Lewin and Morton Deutsch, the premise may be made that the type of interdependence structured among students determines how they interact with each other, which in turn largely determines instructional outcomes. The quality of peer relationships, furthermore, has widespread and powerful impact on individuals' cognitive and social development. In this chapter, therefore, the importance of high-quality peer relationships, student-student interaction patterns, and the instructional outcomes promoted by the three goal structures are discussed.

> Let us put our minds together . . . and see what life we can make for our children. —*Sitting Bull*

IMPORTANCE OF PEER RELATIONSHIPS

Children and adolescents live in an expanding social world. From relating primarily to adult caretakers, young children begin interacting with other adults and with other children. As children become older, they have more interaction with other children and less interaction with adults. Yet, traditionally, adults in the United States have viewed the interactions between adults and children as the most important vehicle for ensuring the effective socialization and development of children and adolescents. Child-child relationships have been assumed to be, at best, relatively unimportant and, at worst, unhealthy influences.

This adult-centric view is reflected in the policies of American schools. Most legitimate peer interaction among students has been limited to extracurricular activities. These activities rarely deal directly with the basic issues of classroom life. The system of instruction emphasizes teacher lectures and seatwork done by students individualistically. Student attempts to interact with each other are seen as disruptive of this system. Furthermore, the rigid age segregation usually applied in school classrooms (and also fostered by the subdividing of school programs for administrative purposes into elementary, junior, and senior high schools) often limits peer interaction within a narrowly confined age span. Finally, educators systematically fail to train students in the basic social skills necessary for interacting effectively with peers (in this chapter the word *peer* means a wide range of other children or adolescents). These skills are not considered pedagogically useful. Essentially, the typical adult-child dyadic view of teaching and learning has deemphasized student-student relationships in the classroom.

Despite these patterns of deemphasis, *peer relationships are a critical element in the development and socialization of children and adolescents* (Hartup, Glazer, & Charlesworth, 1976; Johnson, 1980). In fact, the primary relationships in which development and socialization may take place may be with peers. Compared with interactions with adults, interactions with peers tend to be more frequent, intense, and varied throughout childhood and adolescence. Experiences with peers are not superficial luxuries to be enjoyed during lunch or on a Saturday afternoon. Constructive relationships with peers are a necessity.

There are numerous ways in which peer relationships contribute to (1) social and cognitive development and (2) socialization. Some of the more important consequences correlated with peer relationships are as follows (the specific supporting evidence may be found in Johnson, 1989, and Johnson & Johnson, 1989a):

1. *In their interactions with peers, children and adolescents directly learn attitudes, values, skills, and information unobtainable from adults.* In their interactions with each other, children and adolescents imitate each other's behavior and identify with friends possessing admired competencies. Through providing models, reinforcement, and direct learning, peers shape a wide variety of social behaviors, attitudes, and perspectives.

2. *Interaction with peers provides support, opportunities, and models for prosocial behavior.* It is within interactions with other children and adolescents that one helps, comforts, shares with, takes care of, assists, and gives to others. Without peers with whom to engage in such behaviors, many forms of prosocial values and commitments could not be developed. Conversely, whether adolescents engage in problem or transition behavior, such as the use of illegal drugs and delinquency, is related to the perceptions of their friends' attitudes toward

such behaviors. Being rejected by one's peers tends to result in antisocial behavioral patterns characterized by aggressiveness, disruptiveness, and other negatively perceived behavior.

3. Children and adolescents frequently lack the time perspective needed to tolerate delays in gratification. As they develop and are socialized, the focus on their own immediate impulses and needs is replaced with the ability to take longer perspectives. *Peers provide models of, expectations of, directions for, and reinforcements of learning to control impulses.* Aggressive impulses provide an example. Peer interaction involving such activities as rough-and-tumble play promotes the acquisition of a repertoire of effective aggressive behaviors and helps establish the necessary regulatory mechanisms for modulating aggressive effect.

4. *Children and adolescents learn to view situations and problems from perspectives other than their own through their interaction with peers.* Such perspective taking is one of the most critical competencies for cognitive and social development. All psychological development may be described as a progressive loss of egocentrism and an increase in ability to take wider and more complex perspectives. It is

A human being is a part of the whole, called by us "Universe," a part limited in time and space. He experiences himself, his thoughts and feelings as something separated from the rest—a kind of optical delusion of consciousness. This delusion is a kind of prison for us, restricting us to our personal desires and to affection for a few persons nearest to us. Our task must be to free ourselves from this prison by widening our circle of compassion to embrace all living creatures and the whole nature in its beauty. —*Albert Einstein* primarily in interaction with peers that egocentrism is lost and increased perspective taking is gained.

5. *Autonomy* is the ability to understand what others expect in any given situation and to be free to choose whether to meet their expectations. Autonomous people are independent of both extreme inner- and outer-directedness. When making decisions concerning appropriate social behavior, autonomous people tend to consider both their internal values and the situational requirements and then respond in flexible and appropriate ways. Autonomy is the result of (1) the internalization of values (including appropriate self-approval) derived from caring and supportive relationships, and (2) the acquisition of social skills and sensitivity. *Relationships with other children and adolescents are powerful influences on the development of the values and the social sensitivity required for autonomy.* Children with a history of isolation from or rejection by peers, furthermore, often are inappropriately other-directed. They conform to group pressures even when they believe the recommended actions are wrong or inappropriate.

6. While adults can provide certain forms of companionship, *children need close and intimate relationships with peers with whom they can share their thoughts and feelings, aspirations and hopes, dreams and fantasies, and joys and pains.* Children need constructive peer relationships to avoid the pain of loneliness.

7. Throughout infancy, childhood, adolescence, and early adulthood, a person moves through several successive and overlapping identities. The physical changes involved in growth, the increasing number of experiences with other people, increasing responsibilities, and general cognitive and social development all cause changes in self-definition. The final result should be a coherent and integrated identity. In peer relationships children and adolescents become aware of the similarities and differences between themselves and others. They experiment with a variety of social roles that help them integrate their own sense of self. In peer relationships values and attitudes are clarified and integrated into an individual's self-definition. *It is through peer relationships that a frame of reference for perceiving oneself is developed.* Gender typing and its impact on one's identity is an example.

8. *Coalitions formed during childhood and adolescence provide help and assistance throughout adulthood.*

9. The ability to maintain interdependent, cooperative relationships is a prime manifestation of psychological health. Poor peer relationships in elementary school predict psychological disturbance and delinquency in high school, and poor peer relationships in high school predict adult pathology. *The absence of any friendships during childhood and adolescence seems to increase the risk of mental disorder.*

10. *In both educational and work settings, peers have a strong influence on productivity.* Greater achievement is typically found in collaborative situations where peers work together than in situations where individuals work alone. Especially when a child or adolescent has poor study skills or is unmotivated, cooperative interaction with peers has powerful effects on productivity. Supportive relationships with peers are also related to using one's abilities in achievement situations.

11. *Student educational aspirations may be more influenced by peers than by any other social influence.* Similarly, ambition in career settings is greatly influenced by peers.

Within instructional situations, peer relationships can be structured to create meaningful interdependence through learning cooperatively with peers. Within cooperative learning situations students experience feelings of belonging, acceptance, support, and caring, and the social skills and social roles required for maintaining interdependent relationships can be taught and practiced.

Through repeated cooperative experiences students can develop social sensitivity concerning the behavior expected of others and the actual skills and autonomy to meet such expectations if they so desire. Through holding each other accountable for appropriate social behavior, students can greatly influence the values they internalize and the self-control they develop. It is through belonging to a series of interdependent relationships that values are learned and internalized. It is through prolonged cooperative interaction with other people that healthy social development, with an overall balance favoring trust rather than distrust of other people, the ability to view situations and problems from a variety of perspectives, a meaningful sense of direction and purpose in life, an awareness of mutual interdependence with others, and an integrated and coherent sense of personal identity, takes place (Johnson, 1979; Johnson & Matross, 1977).

In order for peer relationships to be constructive influences, they must promote feelings of belonging, acceptance, support, and caring, rather than feelings of hostility and rejection (Johnson, 1980). Being accepted by peers is related to willingness to engage in social interaction, utilizing abilities in achievement situations, and providing positive social rewards for peers. Isolation from peers is associated with high anxiety, low self-esteem, poor interpersonal skills, emotional handicaps, and psychological pathology. Rejection by peers is related to disruptive classroom behavior, hostile behavior and negative affect, and negative attitudes toward other students and school. In order to promote constructive peer influences, therefore, teachers must first ensure that students interact with each other and, second, must ensure that the interaction takes place within a cooperative context.

Advice to Teachers

Educators who wish to promote constructive relationships among students will wish to do the following (Johnson, 1980):

1. Structure cooperative situations in which children and adolescents work with peers to achieve a common goal.
2. Emphasize joint rather than individual products whenever possible.
3. Directly teach the interpersonal skills needed to build and maintain collaborative relationships with peers.

4. Give children and adolescents meaningful responsibility for the well-being and success of their peers.

5. Encourage the feelings of support, acceptance, concern, and commitment that are part of collaborative situations.

6. Hold children and adolescents accountable for fulfilling their obligations and responsibilities to their collaborators and give them mutual authority over each other.

7. Ensure that students experience success in working cooperatively with peers.

INTERACTION PATTERNS

Simply placing students near each other and allowing interaction to take place does not mean that high-quality peer relationships will result and that learning will be maximized. The nature of interaction is important. Some interaction leads to students rejecting each other and defensively avoiding being influenced by peers. When student-student interaction leads to relationships characterized by perceived support and acceptance, then the potential effects described in the previous section are likely to be found.

There have been several hundred studies comparing the effects of cooperative, competitive, and individualistic goal structures on aspects of interpersonal interaction important for learning (see Johnson & Johnson, 1989a). A cooperative goal structure leads to a promotive interaction pattern among students. *Promotive interaction* occurs when individuals encourage and facilitate each other's efforts to achieve. It is characterized by personal and academic acceptance and support, exchange of information, mutual help and assistance, high intrinsic achievement motivation, and high emotional involvement in learning.

A competitive goal structure results in an oppositional pattern of student-student interaction. *Oppositional interaction* occurs when individuals discourage and obstruct each other's efforts to achieve. It results in rejection of classmates, obstruction of each other's work, avoidance of information exchange or communication, low achievement motivation, and psychological withdrawal and avoidance. The negative interdependence created by a competitive goal structure results in students having a vested interest in obstructing one another's learning. There are two ways to win in a competition—to do better than anyone else or to prevent anyone else from doing better than you. These strategies are known as a good offense and a good defense. In a classroom, however, preventing one's classmates from learning more than oneself can create destructive interaction patterns that decrease learning for everyone.

An individualistic goal structure results in no interaction among students. *No interdependence* exists when individuals work independently without any interchange with each other. Students work alone without bothering their classmates. Such a goal structure minimizes peer relationships and interaction in learning situations.

Acceptance, Support, Trust, Liking

If you want students to encourage and support each other's efforts to achieve, and if you wish students to accept and trust each other, cooperative learning should dominate your classroom. Cooperative learning experiences, compared with competitive and individualistic ones, have been found to result in stronger beliefs that other students (and teachers) care about how much one learns and want to help one learn (Johnson & Johnson, 1989a). Furthermore, cooperative attitudes are related to mutual acceptance, respect, liking, and trust among students.

> Cooperation, not conflict, was evidently the selectively most valuable form of behavior for man taken at any stage of his evolutionary history, and surely, quite as evidently never more so than today. . . . It is essentially the experience, the means, that fits human beings not to their external environment so much as to one another. It must never be forgotten that society is fundamentally, essentially, and in all ways a cooperative enterprise, an enterprise designed to keep men in touch with one another. Without the cooperation of its members society cannot survive, and the society of man has survived because the cooperativeness of its members made survival possible—it was not an advantageous individual here and there who did so, but the group. In human societies the individuals who are most likely to survive are those who are best enabled to do so by their group. —*Ashley Montagu (1965)*

From Table 2.1 (see p. 40) it may be seen that cooperation resulted in greater social support than did competitive or individualistic efforts (effect sizes of 0.59 and 0.71, respectively). Social support tends to be related to the following factors (see Johnson & Johnson, 1989a):

1. Achievement, successful problem solving, persistence on challenging tasks under frustrating conditions, lack of cognitive interference during problem solving, lack of absenteeism, academic and career aspirations, more appropriate seeking of assistance, retention, job satisfaction, high morale, and greater compliance with regimens and behavioral patterns that increase health and productivity.

2. Living a longer life, recovering from illness and injury faster and more completely, and experiencing less severe illnesses.

3. Psychological health and adjustment, lack of neuroticism and psychopathology, reduction of psychological distress, coping effectively with stressful situations, self-reliance and autonomy, a coherent and integrated self-identity, greater psychological safety, higher self-esteem, increased general happiness, and increased interpersonal skills.

4. Effective management of stress by providing the caring, information, resources, and feedback individuals need to cope with stress, by reducing the number and severity of stressful events in an individual's life, by reducing anxiety, and by helping one appraise the nature of the stress and one's ability to deal with it constructively.

5. The emotional support and encouragement individuals need to cope with the risk that is inherently involved in challenging one's competence and striving to grow and develop.

The importance of social support in education has been ignored over the past thirty years. A general principle to keep in mind is that the pressure to achieve should always be matched with an equal level of social support. Challenge and support must be kept in balance. Whenever increased demands and pressure to be productive are placed on students (and teachers), a corresponding increase in social support should be structured.

Exchange of Information

The seeking of information, together with utilizing it in one's learning, is essential for academic achievement. Students working within a cooperative goal structure (Johnson & Johnson, 1989a).

1. Seek significantly more information from each other than do students working within a competitive goal structure.
2. Are less biased and have fewer misperceptions in comprehending the viewpoints and positions of other individuals.
3. More accurately communicate information by verbalizing ideas and information more frequently, attending to others' statements more carefully, and accepting others' ideas and information more frequently.
4. Are more confident about the value of their ideas.
5. Make optimal use of the information provided by other students.

Motivation

Motivation is most commonly viewed as a combination of the perceived likelihood of success and the perceived incentive for success. The greater the likelihood of success and the more important it is to succeed, the higher the motivation. Success that is intrinsically rewarding is usually seen as being more desirable for learning than is having students believe that only extrinsic rewards are worthwhile. There is greater perceived likelihood of success and success is viewed as more important in cooperative than in competitive or individualistic

learning situations (Johnson & Johnson, 1989a). In addition, cooperative learning tends to generate intrinsic motivation to learn, while competitive and individualistic learning tend to be fueled by extrinsic motivation. Finally, students tend to be more emotionally involved in cooperative than in competitive or individualistic learning activities.

LEARNING OUTCOMES

Different learning outcomes result from the student-student interaction patterns promoted by the use of cooperative, competitive, and individualistic goal structures (Johnson & Johnson, 1989a). Though space is too short here to review all of the research, some of the major findings are discussed in the following subsections.

Cooperative Efforts and Achievement/Productivity

The highest and best form of efficiency is the spontaneous cooperation of a free people.

Woodrow Wilson

How successful competitive, individualistic, and cooperative efforts are in promoting productivity and achievement is the first question pragmatists ask about social interdependence. More than 375 studies during the past 90 years have attempted to find an answer (Johnson & Johnson, 1989a). When all of the studies were included in the analysis, the average cooperator performed at about two-thirds of a standard deviation above average student learning within a competitive situation (effect size = 0.66) or an individualistic situation (effect size = 0.63). When only the high-quality studies were included in the analysis, the effect sizes were 0.86 and 0.59, respectively. Cooperative learning, furthermore, resulted in more higher-level reasoning, more frequent generation of new ideas and solutions (i.e., process gain), and greater transfer of what is learned within one situation to another (i.e., group-to-individual transfer) than did competitive or individualistic learning.

Some cooperative learning procedures contained a mixture of cooperative, competitive, and individualistic efforts, while others were "pure." The original jigsaw procedure (Aronson et al., 1978), for example, is a combination of resource interdependence (cooperative) and individual reward structures (individualistic). Teams-games-tournaments (DeVries and Edwards, 1974) and student-teams achievement divisions (Slavin, 1980) are mixtures of cooperation and intergroup competition. Team-assisted instruction (Slavin, Leavey, & Madden, 1982) is a mixture of individualistic and cooperative learning. When the results of

TABLE 2.1 Social Interdependence: Weighted Findings

	MEAN	S.D.	N
Achievement			
Cooperative vs. Competitive	0.66	0.94	128
Cooperative vs. Individualistic	0.63	0.81	182
Competitive vs. Individualistic	0.30	0.76	39
Interpersonal Attraction			
Cooperative vs. Competitive	0.65	0.47	88
Cooperative vs. Individualistic	0.62	0.59	59
Competitive vs. Individualistic	0.08	0.70	15
Social Support			
Cooperative vs. Competitive	0.59	0.39	75
Cooperative vs. Individualistic	0.71	0.45	70
Competitive vs. Individualistic	−0.12	0.37	18
Self-Esteem			
Cooperative vs. Competitive	0.60	0.56	55
Cooperative vs. Individualistic	0.44	0.40	37
Competitive vs. Individualistic	−0.19	0.40	18

Source: D. W. Johnson, R. Johnson, & E. Holubec: *Circles of learning: Cooperation in the classroom* (rev. ed.) Edina, MN. Interaction, 1990, p. 32. Reprinted with permission.

"pure" and "mixed" operationalizations of cooperative learning were compared, the "pure" operationalizations produced higher achievement.

Since research participants have varied widely as to economic class, age, sex, and cultural background, since a wide variety of research tasks and measures of the dependent variables have been used, and since the research has been conducted by many different researchers with markedly different orientations working in different settings and in different decades, the overall body of research on social interdependence has considerable generalizability.

That working together to achieve a common goal produces higher achievement and greater productivity than does working alone is so well confirmed by so much research that it stands as one of the strongest principles of social and organizational psychology. Cooperative learning is indicated whenever the learning goals are highly important, mastery and retention are important, the task is complex or conceptual, problem solving is desired, divergent thinking or creativity is desired, quality of performance is expected, and higher-level reasoning strategies and critical thinking are needed.

What Mediates?

Why does cooperation result in higher achievement—what mediates? The critical issue in understanding the relationship between cooperation and achievement is specifying the variables that mediate the relationship. Simply placing students in groups and telling them to work together does not in and of itself promote higher achievement. It is only under certain conditions that group efforts may be expected to be more productive than individual efforts. Those conditions are as follows:

1. Clearly perceived positive interdependence. From the research, it may be concluded that positive interdependence provides the context within which promotive interaction takes place, that group membership and interpersonal interaction among students do not produce higher achievement unless positive interdependence is clearly structured, that the combination of goal and reward interdependence increases achievement over goal interdependence alone, and that resource interdependence does not increase achievement unless goal interdependence is present also (Johnson & Johnson, 1989a).

2. Considerable promotive (face-to-face) interaction. Within cooperative learning, compared with competitive and individualistic learning, students (a) provide others with efficient and effective help and assistance, (b) exchange needed resources such as information and materials and process information more efficiently and effectively, (c) provide each other with feedback in order to improve their subsequent performance on assigned tasks and responsibilities, (d) challenge each other's conclusions and reasoning in order to promote higher-quality decision making and greater insight into the problems being considered, (e) advocate exerting efforts to achieve mutual goals, (f) influence each other's efforts to achieve mutual goals, (g) act in trusting and trustworthy ways, (h) are motivated to strive for mutual benefit, and (i) feel less anxiety and stress (Johnson & Johnson, 1989a).

3. Felt personal responsibility (individual accountability) to achieve the group's goals. When groups work on tasks where it is difficult to identify members' contributions, when there is an increased likelihood of redundant efforts, and when there is lessened responsibility for the final outcome, some members will contribute less to goal achievement. If, however, there is high individual accountability and it is clear how much effort each member is contributing, if redundant efforts are avoided, and if every member is responsible for the final outcome, then the social loafing effect vanishes (Johnson & Johnson, 1989a). The smaller the size of the group, the greater the individual accountability may be.

4. Frequent use of relevant interpersonal and small group skills. Social skills and competencies tend to increase more within cooperative rather than in competitive or individualistic situations (Johnson & Johnson, 1989a). Working together to get the job done requires students to provide leadership, build and maintain trust, communicate effectively, and manage conflicts constructively. The more socially skillful students are, and the more attention teachers pay to teaching and rewarding the use of social skills, the higher the achievement that can be expected within cooperative learning groups. In their studies on the long-term implementation of cooperative learning, Lew and Mesch (Lew, Mesch, Johnson, & Johnson, 1986a, 1986b; Mesch, Johnson, & Johnson, 1988; Mesch, Lew, Johnson, & Johnson, 1986) investigated the impact of a reward contingency for using social skills as well as positive interdependence and a contingency for academic achievement on performance within cooperative learning groups. In the cooperative skills conditions students were trained weekly in four social skills, and each member of a cooperative group was given two bonus points toward the quiz grade if all group members were observed by the teacher to demonstrate three out of four cooperative skills. The results indicated that the combination of positive interdependence, an academic contingency for high performance by all group members, and a social skills contingency promoted the highest achievement.

5. *Periodic and regular group processing.*   Stuart Yager examined the impact on achievement of (a) cooperative learning in which members discussed how well their group was functioning and how they could improve its effectiveness, (b) cooperative learning with any group processing, and (c) individualistic learning (Yager, Johnson & Johnson, 1985). The results indicate that the high-, medium-, and low-achieving students in the cooperation with group processing condition achieved higher on daily achievement, postinstructional achievement, and retention measures than did the students in the other two conditions. Students in the cooperation without group processing condition, furthermore, achieved higher on all three measures than did the students in the individualistic condition. Johnson, Johnson, Stanne, and Garibaldi (in press) conducted a follow-up study comparing cooperative learning with no processing, cooperative learning with teacher processing (the teacher specified cooperative skills to use, observed, and gave whole class feedback as to how well students were using the skills), cooperative learning with teacher and student processing (teacher specified cooperative skills to use, observed, gave whole class feedback as to how well students were using the skills, and had learning groups discuss how well they interacted as a group), and individualistic learning. Forty-nine high-ability black American high school seniors and newly registered college freshmen at Xavier University participated in the study. A complex computer-assisted problem-solving assignment was given to all students. All three cooperative conditions performed higher than did the individualistic condition. The combination of teacher and student processing resulted in greater problem-solving success than did the other cooperative conditions.

This is the confession of a half-educated man. My education prepared me superbly for a bird's-eye view of the world; it taught me how to recognize easily and instantly the things that differentiate one place or people from another. But my education failed to teach me that the principal significance of such differences is that they are largely without significance. My education failed to grasp the fact that beyond the differences are realities scarcely comprehended because of their shattering simplicity. And the simplest reality of all is that the human community is one—greater than any of its parts, greater than the separateness imposed by actions, greater than the divergent faiths and allegiances or the depth and color of varying cultures. —*Norman Cousins*

Critical Thinking Competencies

In many subject areas related to science and technology the teaching of facts and theories is considered to be secondary to the teaching of critical thinking and the use of higher-level reasoning strategies. The aim of science education, for example, has been to develop individuals "who can sort sense from nonsense," or who have the critical thinking abilities of grasping information, examining it, evaluating it for soundness, and applying it appropriately. Cooperative learning promotes a greater use of higher reasoning strategies and critical thinking than do competitive and individualistic learning strategies (Johnson & Johnson, 1989a).

Students in the United States frequently believe that a learning task is completed when they have an answer in every blank in a worksheet. Sustained effort to comprehend material deeply seems to be rare. The Japanese, on the other hand, view academic success as a matter of disciplined, enduring effort aimed at achieving *satori,* or the sudden flash of enlightenment that comes after long, intensive, but successful effort. The achievement of satori is much more likely after a discussion in cooperative learning groups than after working alone, or competitively to complete an assignment.

Attitudes Toward Subject Area

Cooperative learning experiences, compared with competitive and individualistic ones, promote more positive attitudes toward the subject area, more positive attitudes toward the instructional experience, and more continuing motivation to learn more about the subject area being studied (Johnson & Johnson, 1989a). These findings have important implications, for example, for influencing female and minority students to enter science- and math-oriented careers.

INTERPERSONAL RELATIONSHIPS

Cooperative learning experiences, compared with competitive, individualistic, and "traditional instruction," promote considerably more liking among students (effect sizes = 0.65 and 0.62, respectively) (Johnson & Johnson, 1989a; Johnson, Johnson, & Maruyama, 1983). This statement is true regardless of differences in ability level, sex, handicapping conditions, ethnic membership, social class differences, or task orientation. Students who collaborate on their studies develop considerable commitment and caring for each other no matter what their initial impressions of and attitudes toward each other were. They also like the teacher better and perceive the teacher as being more supportive and accepting academically and personally.

In order to be productive, a class of students (or a school faculty) has to cohere and have a positive emotional climate. As relationships become more positive, absenteeism decreases, and increases may be expected in student commitment to learning, feelings of personal responsibility to do the assigned work, willingness to take on difficult tasks, motivation and persistence in working on learning tasks, satisfaction and morale, willingness to endure pain and frustration to succeed, willingness to defend the school against external criticism or attack, willingness to listen to and be influenced by peers, commitment to peers' success and growth, and productivity and achievement (Johnson & F. Johnson, 1987; Watson & Johnson, 1972). In addition, when students are heterogeneous with regard to ethnic, social class, language, and ability differences, cooperative learning experiences are a necessity for building positive peer relationships.

The fundamental facts that brought about cooperation, society, and civilization and transformed the animal man into a human being are the facts that work performed under the division of labor is more productive than isolated work and that man's reason is capable of recognizing this truth. But for these facts men would have forever remained deadly foes of one another, irreconcilable rivals in their endeavors to secure a portion of the scarce supply of means of sustenance provided by Nature. Each man would have been forced to view all other men as his enemies; his craving for the satisfaction of his own appetites would have brought him into an implacable conflict with all his neighbors. No sympathy could possibly develop under such a state of affairs. . . . We may call consciousness of kind, sense of community, or sense of belonging together the acknowledgement of fact that all other human beings are potential collaborators in the struggle for survival because they are capable of recognizing the mutual benefits of cooperation. . . .
—*Ludwig Von Mises (1949)*

Psychological Health

When students leave school, we would hope that they have the psychological health and stability required to build and maintain career, family, and community relationships, to establish a basic and meaningful interdependence with other people, and to participate effectively in society. Our studies (Johnson & Johnson, 1989a) indicate that *cooperativeness* is positively related to a number of indices of psychological health, namely: emotional maturity, well-adjusted social relations, strong personal identity, and basic trust in and optimism about people. *Competitiveness* seems also to be related to a number of indices of psychological health, while *individualistic attitudes* tend to be related to a number of indices of psychological pathology, emotional immaturity, social maladjustment, delinquency, self-alienation, and self-rejection. To the degree that schools can contribute to a student's psychological well-being, they should be organized to reinforce those traits and tendencies that promote it.

Accuracy of Perspective Taking

Social perspective taking is the ability to understand how a situation appears to another person and how that person is reacting cognitively and emotionally to the situation. The opposite of perspective taking is *egocentrism*, the embeddedness in one's own viewpoint to the extent that one is unaware of other points of view and of the limitations of one's own perspectives. Cooperative learning experiences tend to promote greater cognitive and affective perspective taking than do competitive or individualistic learning experiences (Johnson & Johnson, 1989a).

Self-esteem

The data in Table 2.1 indicate that cooperation produced higher levels of self-esteem than did competitive and individualistic efforts (effect-sizes of 0.60 and 0.44, respectively). Individuals with low self-esteem tend to have the following characteristics (Johnson & Johnson, 1989a):

1. They have low productivity because they set low goals for themselves, lack confidence in their ability, and assume that they will fail no matter how hard they try.
2. They are critical of others as well as themselves; they look for flaws in others and try to "tear them down."
3. They withdraw socially because they feel awkward, self-conscious, and vulnerable to rejection.
4. They are conforming, agreeable, highly persuasible, and highly influenced by criticism.

5. They develop psychological problems such as anxiety, nervousness, insomnia, depression, and psychosomatic symptoms more frequently.

Within *competitive* situations self-esteem tends to be based on a contingent view of one's competence; that is, "If I win, then I have worth as a person, but if I lose, then I have no worth." Winners attribute their success to superior ability and attribute the failure of others to lack of ability, both of which contribute to self-aggrandizement. Losers, who are the vast majority, defensively tend to be self-disparaging and apprehensive about evaluation, and tend to withdraw psychologically and physically. Within *individualistic* situations, students are isolated from one another, receive little direct comparison with or feedback from peers, and perceive evaluations as inaccurate and unrealistic. A defensive avoidance, evaluation apprehension, and distrust of peers result. Within *cooperative* situations, individuals tend to interact, promote each other's success, form multidimensional and realistic impressions of each other's competencies, and give accurate feedback. Such interaction tends to promote a basic self-acceptance of oneself as a competent person.

Understanding Interdependence

Cooperative learning simultaneously models interdependence and provides students with the experiences they need to understand the nature of cooperation (Johnson & Johnson, 1989a). The future of the world depends on the constructive and competent management of world interdependence as well as interdependence in family, work, community, and societal settings. Students who have had twelve to twenty years of cooperative learning will be better able to perceive the importance of interdependence than will students who have had twelve to twenty years of competitive and individualistic learning.

The more cooperative students' attitudes are, the more they see themselves as being intrinsically motivated: They persevere in pursuit of clearly defined learning goals; believe that it is their own efforts that determine their school success; want to be good students and get good grades; and believe that ideas, feelings, and learning new ideas are important and enjoyable. These studies also indicate that the more competitive students' attitudes are, the more they see themselves as being extrinsically motivated in elementary and junior high schools. Competitive attitudes, however, are somewhat related to intrinsic motivation, to being a good student, and to getting good marks in senior high school. Individualistic attitudes tend to be unrelated to all measured aspects of the motivation to learn. Being part of a cooperative learning group has been found to be related to a high subjective probability of academic success and continuing motivation for further learning by taking more advanced courses in the subject area studied. There is also experimental evidence that indicated that cooperative learning experiences, compared with individualistic ones, will result in more intrinsic motivation, less extrinsic motivation, and less need for teachers to set clear goals for the students.

RELATIONSHIPS AMONG OUTCOMES

There are bidirectional relationships among achievement, quality of interpersonal relationships, and psychological health, as shown in Figure 2.1 (Johnson & Johnson, 1989a). Each factor influences the others. Caring and committed friendships come from a sense of mutual accomplishment, mutual pride in joint work, and the bonding that results from joint efforts. The more students care about each other, on the other hand, the harder they will work to achieve mutual learn-

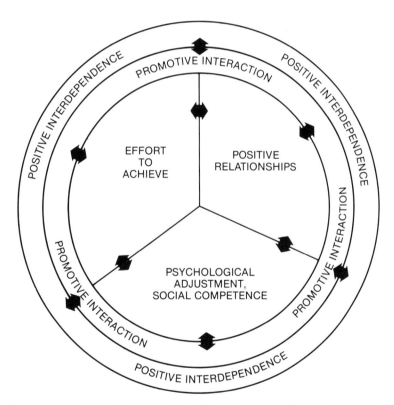

FIGURE 2.1 Outcomes of cooperation. (*Source:* D. W. Johnson & R. Johnson: *Cooperation and competition: Theory and research.* Edina, MN. Interaction, 1989. Reprinted with permission.)

ing goals. Long-term and persistent efforts to achieve do not come from the head, they come from the heart (Johnson & Johnson, 1989b). Individuals seek out opportunities to work with those they care about. As caring increases, so do feelings of personal responsibility to do one's share of the work, willingness to take on difficult tasks, motivation and persistence in working toward goal achievement, and willingness to endure pain and frustration on behalf of the group. All these contribute to group productivity.

In addition, the joint success experienced in working together to get the job done enhances social competencies, self-esteem, and general psychological health. The healthier individuals are psychologically, on the other hand, the better able they are to work with others to achieve mutual goals. Joint efforts require coordination, effective communication, leadership, and conflict management. States of depression, anxiety, guilt, shame, and anger decrease the energy available to contribute to a cooperative effort.

Finally, the more positive interpersonal relationships are, the greater is the psychological health of the individuals involved. Through the internalization of positive relationships, direct social support, shared intimacy, and expressions of caring, psychological health and the ability to cope with stress are built. The absence of caring and committed relationships and the presence of destructive relationships tend to increase psychological pathology. On the other hand, states of depression, anxiety, guilt, shame, and anger decrease individuals' ability to build and maintain caring and committed relationships. The healthier individuals are psychologically, the more meaningful and caring are the relationships they can build and maintain.

REDUCING THE DISCREPANCY

With the amount of research evidence available, it is surprising that classroom practice is primarily oriented toward individualistic and competitive learning and that schools are dominated by a competitive and individualistic structure. *It is time to reduce the discrepancy between what research indicates is effective in teaching and what teachers actually do.* In order to do so, educators must understand the role of the teacher in implementing cooperative learning experiences. That is the focus of the next chapter.

FINAL NOTE

Despite the overwhelming evidence of the power and importance of cooperative learning experiences, and the lack of clear evidence as to when competitive and individualistic goal structures can be beneficially used in the classroom, the current research findings are incomplete. The appropriate use of competitive and individualistic goal structures has not been sufficiently explored. Teachers should use all three goal structures in an integrated way, and students should be taught the skills necessary to function in all three types of situations. In the next three chapters, therefore, the conditions under which each goal structure can be appropriately used are discussed.

3

Structuring Cooperative Learning

INTRODUCTION

It is 12,896 B.C. A small group of hunters surround a band of reindeer as they ford an icy river. The hunters are armed with harpoons tipped with spearheads carved from reindeer antlers. As the reindeer wallow in the water, the hunters run in and slaughter them. It is the coordinated action of the group of Cro-Magnon hunters that makes them more successful then their Neanderthal cousins, who hunt as individuals.

Our origins are somehow linked with the fate of the Neanderthals. We have never been proud of our extinct predecessors, partly because of their looks. Nevertheless, the Neanderthals represent a high point in the human story. Their lineage goes back to the earliest members of the genus *Homo*. They were the original pioneers. Over thousands of years Neanderthals moved out of Africa by way of the Near East into India and China and Malaysia, and into southern Europe. In recent times, 150,000 or so years ago, they pioneered glacial landscapes. The Neanderthals were the first to cope with climates hospitable only to woolly mammoths and reindeer.

There is no anatomical evidence that the Neanderthals were inferior to us (the Cro-Magnons) cerebrally, and no doubt whatever that they were our physical superiors. Their strongest individuals could probably lift weights of half a ton or so. Physically, we are quite puny in comparison. But we gradually replaced the Neanderthals during an overlapping period of a few thousand years. It may have mainly been a matter of attrition and population pressure. As the glaciers from

Scandinavia advanced, northern populations of Neanderthals moved south while our ancestors were moving north out of Africa. We met in Europe. They vanished about 30,000 years ago.

There are numerous explanations for the disappearance of the Neanderthals. Perhaps they evolved into us. Perhaps we merged. Perhaps there was an intergroup competition for food, with the Neanderthals unable to meet our challenge and dying off in marginal areas. Perhaps the Neanderthals were too set in their ways and were unable to evolve and refine better ways to cooperate while we were continually organizing better cooperative efforts to cope with changing climatic conditions. There seems to be little doubt that we were more able to form and maintain cooperative efforts within small groups.

During the time we (the Cro-Magnons) overlapped with the Neanderthals, our ancestors developed highly sophisticated cooperative efforts characterized by social organization, group-hunting procedures, creative experimentation with a variety of materials, sharing of knowledge, divisions of labor, trade, and transportation systems. We sent out scouts to monitor the movements of herds of animals we preyed on. The Neanderthals probably did not. We cached supplies and first aid materials to aid hunting parties far away from our home bases. The Neanderthals did not. Neanderthals apparently engaged their prey chiefly in direct combat. We learned more efficient ways of hunting, such as driving animals over cliffs, that changed fundamentally our relationship with the rest of the animal kingdom (i.e., instead of behaving like lions and other carnivores, going after young and old and sick animals to weed out the less fit, our ancestors conducted large-scale game drives that wiped out entire herds and perhaps entire species). We developed more sophisticated tools and weapons to kill from a distance, such as the spear-thrower and the bow and arrow. The Neanderthals probably did not. The Neanderthals used local materials to develop tools. We were more selective, often obtaining special fine-grained and colorful flints from quarries as far as 250 miles away. This took a level of intergroup cooperation and social organization that Neanderthals did not develop. We improved the tool-making process through experimentation and sharing knowledge. The Neanderthals did not. The Neanderthals used stone almost exclusively for tools. We used bone and ivory to make needles and other tools. We "tailored" our clothes and made ropes and nets. Our ability to obtain more food than we needed resulted in trading and the formation of far-ranging social networks. Status hierarchies, the accumulation of wealth, artistic efforts, laws, and storytelling to preserve traditions followed, as more complex forms of cooperation were developed. Whether we replaced or evolved from the Neanderthals, our ingenuity was especially evident in organizing cooperative efforts to increase our standard of living and the quality of our lives. We excelled at organizing effective small-group efforts.

Humans are small-group beings. We always have been and we always will be. As John Donne said, "No man is an island, entire of itself." Throughout the history of our species we have lived in small groups. For 200,000 years humans lived in small hunting and gathering groups. For 10,000 years humans lived in small farming communities. It is only recently, during the past 100 years or so, that large cities have become the rule rather than the exception.

WHEN COOPERATION FAILS

Simply placing individuals in groups and telling them to work together does not in and of itself promote productivity. There are many ways in which group efforts may go wrong. Less able members sometimes "let George do it" to complete the group's tasks, thus creating a *free rider* effect (Kerr & Bruun, 1983) whereby group members expend decreasing amounts of effort and just go through the teamwork motions. At the same time, the more able group member may expend less effort to avoid the *sucker effect* of doing all the work (Kerr, 1983). High-ability group members may be deferred to and may take over the important leadership roles in ways that benefit them at the expense of the other group members (the *rich-get-richer* effect). In a learning group, for example, a more able group member may give all the explanations of what is being learned. Since the amount of time spent explaining correlates highly with the amount learned, more able members learn a great deal while the less able members flounder as a captive audience. The time spent listening in group brainstorming can reduce the amount of time available for individuals to state their own ideas (Hill, 1982; Lamm & Trommsdorff, 1973). Group efforts can be characterized by self-induced helplessness (Langer & Benevento, 1978), diffusion of responsibility and social loafing (Latane, Williams, & Harkins, 1979), ganging up against a task, reactance (Salomon, 1981), dysfunctional divisions of labor ("I'm the thinkist and you're the typist") (Sheingold, Hawkins, & Char, 1984), inappropriate dependence on authority (Webb, Ender, & Lewis, 1986), destructive conflict (Collins, 1970; Johnson & Johnson, 1979), and other patterns of behavior that debilitate group performance.

It is only when the essential components of cooperative learning are carefully structured that cooperative efforts may be expected to be more productive than competitive and individualistic efforts (Johnson & Johnson, 1989a).

TYPES OF COOPERATIVE LEARNING GROUPS

Cooperative learning may be incorporated into courses through the use of *formal learning groups,* which are more structured and stay together until the task is done (e.g., a triad that ensures that all members master the information assigned about the Revolutionary War); *informal learning groups,* which are short-term and less structured (check the person next to you to see if he or she understood); and *base groups,* which are long-term groups whose role is primarily one of peer support and long-term accountability. Of the three types of cooperative learning groups, it is the use of formal cooperative learning groups that provides the basis for teachers to gain expertise in using cooperative learning procedures and provides the foundation for the other two. This chapter focuses on formal cooperative learning groups. Informal cooperative learning groups and base groups are discussed in Chapter 8.

ESSENTIAL COMPONENTS OF COOPERATIVE LEARNING

In Roy Smith's junior high school English class in Hingham, Massachusetts, students are given the assignment of writing thesis essays on a story, "The Choice," which discusses the experience of a time traveler who goes into the future and returns. The class is divided into groups of four, with high-, medium-, and low-achieving students and both male and female students in each group. Seven instructional tasks are assigned over a four-day unit:

1. A prereading discussion on what should be taken on a time-travel trip into the future, what should be found out, and what should be told to others on one's return.
2. Each student writes a letter/proposal requesting funding for a time-travel into the future.
3. Group members edit each other's letter/proposals, give suggestions for improvement, and mark any errors that need correcting. All revised letter/proposals are handed in with the signatures of the group members who edited them.
4. Each member reads the story "The Choice" and makes a tentative interpretation of its meaning.
5. Group members discuss the story and reach consensus on the answers to seven questions about its content.
6. Each student writes a composition, taking the position that the decision made by Williams was correct or incorrect and presenting a convincing rationale as to why his or her position is valid.
7. Group members edit two other members' compositions. Careful editing for spelling, punctuation, and the components of thesis essays is emphasized. All revised compositions are handed in with the signatures of the group members who edited them.

Within this lesson *positive interdependence* is structured by having each group start out with 100 points and subtracting 5 points for every spelling or punctuation error and every failure to include the essential components of thesis essays. The group is given 20 bonus points if every member clearly articulates an interpretation of the story and supports it with valid reasoning. Students discuss the assignment and help and assist each other in a *face-to-face promotive interaction*. *Individual accountability* is ensured by requiring each student to write the letter/proposal and essay and revise them to meet the standards of his or her groupmates. The *cooperative skill* of criticizing ideas without criticizing the person is explained by the teacher and practiced by the students. Finally, the group spends some time during the final class session *processing* how well they worked together and what they could do in the future to be even more effective group members. This lesson illustrates the essential components of cooperative learning.

Many educators who believe that they are using cooperative learning are, in fact, missing its essence. There is a crucial difference between simply putting students into groups to learn and in structuring cooperation among students.

Cooperation is *not* having students sit side-by-side at the same table to talk with each other as they do their individual assignments. Cooperation is *not* assigning a report to a group of students where one student does all the work and the others put their names on the product as well. Cooperation is much more than being physically near other students, discussing material with other students, helping other students, or sharing material among students, although each of these is important in cooperative learning. Five components must be included for small-group learning to be truly cooperative. These essential elements are discussed in the following subsections.

Positive Interdependence

All for one and one for all.

Alexandre Dumas

In a football game the quarterback who throws the pass and the receiver who catches the pass are positively interdependent. The success of one depends on the success of the other. It takes two to complete a pass. One player cannot succeed without the other. Both have to perform competently if their mutual success is to be assured. They sink or swim together.

The first requirement for an effectively structured cooperative lesson is that students believe that they "sink or swim together." Within cooperative learning situations students have two responsibilities: learn the assigned material and ensure that all members of their group learn the assigned material. The technical term for that dual responsibility is positive interdependence. *Positive interdependence* exists when students perceive that they are linked with groupmates in such a way that they cannot succeed unless their groupmates do (and vice versa), or that they must coordinate their efforts with the efforts of their groupmates to complete a task. Positive interdependence promotes a situation in which students see that their work benefits groupmates and vice versa, and students work together in small groups to maximize the learning of all members by sharing their resources, providing mutual support, and celebrating their joint success.

When positive interdependence is clearly understood, it highlights these factors:

1. Each group member's efforts are required and indispensable for group success (i.e., there can be no "free riders").
2. Each group member has a unique contribution to make to the joint effort because of his or her resources and role and task responsibilities.

There are a number of ways of structuring positive interdependence within a learning group (goal, reward, resource, and role interdependence). To ensure that students believe they sink or swim together and care about how much each other learns, you (the teacher) have to structure a clear *group or mutual goal*, such as "Learn the assigned material, and make sure that all members of your group learn the assigned material." The group goal always has to be part of the lesson. To supplement goal interdependence, you may wish to add *joint rewards* (if all members of the group score 90 percent correct or better on the test, each will receive 5 bonus points), *divided resources* (giving each group member a part of the total information required to complete an assignment), and *complementary roles* (reader, checker, encourager, elaborator).

Face-to-Face Promotive Interaction

In an industrial organization it's group effort that counts. There's really no room for stars in an industrial organization. You need talented people, but they can't do it alone. They have to have help.

John F. Donnelly, President, Donnelly Mirrors

The second component is *face-to-face promotive interaction* among group members. Cooperative learning requires face-to-face interaction among students within which they promote each other's learning and success. There is no magic in positive interdependence in and of itself. It is the interaction patterns and verbal interchange among students promoted by the positive interdependence that affect education outcomes.

Within cooperative lessons, you need to maximize the opportunity for students to promote each other's success by helping, assisting, supporting, encouraging, and praising each other's efforts to learn. Such promotive interaction has a number of effects. First, there are cognitive activities and interpersonal dynamics that occur only when students explain to each other how the answers to assignments are derived. These include orally explaining how to solve problems, discussing the nature of the concepts being learned, teaching one's knowledge to groupmates, and explaining how present learning is connected with past learning. Second, it is within face-to-face interaction that the opportunity for a wide variety of social influences and patterns emerge. Helping and assisting take place. Accountability to peers, influencing each other's reasoning and conclusions, social modeling, social support, and interpersonal rewards all increase as the face-to-face interaction among group members increases, Third, the verbal and nonverbal responses of other group members provide important feedback concerning each other's performance. Fourth, it provides an opportunity for peers to pressure unmotivated group members to achieve. Fifth, it is the interaction involved in completing the work that allows students to get to know each other as persons, which in turn forms the basis for caring and committed relationships among members.

To obtain meaningful face-to-face interaction, the size of groups needs to be small (from two to six members), because the perception that one's participation and efforts are needed increases as the size of the group decreases. On the other hand, as the size of the group increases, the amount of pressure peers may place on unmotivated group members increases. Whatever the size, the effects of social interaction cannot be achieved through nonsocial substitutes such as instructions and materials.

Individual Accountability and Personal Responsibility

What children can do together today, they can do alone tomorrow.

Lev S. Vygotsky

Among the early settlers of Massachusetts there was a saying, "If you do not work, you do not eat." The third essential component of cooperative learning is *individual accountability,* which exists when the performance of each individual student is assessed and the results given back to the group and the individual. It is important that the group knows who needs more assistance, support, and encouragement in completing the assignment. It is also important that group members know that they cannot "hitchhike" on the work of others.

To ensure that each student is individually accountable to do his or her fair share of the group's work, you need to

1. Assess how much effort each member is contributing to the group's work.
2. Provide feedback to groups and individual students.
3. Help groups avoid redundant efforts by members.
4. Ensure that every member is responsible for the final outcome.

When it is difficult to identify members' contributions, when members' contributions are redundant, and when members are not responsible for the final group outcome, members are likely to loaf and seek a free ride. The smaller the size of the group, furthermore, the greater the individual accountability may be.

The purpose of cooperative learning groups is to make each member a stronger individual. Individual accountability is the key to ensuring that all group members are in fact strengthened by learning cooperatively. After participating in a cooperative lesson, group members should be better able to complete similar tasks by themselves. There is a pattern to classroom learning. First, students learn how to solve the problem or use the strategy in a cooperative group; then, they perform it alone. Common ways to structure individual accountability include giving an individual test to each student, randomly selecting one student's product to represent the entire group, having students teach what they have learned to someone else, and having students explain what they know to the group.

Interpersonal and Small Group Skills

I will pay more for the ability to deal with people than any other ability under the sun.

John D. Rockefeller

The fourth essential component of cooperative learning is the appropriate use of *interpersonal and small group skills*. Placing socially unskilled individuals in a group and telling them to cooperate does not guarantee that they are able to do so effectively. We are not born instinctively knowing how to interact effectively with others. Interpersonal and group skills do not magically appear when they are needed. Persons must be taught the social skills required for high-quality collaboration and be motivated to use them if cooperative groups are to be productive. In order to coordinate efforts to achieve mutual goals, students must (1) get to know and trust each other, (2) communicate accurately and unambiguously, (3) accept and support each other, and (4) resolve conflicts constructively (Johnson, 1990, 1987; Johnson & F. Johnson, 1987). Interpersonal and small-group skills form the basic nexus among students, and if students are to work together productively and cope with the stresses and strains of doing so, they must have a modicum of these skills.

Group Processing

The fifth essential component of cooperative learning is *group processing*, which exists when group members discuss how well they are achieving their goals and maintaining effective working relationships. Effective group work is influenced by whether or not groups reflect on (i.e., process) how well they are functioning.

A *process* is an identifiable sequence of events taking place over time, and the term *process goals* refers to the sequence of events instrumental in achieving outcome goals. *Group processing* may be defined as reflecting on a group session to (a) describe the member actions that were helpful and unhelpful and (b) make decisions about what actions to continue or change. The purpose of group processing is to clarify and improve the effectiveness of the members in contributing to the collaborative efforts to achieve the group's goals. Groups need to describe what member actions were helpful and unhelpful in completing the group's work and make decisions about what behaviors to continue or change. Such processing (1) enables learning groups to focus on maintaining good working relationships among members, (2) facilitates the learning of cooperative skills, (3) ensures that members receive feedback on their participation, (4) ensures that students think on the metacognitive as well as the cognitive level, and (5) provides the means to celebrate the success of the group and reinforce positive behaviors of group members. Some of the keys to successful processing are allowing sufficient time for it to take place, emphasizing positive feedback, making the processing specific rather than vague, maintaining student involvement in processing, reminding students to use their cooperative skills while they process, and communicating clear expectations as to the purpose of processing.

Besides having each learning group process, teachers may lead whole-class processing. When cooperative learning groups are used, the teacher observes the groups, analyzes the problems they have working together, and gives feedback to each group on how well they are working together. An important aspect of both small-group and whole-class processing is group and class celebrations. It is feeling successful, appreciated, and respected that builds commitment to learning and a sense of self-efficacy. See Table 3.1 for a summary of differences between cooperative learning and traditional learning groups.

TABLE 3.1   What Is the Difference?

COOPERATIVE LEARNING GROUPS	TRADITIONAL LEARNING GROUPS
Positive interdependence	No interdependence
Individual accountability	No individual accountability
Heterogeneous membership	Homogeneous membership
Shared leadership	One appointed leader
Responsible for each other	Responsible only for self
Task and maintenance emphasized	Only task emphasized
Social skills directly taught	Social skills assumed and ignored
Teacher observes and intervenes	Teacher ignores groups
Group processing occurs	No group processing

Source: D.W. Johnson, R. Johnson, & E. Holubec: *Circles of learning: Cooperation in the classroom* (3rd ed.) Edina, MN. Interaction, 1990, p. 16. Reprinted with permission of authors.

NATURE AND APPROPRIATE USE
OF COOPERATIVE LEARNING

You have just presented a problem to a group of students by asking how long a candle will burn in a quart jar. Instead of a single answer, the class comes up with a range of answers that are the results of their experiments. You ask why all students did not get the same answer, and the students suggest that the shape of the quart jar and whether or not a previous candle has been burned in the jar might affect the answers. You then ask, "How many things can your group find that make a difference in how long the candle burns?" A large piece of paper is taped to the wall to collect suggestions, and the students are encouraged to check out their ideas with each other and have other students double-check suggestions by repeating the experiment. The goal structure described in this situation is cooperative. In this chapter the conditions under which cooperative learning can be appropriately used are discussed, and the teacher's role in structuring cooperative activities is detailed (see Table 3.2). The skills students need to function effectively within a cooperative learning situation are presented in Chapter 7.

Since cooperative learning has been discussed at some length in Chapters 1 and 2, the discussion of the appropriate use of cooperative learning will be brief.

Interdependence

Cooperative learning exists when students' goal attainments are positively correlated; when one student obtains his or her goal, all other students with whom he

TABLE 3.2 Appropriate Cooperative Learning

Interdependence	Positive
Type of Instructional Activity	Any instructional activity. The more conceptual and complex the task, the greater the superiority of cooperative over competitive or individualistic learning.
Peception of Goal Importance	Goal is perceived to be important.
Teacher-Student Interaction	Teacher monitors and intervenes in learning groups to teach collaborative skills.
Student-Materials Interaction	Materials are arranged according to purpose of lesson.
Student-Student Interaction	Prolonged and intense interaction among students, helping and sharing, oral rehearsal of material being studied, peer tutoring, and general support and encouragement.
Student Expectations	Group to be successful. All members to contribute to success. Positive interaction among group members. All members master the assigned material.
Room Arrangement	Small groups.
Evaluation Procedures	Criterion-referenced.

or she is cooperatively linked obtain their goals (Deutsch, 1949). The learning goal is perceived to be important, and students expect to achieve the goal with some help and assistance from fellow group members.

Appropriate Tasks

Cooperation is appropriate for any instructional task. The more conceptual the task, the more problem solving and decision making required; and the more creative answers need to be, the greater the superiority of cooperative over competitive and individualistic learning. Whenever problem solving is desired, whenever divergent thinking or creativity is desired, whenever quality of performance is expected, whenever higher-level reasoning strategies are needed, whenever long-term retention is desired, whenever the task is complex or conceptual, whenever the learning goals are highly important, and whenever the social development of students is one of the major instructional goals, cooperative learning should be used.

Teacher-Student Interaction

The teacher is used infrequently as a source of ideas and solutions. The teacher monitors the functioning of the learning groups and intervenes to teach collaborative skills and provide task assistance when it is needed. The teacher is more a consultant to promote effective group functioning than a technical expert. Typical statements a teacher may make are, "Check with your group"; "Does anyone in your group know"; "Make sure everyone in your group understands."

Student-Materials Interaction

Depending on the instructional goals, each student may receive an individual set of materials, the group may receive one set of materials, or students may receive part of the required materials and be responsible for teaching their portion to the other group members.

Student-Student Interaction

Other students are perceived to be the major resource for assistance, feedback, reinforcement, and support. Students should be sitting so that each student can see all the other members of the group and can be heard without needing to shout (and disturb the other groups). These small groups should be spaced in the classroom in such a way as to maximize the distance between them.

Student Role Expectations

Students expect to interact with other students, sharing ideas and materials, supporting and encouraging academic achievement, and holding each other accountable for learning. Students will expect their group to be successful and for every member to contribute in some way to that success.

Evaluation System

A criterion-referenced evaluation system is used within cooperative learning situations.

ESTABLISHING A COOPERATIVE STRUCTURE

There is more to the teacher's role in structuring cooperative learning situations, however, than structuring cooperation among students. The teacher's role includes five major sets of strategies (Johnson, Johnson, & Holubec, 1990):

1. Clearly specifying the objectives for the lesson.
2. Making certain decisions about placing students in learning groups before the lesson is taught.
3. Clearly explaining the task and goal structure to the students.
4. Monitoring the effectiveness of the cooperative learning groups and intervening to provide task assistance (such as answering questions and teaching task skills) or to increase students' interpersonal and group skills.
5. Evaluating the students' achievement and helping students discuss how well they collaborated with each other.

The following nineteen steps elaborate these strategies and detail a procedure for structuring cooperative learning. Specific examples of lessons may be found in Johnson, Johnson, and Holubec (1987). There are also two films available demonstrating the use of cooperative learning procedures (*Belonging* and *Circles of Learning*).

Specifying the Instructional Objectives

There are two types of objectives that a teacher needs to specify before the lesson begins. The *academic objective* needs to be specified at the correct level for the students and matched to the right level of instruction according to a conceptual or task analysis. The *collaborative skills objective* details the collaborative skills that will be emphasized during the lesson. A common error many teachers make is to specify only academic objectives and to ignore the collaborative skills needed to train students to cooperate with each other.

Deciding on the Size of the Group

Once the objectives of the lesson are clear, the teacher must decide which size of learning group is optimal. Cooperative learning groups tend to range in size from two to six. A number of factors should be considered in selecting the size of a cooperative learning group:

1. As the size of the learning group increases, the range of abilities, expertise, and skills increases, as does the number of minds available for acquiring and processing information. The more group members you have, the more chance to have someone who has special knowledge helpful to the group and the more willing hands and talents are available to do the task.

2. The larger the group, the more skillful group members must be in providing everyone with a chance to speak, coordinating the actions of group members, reaching consensus, ensuring explanation and elaboration of the material being learned, keeping all members on task, and maintaining good working relationships. Within a pair students have to manage two interactions. Within a group of three there are six interactions to manage. Within a group of four there are twelve interactions to manage. As the size of the group increases, the interpersonal and small group skills required to manage the interactions among group members become far more complex and sophisticated. Very few students have the social skills needed for effective group functioning even for small groups. A common mistake made by many teachers is to have students work in groups of four, five, and six members before the students have the skills to do so competently.

3. The materials available or the specific nature of the task may dictate a group size.

4. The shorter the period of time available, the smaller the learning group should be. If there is only a brief period of time available for the lesson, then smaller groups will be more effective because they take less time to get organized, they operate faster, and there is more "air time" per member.

Our best advice to beginning teachers is to start with pairs or threesomes. When students become more experienced and skillful, they will be able to manage larger groups. Six may be the upper limit for a cooperative learning group. More members would be cumbersome even for very socially skilled students. In one classroom we recently observed, the teacher had divided the class into "committees" of eight. In the typical committee some students were being left out, others were passive, and some were engaged in a conversation with only one or two members. Cooperative learning groups have to be small enough that everyone is engaged in mutual discussion while achieving the group's goals. So be cautious about group size. Some students will not be ready for a group as large as four.

Assigning Students to Groups

Teachers often ask four basic questions about assigning students to groups:

1. Should students be placed in learning groups homogeneous or heterogeneous in member ability?   There are times when cooperative learning groups that are homogeneous in ability may be used to master specific skills or to achieve certain instructional objectives. Generally, however, we recommend that teachers maximize the heterogeneity of students, placing high-, medium-, and low-ability students within the same learning group. More elaborative thinking, more frequent giving and receiving of explanations, and greater perspective taking in discussing material seem to occur in heterogeneous groups, all of which increase the depth of understanding, the quality of reasoning, and the accuracy of long-term retention.

2. Should nontask-oriented students be placed in learning groups with task-oriented peers or be separated?   To keep nonacademically oriented students on task, it often helps to place them in a cooperative learning group with task-oriented peers.

3. Should students select whom they want to work with, or should the teacher assign students to groups?   Teacher-made groups often have the best mix, since teachers can put together optimal combinations of students. Random assignment, such as having students "count off" is another possibility for getting a good mix of students in each group. Having students select their own groups is often not very successful. Student-selected groups often are homogeneous with high-achieving students working with other high-achieving students, white students working with other white students, minority students working with other minority students, and males working with other males. Often there is less on-task behavior in student-selected than in teacher-selected groups. A useful modification of the "select your own group" method is to have students list whom they would like to work with and then place them in a learning group with one person they choose and one or two or more students that the teacher selected.

4. How long should the groups stay together?   Actually, there is no formula or simple answer to this question. Some teachers keep cooperative learning groups together for an entire year or semester. Other teachers like to keep a learning group together only long enough to complete a unit or chapter. In some schools student attendance is so unpredictable that teachers form new groups every day. Sooner or later, however, every student should work with every other classmate. An elementary setting allows students to be in several different learning groups during the day. Our best advice is to allow groups to remain stable long enough for them to be successful. Breaking up groups that are having trouble functioning effectively is often counterproductive because the students do not learn the skills they need to resolve problems in collaborating with each other.

There is merit in having students work with everyone in their class during a semester or school year. Building a strong positive feeling of collaboration across an entire class and giving students opportunities to practice the skills needed to begin new groups can add much to a school year. Never underestimate the power of heterogeneous cooperative learning groups in promoting high-quality, rich, and involved learning.

Arranging the Room

How the teacher arranges the room is a symbolic message of what is appropriate behavior, and it can facilitate the learning groups within the classroom. Members of a learning group should sit close enough to each other that they can share materials, maintain eye contact with all group members, and talk to each other quietly without disrupting the other learning groups. Circles are usually best. The teacher should have a clear access lane to every group. Common mistakes that teachers make in arranging a room are to (1) place students at a rectangular table where they cannot have eye contact with all the other members and (2) move several desks together, which may place students too far apart to communicate quietly with each other and share materials. Within each learning group students need to be able to see all relevant task materials, see each other, converse with each other without raising their voices, and exchange ideas and materials in a comfortable atmosphere. "Knee-to-knee and eye-to-eye"—the closer the better. The groups, of course, need to be far enough apart so that they do not interfere with each other's learning.

Planning the Instructional Materials to Promote Interdependence

Materials need to be distributed among group members so that all members participate and achieve. When a group is mature and experienced and group members have a high level of collaborative skills, the teacher may not have to arrange materials in any specific way. When a group is new or when members are not very skilled, however, teachers may wish to distribute materials in carefully planned ways to communicate that the assignment is to be a joint (not an individual) effort and that the students are in a "sink or swim together" learning situation. Three of the ways of doing so are as follows:

1. *Materials interdependence:* Give only one copy of the materials to the group. The students will then have to work together in order to be successful. This method is especially effective the first few times the group meets. After students are accustomed to collaborating with each other, teachers will wish each student to have an individual copy of the materials.

2. *Information interdependence:* Group members may each be given different books or resource materials to be synthesized. Or the materials may be arranged like a jigsaw puzzle so that each student has part of the materials needed to complete the task. Such procedures require that every member participate in order for the group to be successful.

3. *Interdependence from outside enemies:* Materials may be structured into a tournament format with intergroup competition as the basis for a perception of interdependence among group members. Such a procedure was introduced by DeVries and Edwards (1973). In the teams-games-tournament format students are divided into heterogeneous cooperative learning teams to prepare members for a tournament in which they compete with the other teams. During the intergroup competition

the students individually compete against members of about the same ability level from other teams. The team whose members do the best in the competition is pronounced the winner by the teacher.

All of these procedures may not be needed simultaneously. They are alternative methods of ensuring that students perceive that they are involved in a "sink or swim together" learning situation and behave collaboratively.

Assigning Roles to Ensure Interdependence

Positive interdependence may also be arranged through the assignment of complementary and interconnected roles to group members. Each group member is assigned a responsibility that must be fulfilled for the group to work effectively. Such roles include a *summarizer* (who restates the group's major conclusions or answers), a *checker* (who ensures that all group members can explicitly explain how to arrive at an answer or conclusion), an *accuracy coach* (who corrects any mistakes in another member's explanations or summaries), a *relater/elaboration seeker* (who asks members to relate current concepts and strategies to material studied previously), a *researcher-runner* (who gets needed materials for the group and communicates with the other learning groups and the teacher), a *recorder* (who writes down the group's decisions and edits the group's report), an *encourager* (who reinforces members' contributions), and an *observer* (who keeps track of

One can acquire everything in solitude—except character. —*Henri Beyle*

No man is an island, entire of itself; every man is a piece of the continent, a part of the main. —*John Donne*

Not vain the weakest, if their force unite. —*Homer*

United we stand, divided we fall. —*Aesop*

Union gives strength. —*Aesop*

Two heads are better than one. —*Heywood*

All for one, one for all, that is our device. —*Alexandre Dumas*

The true security is to be found in social solidarity rather than in isolated individual effort. —*Fyodor Dostoyevsky*

If we would seek for one word that describes society better than any other, the word is *cooperation.* —*Ashley Montagu*

There is no violent struggle between plants, no warlike mutual killing, but a harmonious development on a share-and-share-alike basis. The cooperative principle is stronger than the competitive one. —*Frits W. Went,* Plants how well the group is collaborating). Assigning such roles is an effective method of teaching students collaborative skills and fostering positive interdependence.

Explaining the Academic Task

Teachers explain the academic task so that students are clear about the assignment and understand the objectives of the lesson. Direct teaching of concepts, principles, and strategies may take place at this point. Teachers may wish to answer any questions students have about the concepts or facts they are to learn or apply in the lesson. Teachers need to consider several aspects of explaining an academic assignment to students:

1. *Set the task so that students are clear about the assignment.* Most teachers have considerable practice in this area already. Instructions that are clear and specific are crucial in warding off student frustration. One advantage of cooperative learning groups is that they can handle more ambiguous tasks (when they are appropriate) than can students working alone. In cooperative learning groups students who do not understand what they are to do will ask their group for clarification before asking the teacher.

2. *Explain the objectives of the lesson and relate the concepts and information to be studied to students' past experience and learning to ensure maximum transfer and retention.* Explaining the intended outcomes of the lesson increases the likelihood that students will focus on the relevant concepts and information throughout the lesson.

3. *Define relevant concepts, explain procedures students should follow, and give examples to help students understand what they are to learn and do in completing the assignment.* To promote positive transfer of learning, point out the critical elements that separate this lesson from past learning.

4. *Ask the class specific questions to check the students' understanding of the assignment.* Such questioning ensures thorough two-way communication, ensures that the assignment has been given effectively, and ensures that the students are ready to begin completing it.

Structuring Positive Goal Interdependence

Communicate to students that they have a group goal and must work collaboratively. We cannot overemphasize the importance of communicating to students that they are in a "sink or swim together" learning situation. In a cooperative learning group students are responsible for learning the assigned material, making sure that all other group members learn the assigned material, and making sure that all other class members successfully learn the assigned material, in that order. Teachers can do this a couple of ways:

1. *Ask the group to produce a single product, report, or paper.* Each group member should sign the paper to indicate that he or she agrees with the answers and can explain

why the answers are appropriate. Each student must know the material. When a group is producing only one product, it is especially important to stress individual accountability. Teachers may pick a student at random from each group to explain the rationale for their answers.

2. *Provide group rewards.* Bonus points and a total group score are ways to give students the "sink or swim together" message. An example is a spelling group where members work with each other during the week to make sure that all members learn their words correctly. They then take the test individually and are rewarded on the basis of the total number of words spelled correctly by all group members. Math lessons can be structured so that students work in cooperative learning groups, take a test individually, receive their individual score, and be given bonus points on the basis of how many group members reach a preset level of excellence. Some teachers have students work in cooperative learning groups, give individual tests, give students individual grades on the basis of their scores, and then reward groups where all members reach a preset criterion of excellence with free time or extra recess.

Positive interdependence creates peer encouragement and support for learning. Such positive peer pressure influences underachieving students to become academically involved. Members of cooperative learning groups should give interrelated messages, "Do your work—we're counting on you!" and "How can I help you to do better?"

Structuring Individual Accountability

The purpose of a cooperative group is to maximize the learning of each member. A group is not truly cooperative if members are "slackers" who let others do all the work. To ensure that all members learn and that groups know which members to provide with encouragement and help, teachers need to assess frequently the level of performance of each group member. Practice tests; randomly selecting members to explain answers; having members edit each other's work, teach what they know to someone else, and use what they have learned on a different problem; and randomly picking one paper from the group to grade are ways to structure individual accountability.

Structuring Intergroup Cooperation

The positive outcomes found within a cooperative learning group can be extended throughout a whole class by structuring intergroup cooperation. Bonus points may be given if all members of a class reach a preset criterion of excellence. When a group finishes its work, the teacher should encourage the members to help other groups complete the assignment.

Explaining Criteria for Success

Evaluation within cooperatively structured lessons needs to be criterion-referenced. Criteria must be established for acceptable work (rather than grading on a curve). Thus at the beginning of the lesson teachers should clearly explain the criterion by which the students' work will be evaluated. The criterion for success must be structured so that students may reach it without penalizing other students and so that groups may reach it without penalizing other groups. For some learning groups all members can be working to reach the same criterion. For other learning groups different members may be evaluated according to different criteria. The criterion should be tailored to be challenging and realistic for each individual group member. In a spelling group, for example, some members may not be able to learn as many as 20 words, and their number can be reduced accordingly. Teachers may structure a second level of cooperation by not only keeping track of how well each group and its members are performing, but also setting a criterion for the whole class to reach. Thus the number of words the total class spells correctly can be recorded from week to week with an appropriate criterion being set to promote classwide collaboration and encouragement. Criteria are important to give students information about what constitutes "doing well" on assigned tasks, but the criteria do not always have to be as formal as counting the number correct. On some assignments, simply completing the task may be adequate for a criterion. Or simply doing better this week than last may be the criterion of excellence.

Setting Up Group Contingencies

At times a teacher may wish to reward students using extrinsic reinforcements such as tokens or privileges within the school. When extrinsic reinforcements are used, they are made contingent upon certain behaviors and level of performances of students. Three basic alternative group contingencies may be used to promote cooperative behavior and achievement. The first is the *average performance group contingency*. All members of a group are reinforced on the basis of the average performance of all of the group members. Alternatively, the group may be reinforced on the basis of the high performances in the group. Thus, the highest scores of one-quarter of the group may be used as a basis for determining reinforcements. This procedure is referred to as a *high-performance group contingency*. Finally, a group may be reinforced on the basis of the low performances in the group; the lowest scores of one-quarter of the group are used as a basis for determining reinforcements under a *low performance group contingency*. Research on the use of these three types of group contingencies indicates that the most fruitful is the low performance group contingency. The performance of poor students is greatly raised, both through increased motivation to help their group and through tutoring by the more gifted students. The performance of the more gifted students is not hampered by the use of this group contingency. The overall performance of the group will be the highest when the low performance group contingency is used.

Specifying Desired Behaviors

The word *cooperation* has many different connotations and uses. Teachers will need to define cooperation operationally by specifying the behaviors that are appropriate and desirable within the learning groups. There are beginning behaviors, such as "stay with your group and do not wander around the room," "use quiet voices," "take turns," and "use each other's names." When groups begin to function effectively, expected behaviors may include

1. Having each member explain how to get the answer.
2. Asking each member to relate what is being learned to previous learning.
3. Checking to make sure everyone in the group understands the material and agrees with the answers.
4. Encouraging everyone to participate.
5. Listening accurately to what other group members are saying.
6. Not changing your mind unless you are logically persuaded (majority rule does not promote learning).
7. Criticizing ideas, not people.

Teachers should not make the list of expected behaviors too long. One or two behaviors to emphasize for a few lessons is enough. Students need to know what behavior is appropriate and desirable within a cooperative learning group, but they should not be subjected to information overload.

Monitoring Students' Behavior

The teacher's job begins in earnest when the cooperative learning groups start working. Resist that urge to go get a cup of coffee or grade some papers. Just because the teacher instructs students to cooperate and places them in learning groups does not mean that they will always do so. So, much of the teacher's time in cooperative learning situations should be spent observing group members in order to see what problems they are having in completing the assignment and in working collaboratively. A variety of observation instruments and procedures that can be used for these purposes can be found in Johnson and F. Johnson (1991).

Whenever possible, teachers should use a formal observation sheet to count the number of times they observe appropriate behaviors being used by students. The more concrete the data are, the more useful they are to the teacher and to students. Teachers should not try to count too many different behaviors at one time, especially when they first start formal observation. At first they may want just to keep track of who talks in each group to get a participation pattern for the groups. Our current list of behaviors (though rather long) includes contributing ideas, asking questions, expressing feelings, active listening, expressing support and acceptance (toward ideas), expressing warmth and liking (toward group members and group), encouraging all members to participate, summarizing, checking for understanding, relieving tension by joking, and giving direction to the group's work. All the behaviors we look for are positive behaviors that are to be praised when they are appropriately present and are a cause for discussion when they are missing. It is also a good idea for the teacher to collect notes on specific student behaviors so that the frequency data are extended. Especially useful are skillful interchanges that can be shared with students later as objective praise and perhaps with parents in conferences or telephone conversations.

Student observers can be used to get even more extensive data on each group's functioning. For very young students the system must be kept very simple, perhaps only "Who talks?" Many teachers have had good success with student observers, even in kindergarten. One of the more important things to do is for the teacher to make sure that the class is given adequate instructions (and perhaps practice) on gathering the observation data and sharing them with the group. The observer is in the best position to learn about the skills of working in a group. We can remember one first-grade teacher who had a student who talked all the time (even to himself while working alone). He tended to dominate any group he was in. When she introduced student observers to the class she made him an observer. One important rule for observers was not to interfere in the task but to gather data without talking. He was gathering data on who talks, and he did a good job, noticing that one student had done quite a bit of talking in the group while another had talked very little. The next day when he was a group member, and there was another observer, he was seen starting to talk, clamping his hand over his mouth, and glancing at the observer. He knew what skill was being observed and he didn't want to be the only one marked for talking. The teacher said he may have listened for the first time in the year. So the observer often benefits in learning about group skills.

When teachers are worried about losing the lesson content (observers, however, often know quite a bit about the lesson), then they can have the group as a last review take the observer through the material and see if they can get her signature on the paper as well. Often important changes are made during this review.

It is not necessary to use student observers all the time, and we would not recommend their use until cooperative learning groups are used a few times. It is enough for teachers just to structure the groups to be cooperative in the beginning without having to worry about structuring student observers, too. Whether student observers are used or not, however, teachers should always do some observing and spend some time monitoring the groups. Sometimes a simple checklist is helpful in addition to a systematic observation form. Some questions to ask on the checklist might include the following:

1. Do students understand the task?
2. Have students accepted the positive interdependence and the individual accountability?

3. Are students working toward the criteria, and are those criteria for success appropriate?

4. Are students practicing the specified behaviors, or not?

Providing Task Assistance

In monitoring the groups as they work, teachers will wish to clarify instructions, review important procedures and strategies for completing the assignment, answer questions, and teach task skills as necessary. In discussing the concepts and information to be learned, teachers will wish to use the language or terms relevant to the learning. Instead of saying, "Yes, that is right," teachers will wish to say something more specific to the assignment, such as, "Yes, that is one way to find the main idea of a paragraph." The use of the more specific statement reinforces the desired learning and promotes positive transfer by helping the students associate a term with their learning.

Intervening to Teach Collaborative Skills

While monitoring the learning groups teachers will also find students who do not have the necessary collaborative skills and groups where problems in collaborating have arisen. In these cases the teacher will wish to intervene to suggest more effective procedures for working together and more effective behaviors for students to engage in. Teachers may also wish to intervene and reinforce particularly effective and skillful behaviors that they notice. At times the teacher becomes a consultant to a group in order to help it function more effectively. When it is obvious that group members lack certain social skills they need in order to cooperate with each other, the teacher will want to intervene in order to help the members learn the collaborative skills. The social skills required for productive group work, along with activities that may be used in teaching them, are covered in Johnson and F. Johnson (1987) and Johnson (1990, 1987).

Teachers should not intervene any more than is absolutely necessary in the groups. Most of us as teachers are geared to jumping in and solving problems for students to get them back on track. With a little patience we would find that cooperative groups can often work their way through their own problems (task and maintenance) and acquire not only a solution, but also a method of solving similar problems in the future. Choosing when to intervene and when not to is part of the art of teaching and with some restraint, teachers can usually trust their intuition. Even when intervening, teachers can turn the problem back to the group to solve. Many teachers intervene in a group by having members set aside their task, pointing out the problem, and asking the group to come up with an adequate solution. (The last thing teachers want to happen is for the students to learn to come running to the teacher with every problem.)

In one third-grade class, the teacher noticed when passing out papers that one student was sitting back away from the other three. A moment later the teacher glanced over and only three students were sitting where four were a moment before. As she watched, the three students came marching over to her and complained that Johnny was under the table and wouldn't come out. "Make him come out!" they insisted (the teacher's role: police officer, judge, and executioner). The teacher told them that Johnny was a member of their group and asked how they had tried to solve their problem. "Tried?" was the puzzled reply. "Yes, have you asked him to come out?" the teacher suggested. The group marched back, and the teacher continued passing out papers to groups. A moment later the teacher glanced over to their table and saw no heads above the table (which is one way to solve the problem). After a few more minutes, four heads came struggling out from under the table and the group (including Johnny) went back to work with great energy. We don't know what happened under that table, but whatever it was, it was effective. What makes this story even more interesting is that the group received 100 percent on the paper, and later, when the teacher was standing by Johnny's desk, she noticed he had the paper clutched in his hand. The group had given Johnny the paper, and he was taking it home. He confided to the teacher that this was the first time he could ever remember earning 100 percent on anything in school. (If that was your record, you might slip under a few tables yourself.)

The best time to teach cooperative skills is when the students need them. Intervening should leave a cooperative learning group with new skills that will be useful in the future. It is important that the cooperative skills be taught in the context of the class where they are going to be used, or are practiced in that setting, because transfer of skill learning from one situation to another cannot be assumed. Students learn about cooperative skills when they are taught them, and learn cooperative skills when applying them in the midst of science, math, or English. The good news about cooperative skills is that they are taught and learned like any other skill. At a minimum,

1. Students need to recognize the need for the skill.
2. The skill must be defined clearly and specifically, including what students should say when engaging in the skill.
3. The practice of the skill must be encouraged. Sometimes just the teacher standing there with a clipboard and pencil will be enough to promote student enactment of the skill.
4. Students should have the time and procedures for discussing how well they are using the skill. Students should persevere in the practice until the skill is appropriately internalized. We never drop a skill, we only add on.

For older students (upper elementary school and above) the skills have been well described in *Joining Together* (Johnson & F. Johnson, 1991) and *Reaching Out* (Johnson, 1990). For younger students, teachers may need to revise and rename cooperative skills. Some primary teachers use symbols like traffic signs with a "green light" to represent encouraging participation, a "stop sign" to mean time to summarize, and "slippery when wet" to mean "say that over again, I don't quite understand." Sometimes a more mechanistic structure is beneficial for young students. In one first-grade class the teacher had a number of students who liked to take over the group and dominate. One day in frustration, she formed groups and handed out five poker chips to each group member, with a different color for each group member. The students were instructed to place a chip in the box every time they spoke while they worked on the worksheet. When a student had "spent" all his or her chips, he or she could not speak. When all the chips were in the box, they could get their five colored chips back and start again. There were several surprised students when their five chips were the only chips in the box! Teachers only have to use this device once or twice to get the message across (although first-grade students can get addicted to chips, so watch out). This technique was later used in a monthly principals' meeting. As the principals came in, each was handed several colored strips of paper. When they spoke . . .

Teaching your students how to work together effectively is a necessary part of implementing cooperative learning in your classroom. We would recommend that only a few skills be taught in one semester. Most of the curriculum programs with cooperative learning groups written into them feature about five to eight cooperative skills for a year.

Providing Closure to the Lesson

At the end of the lesson students should be able to summarize what they have learned and to understand where they will use it in future lessons. Teachers may wish to summarize the major points in the lesson, ask students to recall ideas or give samples, and answer any final questions students have.

Evaluating the Quality and Quantity of Students' Learning

The product required from the lesson may be a report, a single set of answers that all members of the group agree to, the average of individual examination scores, or the number of group members reaching a specific criterion. Whatever the measure, the learning of group members needs to be evaluated by a criterion-referenced system. Besides assessing students on how well they learn the assigned concepts and information, group members should also receive feedback on how effectively they collaborated. Some teachers give two grades, one for achievement and one for collaborative behavior.

Assessing How Well the Group Functioned

An old observational rule is, *If you observe, you must process your observations with the group.* Even if class time is limited, some time should be spent talking about how well the groups functioned today, what things were done well, and what things could be improved. Each learning group may have its own observer and spend time discussing how effectively members are working together. Teachers may also wish to spend some time in *whole-class processing*, in which they give the class feedback, have students share incidents that occurred in their groups, and have the students describe how problems were solved. Names do not need to be used, but the feedback should be as specific as possible.

Discussing group functioning is essential. A common teaching error is to provide too brief a time for students to process the quality of their collaboration. Students do not learn from experiences that they do not reflect on. If the learning groups are to function better tomorrow than they did today, members must receive feedback, reflect on how their actions may be more effective, and plan how to be even more skillful during the next group session.

Every small group has two primary goals: (1) to accomplish the task successfully, and (2) to build and maintain constructive relationships in good working order for the next task. Learning groups are often exclusively task-oriented and ignore the importance of maintaining effective working relationships among members. Group sessions should be enjoyable, lively, and pleasant experiences. If no one is having fun, something is wrong. Problems in collaborating should be brought up and solved, and there should be a continuing emphasis on improving the effectiveness of the group members in collaborating with each other.

Often during the "working" part of the class period, students will be very task-oriented, and the "maintenance" of the group may suffer. During the processing time, however, the emphasis is on maintenance of the group, and the students leave the room ready for (a better?) tomorrow. If no processing is done, teachers may find the group's functioning decaying and important relationship issues left undiscussed. Processing may not need to occur each day in depth, but it should happen often. Processing the functioning of the group needs to be taken as seriously as accomplishing the task. The two are very much related. Teachers often have students turn in a "process sheet" along with the paper from the task assignment.

Group processing provides a structure for group members to hold each other accountable for being responsible and skillful group members. In order to contribute to each other's learning, group members need to attend class, be prepared (i.e., have done the necessary homework), and contribute to the group's work. A student's absenteeism and lack of preparation often demoralizes other members. Productive group work requires members to be present and prepared, and there should be some peer accountability to be so. When groups "process," they discuss any member actions that need to be improved in order for everyone's learning to be maximized.

Groups new to processing often need an agenda, including specific questions each group member must address. Inexperienced groups tend to say, "We did fine. Right? Right!" and not deal with any real issues. A simple agenda could be to have each group name two things they did well (and document them) and one thing they need to be even better at, or would like to work harder on.

Structuring Academic Controversies

Within cooperative groups students often disagree as to what answers to assignments should be and how the group should function in order to maximize members' learning. Conflict is an inherent part of learning as old conclusions and conceptions are challenged and modified to take into account new information and broader perspectives. *Controversy* is a type of academic conflict that exists when one student's ideas, information, conclusions, theories, and opinions are incompatible with those of another, and the two seek to reach an agreement. When students become experienced in working cooperatively, and when teachers wish to increase students' emotional involvement in learning and motivation to achieve, teachers may structure controversy into cooperative learning groups by structuring five phases (Johnson & Johnson, 1987; Johnson, Johnson, & Smith, 1986):

1. Assign students to groups of four, then divide the group into two pairs. One pair is given the pro position and the other pair is given the con position on an issue being studied. Each pair prepares their position.
2. Each pair presents its position to the other pair.
3. Students argue the two positions.
4. Pairs reverse perspectives and argue the opposing position.
5. Groups of four reach a decision and come to a consensus on a position that is supported by facts and logic and can be defended by each group member.

Conclusion

These nineteen aspects of structuring learning situations cooperatively blend together to make effective, cooperative learning groups a reality in the classroom. They may be used in any subject area with students of any age. One of the things we have been told many times by teachers who have mastered these strategies and integrated cooperative learning groups into their teaching is, "Don't say it is easy!" We know it's not. It can take years to become an expert. There is a lot of pressure to teach like everyone else, to have students learn alone, and not to let students look at each other's papers. Students will not be accustomed to working together and are likely to have a competitive orientation. You may wish to start small by taking one subject area or one class and use cooperative learning until you feel comfortable, and then expand into other subject areas or other classes. In order to implement cooperative learning successfully, you will need to teach students the interpersonal and small-group skills required to collaborate, structure, and orchestrate intellectual inquiry within learning groups and form collaborative relations with others. Implementing cooperative learning in your classroom is not easy, but it is worth the effort.

WHAT ABOUT SCHOOL STAFF?

Teacher effectiveness is closely related to cooperative efforts. For teachers to improve their instructional effectiveness, they must continually improve their teaching expertise. Teaching expertise begins with mastering teaching strategies conceptually. Teachers must conceptually understand (a) the nature of the strategies they are using, (b) how to implement the strategies step by step, and (c) the results expected from the effective implementation of the strategies. Teachers must also think critically about the strategy and adapt it to their specific students and subject areas. They must retain what they have learned, integrate it into their conceptual networks about teaching, and conceptually combine the new strategy with their existing teaching strategies. Such conceptual understanding is enhanced when teachers *orally summarize, explain, and elaborate* what they know about the teaching strategy to colleagues. Oral reviews consolidate and strengthen what is known and provide relevant feedback about the degree to which mastery and understanding have been achieved. The way people conceptualize material and organize it cognitively is markedly different when they are learning material for their own benefit from when they are learning material to teach to others (Murray, 1983). Material being learned to be taught is learned at a higher conceptual level than is material being learned for one's own use. Such discussions, furthermore, enable the listeners to benefit from others' knowledge, reasoning, and skills. The concept of "gatekeeper," for example, was created to explain the process of information flow through an organization. A *gatekeeper* is a colleague who is sought out to explain what a new strategy is and how it may be used.

Once a strategy has been conceptually mastered, it must be implemented. If teachers are to progress through the initial awkward and mechanical stages to a routine-use, automatic level of mastery, they must (a) receive continual feedback as to the accuracy of their implementation and (b) be encouraged to persevere in their implementation attempts long enough to integrate the new strategy into their ongoing instructional practice. Thus productivity hinges on having colleagues to co-plan and co-teach lessons, observe one's implementation efforts, provide feedback, and encourage one to keep trying until the strategy is used routinely without conscious thought. Needless to say, such procedural learning usually does not take place within competitive and individualistic situations.

BACK TO THE BASICS

The importance of cooperative learning goes beyond maximizing outcomes such as achievement, positive attitudes toward subject areas, and the ability to think critically, although these are worthwhile outcomes. Knowledge and skills are of no use if the student cannot apply them in cooperative interaction with other people. Being able to perform technical skills such as reading, speaking, listening, writing, computing, and problem solving is valuable but of little use if the person cannot apply those skills in cooperative interaction with other people. It does no good to train an engineer, secretary, accountant, teacher, or mechanic if the person does not have the cooperative skills needed to apply the knowledge and technical skills in cooperative relationships on the job.

Much of what students learn in school is worthless in the real world. Schools teach that work means performing tasks largely by oneself, that helping and assisting others is cheating, that technical competencies are the only thing that matters, that attendance and punctuality are secondary to test scores, that motivation is up to the teacher, that success depends on performance on individual tests, and that promotions are received no matter how little one works. In the real world of work, things are altogether different. Most employers do not expect people to sit in rows and compete with colleagues without interacting with them. The heart of most jobs, especially the higher-paying, more interesting jobs, is teamwork, which involves getting others to cooperate, leading others, coping with complex power and influence issues, and helping solve people's problems in working with each other. Teamwork, communication, effective coordination, and divisions of labor characterize most real-life settings. It is time for schools to leave the ivory tower of working alone and sitting in rows to see who is best and more realistically reflect the realities of adult life.

Students increasingly live in a world characterized by interdependence, pluralism, conflict, and rapid change. Because of technological, economic, ecological, and political interdependence, the solution of most problems cannot be achieved by one country alone. The major problems faced by individuals (e.g., contamination of the environment, warming of the atmosphere, world hunger, international terrorism, nuclear war) are increasing ones that cannot be solved by actions taken only at the national level. Our students will live in a complex, interconnected world in which cultures collide every minute and dependencies limit the flexibility of individuals and nations. The internationalization of problems will increase so that there will be no clear division between domestic and international problems. Students need to learn the competencies involved in managing interdependence, resolving conflicts within cooperative systems made up of parties from different countries and cultures, and personally adapting to rapid change.

Quality of life depends on having close friends who last a lifetime, building and maintaining a loving family, being a responsible parent, caring about others, and contributing to the well-being of the world. These are things that make life worthwhile. Grades in school do not predict which students will have a high quality of life after they are graduated. The ability to work cooperatively with others does. The ability of students to work collaboratively with others is the keystone to building and maintaining the caring and committed relationships that largely determine quality of life.

4

Structuring Individualistic Learning

NATURE AND APPROPRIATE USE OF INDIVIDUALISTIC LEARNING

Love many, trust few.
Learn to paddle your own canoe.

Stand on your own two feet.

Horatio Alger

You have just handed out a four-page programmed booklet on how to use a microscope. You explain, "For some of the things we are going to be doing, each student will need to know how to use a microscope. I will give each of you a microscope and the other things you will need to work through this booklet. Take your time and work carefully until you have mastered the tasks outlined in the booklet. Let me know if you need help with anything." You then see that each student has a microscope and set of materials, and you begin to move from student to student to see how they are progressing. The goal structure described in this learning situation is individualistic. In this chapter the conditions under which individualistic learning can be appropriately used are discussed, and the teacher's role in structuring individualistic learning activities is detailed. Finally, the skills students need to function effectively in an individualistic learning situation are discussed.

Interdependence

Individualistic learning exists when the achievement of one student is unrelated to and independent from the achievement of other students; whether or not a student achieves his or her goal has no bearing on whether other students achieve their goals (see Table 4.1). In other words, no interdependence results in a situation in which individuals work alone to reach a preset criterion of excellence. In such a situation, individuals

1. *Recognize that they have an individual fate* unrelated to the fates of their peers.
2. *Strive for self-benefit* to do the best they can irrespective of how their peers perform.
3. *Have a short-term time perspective* focused on maximizing their performance.
4. *Recognize that their identity depends on how their performance compares* with the preset criterion of excellence. Individuals expect to celebrate their individual success by themselves, with only their superiors (manager, teacher, or parent) emotionally involved in their performance. Individuals are basically indifferent to peers' successes or failures. Individuals do not cathect to their peers or the experience.
5. Recognize that their performance is *self-caused* by their own ability and effort. Individuals feel responsibility only to themselves and are invested in only their own

TABLE 4.1   Appropriate Individualistic Learning

Interdependence	None
Instructional Tasks	Simple skill or knowledge acquisition; assignment is clear and behavior specified to avoid confusion and need for extra help
Perception of Goal Importance	Goal is perceived as important for each student; students see task as worthwhile and relevant; and each student expects eventually to achieve the goal.
Student Expectations	Each student expects to be left alone by other students; to work at own pace; to take a major part of the responsibility for completing the task; to take a major part in evaluating own progress and the quality of own efforts toward learning.
	Isolation, self-pacing, self-responsibility, self-evaluation.
Teacher-Student Interaction	Teacher is perceived to be the major source of assistance, feedback, reinforcement, and support.
Teacher Statements	"Do not bother David while he is working." "Raise your hand if you need help." "Let me know when you are finished."
Student-Student Interaction	None; students work on their own with little or no interaction with classmates.
Student-Materials Interaction	Complete set of materials and instructions for each student. Rules, procedures, answers are clear. Adequate space for each student.
Room Arrangement	Separate desks or carrels with as much space between students as can be provided.
Evaluation System	Criterion-referenced.

success. They are obligated to the manager or teacher, but not to their peers. Individuals are not open to influence, are not *inducible* to their peers. Peers' actions do not substitute for individuals' actions.

Working alone does not marshal a number of motives into the service of productivity. Affiliation needs and the desire to be involved in relationships with others may operate directly against productivity in individualistic situations.

ESSENTIAL ELEMENTS OF INDIVIDUALISTIC SITUATIONS

God helps them that help themselves.

Benjamin Franklin

Individuals are more effective when they can appropriately cooperate, compete, and work autonomously on their own. Being able to work individualistically on one's own when it is appropriate is an important competence. Individualistic efforts, however, must be appropriately structured to avoid a number of problems and barriers.

Appropriate Tasks

Individualistic situations are most appropriate when unitary, nondivisible, simple tasks need to be completed, such as the learning of specific facts or the acquisition or the performance of simple skills. The directions for completing the learning task need to be clear and specific so that students do not need further clarification on how to proceed and how to evaluate their work. It is important to avoid confusion as to how the students are to proceed and the need for extra help from the teacher. If several students need help or clarification at the same time, work grinds to a halt. Finally, the learning goal must be perceived as important, and students should expect to be successful in achieving their learning goals.

Importance of Goal: Relation to Cooperative Learning

Individualistically structured learning activities can supplement cooperative learning through a division of labor in which each student learns material or skills to be subsequently used in cooperative activities. Learning facts and simple skills to be used in subsequent cooperative learning projects increases the perceived relevance and importance of individualistic tasks. Within individualistic learning situations it is crucial that students perceive the task as relevant and worthwhile. Self-motivation is a key aspect of individualistic efforts. The more important and relevant students perceive the learning goal to be, the more motivated they will be to learn. Within classrooms, for example, students may individualistically learn facts and simple skills to be used subsequently in a cooperative project. Most divisions of labor are individualistic efforts within the context of an overall cooperative project. The goal must be perceived to be important enough so that concentrated effort is committed to achieving it. It is the overall cooperative effort that provides the meaning to individualistic work. It is contributing to the cooperative effort that makes individualistic goals important.

Be thou thine own home, and in thyself dwell. —*John Donne*

The man who goes alone can start today, but he who travels with another must wait till that other is ready. —*Henry David Thoreau*

"If everybody minded their own business," said the Duchess in a hoarse growl, "the world would go round a deal faster than it does." —*Lewis Carroll*

God helps them that help themselves. —*Benjamin Franklin*

If a man does not keep pace with his companions, perhaps it is because he hears a different drummer. Let him step to the music he hears however measured or far away. —*Henry David Thoreau*

How many a thing which we cast to the ground, when others pick it up becomes a gem! —*George Meredith*

Raphael paints wisdom, Handel sings it, Phidias carves it, Shakespeare writes it, Wren builds it, Columbus sails it, Luther preaches it, Washington arms it, Watt mechanizes it. —*Ralph Waldo Emerson*

Teacher-Student Interaction

Within individualistic learning situations the teacher is the major source of assistance, feedback, reinforcement, and support. Students should expect periodic visits from the teacher, and a great deal of teacher time may be needed to monitor and assist the students.

Student-Materials Interaction

Each student needs a complete set of all necessary materials to complete the work individually. Each student has to be a separate, self-contained learner. Programmed materials, task cards, and demonstrations are among the techniques that can be used to facilitate the task. Provide separate desks or carrels, allowing as much space between students as possible.

Student-Student Interaction

No interaction should occur among students. Students should work on their own without paying attention to or interacting with classmates. Each student should have his or her own space and should be separated from other students. Since each student is working on the task at his or her own pace, student-student interaction is intrusive and not helpful.

Student Role Expectations

Students expect to be left alone by their classmates in order to complete the assigned task, to work at their own pace in their own space, to take responsibility for completing the task, to take a major part in evaluating their own progress and the quality of their efforts, to be successful in achieving the learning goal, and to perceive the learning goal to be important.

Evaluation System

Evaluation should be conducted on a criterion-referenced basis. Students should work on their own toward a criterion that is set so that every student could conceivably be successful. There is an A for everyone if each student earns it individually.

ESTABLISHING AN INDIVIDUALISTIC STRUCTURE

The essence of an individualistic goal structure is giving students individual goals and using a criterion-referenced evaluation system to assign rewards. In a ninth-grade English class, the students have been reading a cluster of novels centering on the building of the railroads in the western United States. The teacher has taught a unit on character analysis covering the need to find out about the appearance, personality, and perspective of major characters in a story. The teacher now explains to the class that the names of several people from the novels are in a box and tells each student to draw a name. The assignment is for students to spend the next few days finding out as much as possible about their characters by reading appropriate passages in the novels and by using any other resources they can find. At the end of the week, there will be a number of discussions about the building of the railroad, and each student will be expected to introduce him- or herself and present the point of view of the selected character. Until the discussion students are to work on their own, each one gathering the necessary information on the fictional character; if students need help, they are to come to the teacher so as not to intrude on the work of classmates. The teacher will work with each student through the next few days to see that each has all the materials needed and has mastered the perspective of the character he or she has drawn, so that all can contribute to the discussions. The specific procedures for teachers to structure such an individualistic learning situation are given in the following paragraphs.

Objectives

1. Specifying instructional objectives. The academic objective needs to be specified at the correct level for each student and matched to the right level of instruction according to a conceptual or task analysis. Often the objective will be to learn specific information or a simple skill to be subsequently used in a cooperative learning situation. Examples include learning the bones and muscles of the arm and shoulder in order to teach it to classmates who are studying other parts of the body, learning the meaning of vocabulary words in order to compose a group story with more understanding, and gathering information for a section of a group report.

Decisions

2. Arranging the classroom. Adequate space must be provided for each student so that he or she can work without being interrupted by others. Examples of isolating students from looking at and being disrupted by classmates include using the perimeter of the classroom by having students face the wall, having students sit back to back, and staggering rows of seats.

3. Planning the instructional materials to promote independence. Structuring the materials to be used in the lesson is especially important for individualistic learning. Each student needs a set of self-contained materials. And usually, the materials need to contain a procedure for students to evaluate their own work. The programmed instruction format is often useful. The materials are the primary resource for learning in the individualistic situation.

Explaining the Task and Goal Structure

4. Explaining the academic task. The academic task needs to be explained in such a way that all students clearly understand what they are supposed to do, realize that they have all the materials they need, feel comfortable that they can do the

task, and realize why they are doing the task. When assigning the academic task, teachers will

a. Set the task so that students are clear about the assignment. Instructions that are clear and specific are crucial in warding off student frustration.

b. Explain the objectives of the lesson and relate the concepts and information to be studied to students' past experiences and learning to maximize transfer and retention. Explaining the intended outcomes of the lesson increases the likelihood that students will focus on the relevant concepts and information throughout the lesson.

c. Define relevant concepts, explain procedures students should follow, and give examples to help students understand what they are to learn and to do in completing the assignment. To promote positive transfer of learning, point out the critical elements that separate this lesson from past learning.

d. Ask the class specific questions to check the students' understanding of the assignment. Such questioning ensures that thorough two-way communication exists, that the assignment has been given effectively, and that the students are ready to begin completing it.

Students must perceive the task as relevant and have some idea of how the information and skills they are learning are going to be useful in future learning situations.

5. Structuring goal independence. Communicate to students that they have individual goals and must work individualistically. The basic individualistic goal is for students to work by themselves, at their own pace, to master the material specifically assigned to them, up to the preset criteria of excellence adjusted for their previous performances. Students should work by themselves without interrupting and interfering with the work of classmates. Students are to ask for assistance from the teacher, not from other students. Students who finish quickly should go beyond the specific assignment and find ways to embellish it.

6 Structuring individual accountability. The purpose of the individualistic goal structure is for students to attend to a specific task and master it on their own. Individual accountability may be structured by the teacher circulating through the room and randomly asking individual students to explain their work.

7. Explaining criteria for success. A criterion for excellence is set to orient students toward the level of mastery required in the lesson. Students need to know specifically what is an acceptable performance on the task that signifies that they have completed the task successfully. Setting a criterion ensures that students are aware that everyone who achieves up to criterion gets an A and, therefore, students are not in competition with each other. Whether one student does or does not learn the material does not affect the success of other students. Each student is rewarded separately on the basis of his or her own work.

8. Specifying desired behaviors.   The word *individualistic* has different connotations and uses. Teachers need to define *individualistic* operationally by specifying the behaviors that are appropriate and desirable within the learning situation, including the following:

a. Work alone without interacting with other students.
b. Focus on the task and tune out everything else.
c. Monitor your time and pace yourself accordingly.
d. Check with the teacher for help.

Students need to know what behaviors are appropriate and desirable within an individualistic learning situation.

Monitoring and Intervening

9. Monitoring students' behavior.   Much of the teacher's time should be spent in observing students in order to see what problems they are having in completing the assignment and in working individualistically. The teacher should move throughout the room, checking students for understanding, answering questions, and checking for the expected student behaviors. The teacher needs to be active while students are working. Some teachers allow students to come to their desk for help, but students may have to wait in line for assistance. It is more efficient to have the teacher periodically circulate through the classroom to assess the students' progress on their assigned tasks, how much the students understand, and what help each student needs to complete the assignment. This method allows teachers to work with students who are not requesting help as well as those who are. The teacher may wish to (a) observe the class as a whole to determine the number of students on task and exerting effort to achieve or (b) observe a few students intensely to obtain the data necessary for individual feedback and constructive suggestions on how to work more efficiently. Systematic observing provides feedback on how well the task is suited for individualistic work and how well students are working individualistically.

10. Providing task assistance.   In monitoring individual students as they work, teachers will wish to clarify instructions, review important procedures and strategies for completing the assignment, answer questions, and teach task skills as necessary. After the materials provided, the teacher is the major resource for student learning. In discussing the concepts and information to be learned, teachers should use the language or terms relevant to the learning. Instead of saying, "Yes, that is right," teachers may wish to say something more specific to the assignment, such as, "Yes, that is the suggested way to solve for the unknown in an equation." The use of specific statements reinforces the desired learning

Reprinted by permission of PLAN Individualized Learning System Division, Westinghouse Learning Corporation.

and promotes positive transfer. Typically, considerable task assistance is required within individualistic learning situations.

11. Intervening to teach individualistic skills. Although it is likely that students have experience in working alone, many students lack some of the basic skills necessary to work well individualistically. While monitoring the class, teachers sometimes find students without the necessary individualistic skills to work effectively on their own. These skills will need to be taught. Some of the basic skills needed in an individualistic learning situation are these:

a. Clarifying the need to learn the material and making a personal commitment to learning it.
b. Tuning out extraneous noise and visual distractions and focusing in on the academic task.
c. Monitoring own progress and pacing self through the material. Charts and records are often helpful in evaluating one's progress.
d. Evaluating one's readiness to apply the material or skills being learned.

It is important that students learn to work autonomously on their own in the school setting. It strengthens cooperative learning when students can learn needed simple skills and factual information individualistically or participate successfully in a division of labor.

In an individualistic situation teachers should intervene as quickly as possible. The amount of time in which students are struggling to work more efficiently should be minimized.

12. Providing closure to the lesson.   At the end of the lesson, students should be able to summarize what they have learned and to understand where they will use it in future lessons. To reinforce student learning, teachers may wish to summarize the major points in the lesson, ask students to recall ideas or give examples, and answer any final questions they may have.

Evaluation and Reinforcement

13. Evaluating and reinforcing the quality and quantity of students' learning.   Student learning needs to be evaluated by a criterion-referenced system. Each student will be evaluated independently of other students. The teacher sets a standard as to how many points a student will receive for mastering the assigned material at different levels of proficiency and gives each student the appropriate grade. Having students mark their progress on a chart is often helpful. Personal reinforcement needs to be given to each student. It is the teacher, not classmates, who gives praise for good work.

Teacher Role Checklist for Individualistic Instruction

1. What are the desired outcomes for the activity of learning specific knowledge and noncomplex skills?

2. Is the classroom arranged so that students
_____ are isolated at separate desks or by a seating arrangement that separates them as much as possible?
_____ are arranged to do their own work without approaching or talking with each other?
_____ have individual sets of self-contained materials?

3. Have you effectively communicated to students that
_____ the instructional goal is an individual goal (each student masters the material on his or her own)?
_____ each student will be rewarded on the basis of how his or her work meets a fixed set of standards for quality and quantity?

4. Have you effectively communicated the expected patterns of student-student interaction? Do student know that they
_____ should not interact with each other?
_____ should work on the assignment alone, trying to ignore completely the other students?
_____ should perceive teacher praise, support, or criticism of other students as irrelevant to their own mastery of the assigned materials?
_____ should go to the teacher for all help and assistance needed?

5. Have you effectively communicated the expected patterns of teacher-student interaction? Do students know that the teacher
_____ wants them to work by themselves and to master the assigned material without paying attention to other students, and will evaluate them on the basis of how their efforts match a fixed set of standards?
_____ will interact with each student individually, setting up learning contracts, viewing student progress, providing assistance, giving emotional support for effort, and answering questions individually?
_____ will praise and support students for working alone and ignoring other students?

INDIVIDUALISTIC SKILLS

Since there is no interaction with other students in an individualistic situation, learning under such a goal structure requires the fewest skills. Students need their own materials, enough space to be isolated from others, and a clear understanding of what they are supposed to do. The primary skill necessary is to be able to work on one's own, ignoring other students, and not being distracted or interrupted by what other students are doing.

Besides being able to "tune out" noises, movement, and distractions, students need to clarify why they need to learn the information or skill, make a personal commitment to do so, and assume responsibility for task completion. Each student must be motivated to complete the task and learn the assigned material on his or her own. Completing a task on one's own depends on the importance one assigns to mastering the material. The importance will probably be greatest when the results of the individualistic efforts are to be contributed to a group project in which students collaborate with each other. Having one's classmates depend on one for certain skills or facts increases one's motivation to learn them.

Third, students must be able to monitor their own progress, pace themselves through the material, and evaluate their own progress. Charts and records are often used to help students evaluate themselves. Self-tests are commonly used. Students must also be able to evaluate their readiness to apply the material or skills being learned.

Finally, students must take a personal pride and satisfaction from successfully completing individualistic assignments. While teachers can provide students some recognition, support, and reinforcement for individualistic success, the students must learn to give themselves needed "pats on the back" for a job well done.

Individualistic Efforts and Personal Autonomy

There is often a confusion between individualistic efforts and personal autonomy. The admiration given to individuals who have a strong sense of personal autonomy and who are able to resist social pressure and act independently is

often directed toward individualistic efforts. As will be discussed in depth in Chapter 10, individualistic efforts do not build personal autonomy. It is social support and caring personal relationships that do so. Individualistic efforts and personal autonomy are quite distinct and separate.

Problems in Implementing Individualistic Efforts

In implementing individualistic efforts there are potential problems that have to be faced and dealt with:

1. *Talking and interacting with others.* The more socializing and discussions that take place within an individualistic situation, the lower the productivity.
2. *Competing with others.* In American society, persons working individualistically in the proximity of others doing similar work begin to compete.
3. *Complex or new tasks.* Individualistic work is most appropriate on simple skill or knowledge acquisition tasks. If the task is new or complex, individualistic efforts are often inadequate.
4. *Unimportant goal.* For many people it is hard to stay motivated while working alone. If the goal is perceived to be unimportant, attention will quickly wane, and effort will be small.
5. *Unclear rules and procedures.* Confusion leads to inaction. In individualistic situations clarification comes from authority figures who may or may not have time to explain the task and procedure again and again until it is understood.
6. *Lack of materials and resources.* In individualistic situations every person must be a self-contained unit. If needed materials and resources are lacking, then individualistic efforts grind to a halt.
7. *Lack of essential skills.*

SUMMARY

The basic elements of an individualistic goal structure include each student working on his or her own toward a set criterion, having his or her own materials and space, perceiving the task as relevant and important, tuning out other students and distractions, and using the teacher as a resource. It is most appropriate to use the individualistic goal structure when the material to be learned is simple, straightforward, and needed for use in the near future. The jigsaw of materials in a cooperative group where each group member is to research a different part of the topic and then help the group synthesize the different aspects of the subject into one group report is an example of where students see a need to learn material on their own. The primary skill necessary is to be able to work on one's own, ignoring other students (that is, not being distracted or interrupted by what other students are doing).

The teacher's role in an individualistic learning situation is to arrange the room so that students will not be distracted by each other, give students their individual set of materials, explain that students are to work alone and check only with the teacher when they need help, set a clear criterion for success that everyone could conceivably reach, ask students to work on their own (clarifying the relevance of the assignment for themselves, tuning out distractions, and monitoring their own progress and pacing), circulating among the students and monitoring their work, intervening to teach skills or help students to refocus on their task, and giving students time to evaluate how well they have learned.

5

Structuring Competitive Learning

INTRODUCTION

After you have spent some time demonstrating how candles burn in jars under different conditions, bring in ten odd-sized and odd-shaped jars. Hold one up and ask, "Who can give me the best estimate of how long a candle will burn in this jar?" Then place the ten jars on tables around the room and assign three students to each jar. Assign the task of predicting how long a candle will burn in the jar, and structure the situation competitively by stating that the three students will be ranked from best to worst on the basis of the accuracy of their predictions. Do not make the reward for winning so important that students will lose the spirit of fun in the competition. Each student studies the jar, writes down the estimate on a slip of paper, and shares it with the two competitors. There is a feeling of excitement as you light each candle and place the jar over it. The students watch both the candle and the clock, timing the duration of its burning. When the candle goes out, there is good-natured congratulating of the winners. In this chapter the conditions under which competitive learning can be appropriately used are discussed, and the teacher's role in structuring competitive learning activities is detailed. Finally, the skills students need to function effectively within a competitive learning situation are given. But first, because many educators have concerns about the instructional use of interpersonal competition, the common criticisms of interpersonal competition are reviewed.

CRITICISMS OF INTERPERSONAL COMPETITION IN SCHOOLS

Historical Roots

In the 1930s an organized advocacy of interpersonal competition in the schools was launched by a combination of various business interests. In 1934, in the midst of the depression, the Liberty League was formed; it united with other business organizations, such as the National Association of Manufacturers, to sell interpersonal competition to educators. Their efforts were so successful that the use of interpersonal competition gained steam in the 1940s and 1950s, and by the 1960s interpersonal competition was considered to be the "traditional" way of structuring student-student interaction. In the 1950s emphasis was placed on norm-referenced evaluation under the rationale that all nature could be fitted on a bell-shaped curve. Social Darwinism, expressed in the myth that it was a "dog-eat-dog" world in which only the fittest survive, became widespread. Observational studies have found that competition and individualistic learning are used 85 to 95 percent of the time in American schools. There is evidence, furthermore, that (1) most students perceive school as being competitive, (2) American children are more competitive than are children from other countries, (3) American children become more competitive the longer they are in school or the older they become, (4) Anglo-American children are more competitive than are other American children (for instance, Mexican-American and black American children), and (5) urban children are more competitive than are rural children (Johnson & Johnson, 1974, 1983a).

> Only a few children in school ever become good at learning in the way we try to make them learn. Most of them get humiliated, frightened, and discouraged. They use their minds, not to learn, but to get out of doing the things we tell them to do—to make them learn. In the short run, these strategies seem to work. They make it possible for many children to get through their schooling even though they learn very little. But in the long run these strategies are self-limiting and self-defeating, and destroy both character and intelligence. The children who use such strategies are prevented by them from growing into more than limited versions of the human beings they might have become. This is the real failure that takes place in school; hardly any children escape. —*John Holt,* How Children Fail *(1964)*

Early Critics

There have been a number of critics of an emphasis on interpersonal competition in the classroom. A large number of educators, psychologists, and popular writers in the 1960s challenged the notion that competition must be an inevitable part of American education and that a large proportion of students experience failure (Glasser, 1969; Holt, 1964; Illich, 1971; Jackson, 1968; Johnson, 1970; Kagan, 1965; Kohl, 1969; Kohn, 1986; Nesbitt, 1967; Postman & Weingartner, 1969; Rathbone, 1970; Rogers, 1970; Silberman, 1971; Walberg & Thomas, 1971; Wilhelms, 1970). Their criticism of the use of interpersonal competition for instructional purposes included the subversion of intrinsic motivation for learning (in competition one learns to win, and knowledge that does not help one win is a waste of time), the valuing of "bettering" others, the joy taken in others' mistakes and failures (because they increase one's own chances for success), the viewing of life as a "rat race" aimed at outshining one's neighbors, the development of a contingent self-acceptance where one is of value only if one wins, feelings of guilt over winning and apprehension about being rejected by the individuals one has defeated, feelings of anger and hostility toward those who defeat one and toward the teacher, the school, and themselves, and in general feelings of anxiety, doubt, and self-orientation. Several of these criticisms are discussed in the following paragraphs.

> There is nothing new in all this. We have heard it before. During the latter half of the 19th century, and during the early part of the 20th century, this viewpoint formed the foundation for the doctrine of "Social Darwinism." It was implied in such ideas as "The Survival of the Fittest" and "The Struggle for Existence," and in such phrases as "The Weakest Go to the Wall," "Competition Is the Life-Blood of a Nation," and the like. Such ideas were not merely taken to explain, but were actually used to justify violence and war. —*Ashley Montagu (1965)*

Most Students Lose Most of the Time

John, a 34-year-old lawyer, was depressed. In trying to explain his depression to his psychotherapist, he stated, "All my life I've failed. I tried my best to be valedictorian of my high school class, and I finished second. I tried my best to be the top of my college class, and I finished third. I entered Harvard Law School and tried my best again to be the top of my class. I failed. I graduated seventh. Now my law firm has made me a partner a year later than I strived for. I've had failure after failure after failure. I'm having trouble sleeping. I'm depressed all the time. Often I feel that life isn't worth living."

Since there can be only one "winner" in a competitive situation, the vast majority of students will experience daily failure. Although there is limited evidence on the effects of prolonged failure, it seems reasonable to assume that a person's self-attitudes and feelings of competence will be affected. In the traditional competitive classroom, the purpose of classroom evaluation is to rank students from the "best" to the "worst" in order to separate the wheat from the chaff. In most classrooms, fairly stable patterns of achievement exist, so that the majority of students always lose and a few students always win. Thus a student may spend twelve years in public schools being confronted daily with the fact that he is a "loser." If the student desires to "win," the daily frustration of failing may be a concomitant of schooling. A sense of helplessness, worthlessness, and incompetence may result from such a situation. "Losers" in a competitive learning situation tend to perceive their learning experiences as boring, unfair, and not fun, and perceive themselves negatively (Crockenberg, Bryant, & Wilce, 1974). Atkinson (1965) predicted from his theory of achievement motivation that students who chronically experience failure will become primarily oriented toward avoiding failure (thus becoming nonachievement oriented). Failure, furthermore, reduces the attraction students feel toward classmates (Ashmore, 1970; Blanchard, Adelman, & Cook, 1975).

Cheating

Rules, the way most coaches see it, are made to be winked at. Education can be sacrificed. Winning is everything, it is the only thing. Coaches' desire to win has no morality.

Anonymous college coach

In a serious competition, winning becomes so important that participants will break the rules to enhance their chances. Richard Turbo (in an article in the *Chicago Tribune Magazine* published on July 31, 1977) stated:

> Admission to the nation's 114 medical schools is so highly prized that the competition among premedical students has reached ruthless levels. Cheating, sabotage, forgery, and academic dishonesty are no longer uncommon among students seeking to enhance their chances. They steal critical books from the library and from each other. They sabotage one another's science experiments in an attempt to gain an advantage in the battle for grades. . . . If they were to help each other, students are afraid that they might give an important edge on exams to their peers. . . . several premedical students told of their malicious activities. "Yes, we cheat," they said. "We try to give the wrong information to other students. We take books from the medical library and destroy parts of them. We don't share information. We sabotage others' chemistry experiments. . . ."

High school students have declared that cheating is universal, necessary, and very easy. Whenever an answer is not known, the students cheat. A survey of students in 61 central Florida elementary schools, high schools, and colleges found that nine out of ten students have cheated on tests or have copied assignments or homework. Cheating has become a part of school experience, a part of the stress on grades, on passing, on good results at all costs. Competition is the reason for cheating, because "if you are not counted among the winners, you are not counted." The Girl Scouts of America conducted a nationwide survey of students in grades 4–12 from 233 public, private, and parochial schools from September 14 to October 30, 1989. Sixty-five percent of the 5,012 students interviewed stated that given the chance, they would cheat on an important examination.

And it is not just the students. A highly regarded school principal in Maryland was recently dismissed for giving his students extra time to finish segments of the Iowa Tests for Educational Development, thus artificially boosting their scores to make himself look successful. The year before another Maryland principal had been forced to resign when it was learned that his students had earned dazzling scores on standardized tests because they had been pretested. Recently a study found that schools in almost all of the United States cheated to increase their students' scores on standardized tests. And it is not only schools. Insider stock trading scandals and fraud within the banking industry are additional examples.

Sport participants, as their competitive experience increases, become more committed to winning at any cost and less committed to values of fairness and justice (Kroll & Peterson, 1965; Loy, Birrell, & Rose, 1976; Webb, 1969). Competition has been found to inhibit empathic responses, and elite athletes, the ones who have weathered years of intense competition, have been found to be aloof and insensitive (Ogilvie & Tutko, 1971). Kleiber and Roberts (1981) found in a two-week study of soccer that crying occurred on three occasions as a result of perceived failure and injustice, and that quarreling took place at regular intervals, with a fistfight following one game. They also found that the participants with the most competitive experience were significantly less likely to behave altruistically and significantly more likely to behave in a rivalrous manner. The emphasis on winning in organized sport may lead children to become more rivalrous in social interactions with other children (Kagan & Madsen, 1972).

Overgeneralization of Results

Within competitions participants often overgeneralize the results. Winning seems to make a person more worthwhile, and losing seems to make a person less worthwhile. Brenda Bryant and her colleagues (Crockenberg, Bryant, & Wilce, 1974) found that children competing to write the best theme tended to see the winners as better students overall and more deserving people.

Interference with Adaptive Problem Solving

Competitive attitudes and behavioral patterns often interfere with individuals' capacity for adaptive problem solving. Nelson and Kagan (1972) found that American students so seldom cooperate spontaneously on the experimental tasks that it appeared that the environment provided for these children was barren of experiences that would sensitize them to the possibility of cooperation. Anglo-American children were found to engage in irrational and self-defeating competition by reducing their own rewards in order to reduce the rewards of peers even more. Nelson and Kagan (1972) stated:

> Anglo-American children are not only irrationally competitive, they are almost sadistically rivalrous. Given a choice, Anglo-American children took toys away from their peers on 78 percent of the trials even when they could not keep the toys for themselves. Observing the success of their actions, some of the children gloated. "Ha! Ha! Now you won't get a toy." Rural Mexican children in the same situation were rivalrous only half as often as the Anglo-American child.

The socialization of American children into competitive attitudes and orientations is so pervasive that Staub (1971) found that American children often believe that helping a person in distress is inappropriate and is disapproved of by others.

High Anxiety Levels

Competition tends to increase anxiety and makes people feel less able to perform. Tseng (1969), for example, found that as rewards increase in value, so do the tension and frustration of failure; children who failed in competitive situations performed poorly in subsequent competitions.

Inappropriate Generalization to Other Areas of People's Lives

The germ that is going around the office does not remain confined to the office for long. Someone brings it home, and the whole family comes down with it. The disease that starts in school or the workplace is carried into living rooms and even bedrooms. The disease is a self-centered, egocentric focus on gratifying one's own needs, even at the expense of others. The disease is a product of individualistic and competitive social structures. Its cure is learning how to cooperate with others.

No Contest

The most comprehensive critique of competition was written by Alfie Kohn (1986). He presents the thesis that gaining success by making others fail is an unproductive way of learning or working. In his book *No Contest,* Kohn summarizes data indicating that competition poisons relationships, causes anxiety, selfishness, self-doubt, poor communication, and aggression among individuals, and generally makes life unpleasant. He believes that the unfortunate consequences of competition are not restricted to "bad" or "excessive" competition; rather, they stem from the basic win/lose structure of competition. Kohn recommends that all competition be ended. Many students would agree. Despite the pervasive use of interpersonal competition there is solid evidence (see Johnson & Johnson, 1983b, 1986) that students actually prefer to work cooperatively with their classmates.

ADVOCATES OF COMPETITION

Not everyone, however, is against competition. The famous coach of the Green Bay Packers, Vince Lombardi, once said, "Winning isn't everything. It's the only thing!" George Allen, the well-known coach of the Washington Redskins, said: "Every time you win, you are reborn. Every time you lose, you die a little." Bill Musselman, the renowned basketball coach, commented: "Defeat is worse than death because you have to live with defeat!" Frank McGuire stated, "In this country, when you finish second, no one knows your name." Leo Durocher offered this advice: "Nice guys finish last!" Finally, even an ex-president of the United States, Gerald Ford, stated, "It isn't enough to compete. Winning is very important. Maybe more important than ever. . . . If you don't win elections you don't play." The feelings of the advocates of competition are as strong as the feelings of the critics.

Despite the strong case against competition, and the strong feelings favoring competition, the proper scientific activity is to identify the conditions under which competition leads to (a) destructive and (b) constructive outcomes. Once the conditions have been identified, the guidelines for the instructional use of competition may be formulated (see Table 5.1)

NATURE AND APPROPRIATE USE
OF COMPETITIVE LEARNING

To say that "winning is everything" is ludicrous. I think it's good to lose every once in a while. I don't think there is anything wrong to having your backside handed to you every once in a while. Because you learn from it. You learn maybe you overlooked something, maybe you got carried away, maybe you were a little bit careless, maybe you did

not make the commitment, or maybe someone is better than you. This is nothing wrong with that. In life you are going to find that some people are better than you.

Joe Paterno, Penn State football coach

In the classroom, competitively structured learning activities can supplement co-operation through entertaining drill-reviews in which a change of pace and a release of energy are desirable. Competition should be used when well-learned material needs to be reviewed. The emphasis should be placed on having an enjoyable drill-review rather than on winning. That the situation described at the beginning of this chapter is appropriately structured is evidenced in the enjoy-ment of the students as they compete with one another in a review of something they have already practiced, in the students' awareness that winning is secondary to having fun, and in the fact that all students believe they have a good chance of winning.

Intergroup Competition Versus Interpersonal Competition

There are two ways in which competition may be used for instructional purposes. Individuals can compete against each other to see who has learned the assigned material the best, or cooperative learning groups can compete to see which group has best mastered the assigned material. While interpersonal competition has many instructional drawbacks, intergroup competition can be used effectively under certain conditions. *Whenever possible, make competition intergroup rather than interpersonal.*

Intergroup competition is a combination of intragroup cooperation and competition between groups. It is important for the teacher to ensure that the intergroup competition does not become so strong that it outweighs the intra-group cooperation. Once competition becomes too serious, all the destructive outcomes of competition will appear, and students resort to bickering, scapegoat-ing, and negative interpersonal relationships. As the saying goes, "It's not whether you win or lose, it's how you play the game." The corollary in this situa-tion would be, "It's not how fiercely you compete with the other groups, it's how comfortably you cooperate with your teammates."

What you lose in using intergroup competition is the flow of ideas and materials between groups and the overall class possibility of a division of labor. What you gain is a change of pace to provide some fun, energy, and variety within the classroom.

Interdependence

In an appropriate competition, clear negative interdependence exists. Formally, *competitive learning* exists when students' goal attainments are negatively corre-lated; when one student obtains his or her goal, all other students with whom he

TABLE 5.1 Appropriate Competitive Learning

Type of Instructional Activity	Skill practice, knowledge recall and review, assignment is clear with rules for competing specified.
Perception of Goal Importance	Goal is *not* perceived to be of large importance to the students, and they can accept either winning or losing.
Student Expectations	Each student expects to have an equal chance of winning; to enjoy the activity, win or lose; to monitor the progress of competitors; to compare ability, skills, or knowledge with peers.
Teacher-Student Interaction	Teacher is perceived to be the major source of assistance, feedback, reinforcement, and support. Teacher available for questions and clarification of the rules; teacher referees disputes and judges correctness of answers; rewards the winners.
Teacher Statements	"Who has the most so far?" "What do you need to do to win next time?"
Student-Materials Interaction	Set of materials for each triad or for each student.
Student-Student Interaction	Observing other students in one's triad. Some talking among students. Students grouped in homogeneous triads to ensure equal chance of winning.
Student Expectations	Review previously learned material. Have an equal chance of winning. Enjoy the activity, win or lose. Monitor the progress of competitors. Follow the rules. Be a good winner and loser.
Room Arrangement	Students placed in triads or small clusters.
Evaluation Procedures	Norm-referenced.

or she is competitively linked fail to obtain their goals (Deutsch, 1949, 1962). Students work against each other to determine who can perform the highest. Competitive learning requires perceived scarcity of goals and winners. The incentive is to win by obtaining the highest score or grade. In their attempts to win, students

1. *Recognize their negatively linked fate.* When one wins, the others lose. Individuals perceive that their success creates failure for others and that obstructing competitors' achievement is beneficial to themselves.

2. *Strive for differential benefit* by trying to gain more than their classmates do. Students recognize that each is trying to defeat the others. Competitors typically attempt to obstruct each other's productivity. There is recognition that what helps a classmate to achieve hurts one's own chances of winning, and vice versa.

3. *Have a short-term time perspective* so that long-term joint productivity is perceived to be of less value than short-term personal advantage.

4. *Develop a relative identity* based on a performance ranking within the situation. One sees oneself as either a "winner" or a "loser" depending on how one compares with others. If one wins (and therefore celebrates), one's competitors lose (and therefore have no reason to celebrate). Winning is celebrated only by the winner. Losing results in feeling inadequate, jealous, and angry about one's failure.

5. *Recognize the relative causation of winning or losing.* In a competition, the outcomes one receives are caused by both one's own performance and the performance of competitors. No matter how well one performs, it is of no use if someone else performs even better. No matter how poorly one performs, it does not matter if all others perform even more poorly. The worse one's competitors perform, the greater one's chances of winning. Thus a person does not have control over his or her outcomes because the productivity of competitors negatively affects his or her chances of winning.

In competitive situations, students are closed to being influenced by each other (i.e., there is a lack of inducibility). The actions of competitors do not substitute for each other, so if one member of the group has taken the action, all others still have to engage in the action even though it may be futile to do so. Once one person has won, for example, all others may have to complete the task knowing that they have lost and that their efforts will not benefit them. Competing, furthermore, creates motives that are contradictory and operate against each other. Affiliation needs and the desire to be involved in relationships with others may operate directly against productivity in competitive situations because someone who makes good grades may not be popular with his or her peers.

To structure lessons competitively, teachers need to make the negative interdependence among groups clear.

Appropriate Tasks

Competition should be used when well-learned skills need to be practiced, when well-learned material needs to be reviewed, or when simple, unitary/nondivisible (i.e., unable to be divided into subtasks), overlearned tasks need to be performed (Miller & Hamblin, 1963; Johnson & Johnson, 1974, 1989a). Competition is frequently used when speed on a very simple task or sheer quantity of performance (i.e., maximizing task) is required. Working in the presence of competitors improves performance on a variety of tasks such as fishing-reel winding (Triplett, 1898), dressing in familiar clothes (Markus, 1978), recognition of salient stimuli (Cottrell, Wack, Sekerak, & Rittle, 1968), negotiating simple mazes (Hunt & Hillery, 1973), and copying simple material (Sanders & Baron, 1975).

When tasks are new or complex, competition is inappropriate. Researchers have found that working in the presence of competitors hampers performance on such tasks as solving difficult anagrams (Green, 1977), dressing in unfamiliar clothes, recognition of novel stimuli, negotiating difficult mazes, and copying difficult material. The underlying reason that has been offered to explain why competition only enhances performance on simple overlearned tasks is that competition increases anxiety, evaluation apprehension, and drive, which in turn increase the likelihood that the dominant or most probable response will occur. If the dominant response includes behaviors that lead to successful performance (as in the case of simple tasks), then people do better when in a high drive state.

If the dominant response primarily includes behaviors that lead to poor performance (as in the case of difficult tasks), then people do worse when in a high drive
state (Zajonc, 1965).

Relation to Cooperative Learning

Competition is first and foremost a cooperative activity. Appropriate competition takes place within a context of cooperation. Competitors have to cooperate
to decide: the nature of the contest, the determination of who wins and who
loses, the rules governing their behavior during the competition, where the competition occurs, and when it begins and ends. This underlying cooperative foundation keeps the competition in perspective and allows participants to enjoy it,
win or lose. The stronger the cooperative foundation, the more constructive the
competition. When it does not matter who wins or who loses, such as when playing tennis with a friend, the cooperative goal of enjoying each other's company
while obtaining exercise dominates. The shared cooperative experience then
dominates. Constructive competition thus provides an enjoyable and exciting
change of pace within ongoing cooperative relationships to demonstrate mastery
of the skills and knowledge required for the cooperative efforts. Intergroup competition is often more constructive than interpersonal competition because
teams tend to handle winning and losing more constructively than do individuals.

Teacher-Student Interaction

The teacher is perceived to be the major source of assistance, feedback, reinforcement, and support. The teacher needs to be available for questions and clarifications of the rules, to referee disputes, to judge the correctness of answers, and to
reward the winners. Common teacher statements are, "Who has the most so far?"
"What do you need to do to win next time?"

Student-Materials Interaction

In order to ensure that all students have appropriate access to the curriculum
materials, a set of materials needs to be provided for each triad or for each student. Clear and specific rules, procedures, and answers are an absolute necessity.
Ambiguity ruins competition because too much time is spent worrying about
what is fair and unfair, what the procedures actually are, and whether or not the
answers are correct.

Student-Student Interaction

Student-student interaction within competitive situations is controlled by clustering students homogeneously, maximizing the number of winners, structuring clear rules and procedures, ensuring that students do not take winning or losing too seriously, and providing an opportunity to monitor the progress of others.

All of us are the inheritors of a tradition of thought, relating to the nature of life, which has been handed down to us from the nineteenth century. Life, this view holds, is struggle, competition, the survival of the fittest. In the jungle, a fight with "Nature, red in tooth and claw"; in society, the claw is perhaps gloved, and the fight is called a "struggle" in which "the race is to the swiftest," in which "the strongest survive and the weakest go to the wall." —*Ashley Montagu (1966)*

All plants and animals are bound together by sharing the same earth, air, and water. They are also linked by a competition for solar energy, on which their lives depend. Once believed to be a ruthless and unbridled battle, more recent study of this struggle for existence suggests that cooperation and interdependence may be more important for the survival of a species than a no-quarter war. —*Peter Farb (1963)*

Homogeneous grouping to motivate competitive efforts. For competition to be constructive, all participants must be motivated to win. Motivation to strive to win depends on being evenly matched with competitors. In order for competition to be an exciting challenge, all participants must believe that they have a good chance to win. Accordingly, competitors should be evenly matched so that they believe they have a reasonable chance of winning. For a competition, therefore, teachers should group students homogeneously. Who wins and who loses should vary. If individuals believe they have little chance of winning, they will not be motivated.

Younger brothers rarely are able to beat older brothers and, therefore, lose all interest in competing. A barrier to constructive competition is having individuals matched against others who are far better or worse than they. In a competition, participants are ranked from best to worst. After a while, fairly stable patterns of achievement often exist, so that the majority of participants lose over and over again and a few individuals always win. *Constant winners tend to work only hard enough to win, and constant losers tend to be unmotivated.* Hurlock (1927) found in an experiment with children that members of a group that was defeated on the first of four days of competition never overcame their initial failure and attained inferior scores for the entire duration of the experiment, even though the groups had been matched on the basis of ability. Matthews (1979) concluded that losers tend to give up and withdraw from the contest. Halisch and Heckhausen (1977) found that children who believed they had a chance of winning increased their speed of response on a simple task when they became aware of being slightly behind a competitor, but children who believed that they had no chance of winning decreased their speed of response in similar circumstances. Finally, Lepley (1937), in a study on whether or not competition enhances speed of performance, placed two rats in a runway and rewarded the fastest runner. The slower runner quickly quit running at all, whereas the faster runner maintained the speed that led to reward.

In compulsory situations, such as school, students may spend up to twelve years being confronted every day with the fact that they are "losers." While winners are almost unanimously fully satisfied with their experiences and themselves, "losers" tend to perceive (a) their learning experiences as boring, unfair, and not fun, and (b) themselves negatively (Crockenberg, Bryant, & Wilce, 1974). If students aspire to be "winners," the daily frustration of failing tends to produce a sense of helplessness, worthlessness, and incompetence. Any stable pattern of winning or losing developed over time among competitors will tend to decrease the performance of all concerned (losers will give up and withdraw from the contest, and winners will only work as hard as needed to win as their less effortful performances will continue to be reinforced).

Atkinson (1965) predicted from his theory of achievement motivation that students who chronically experience failure will become primarily oriented toward avoiding failure (thus becoming nonachievement oriented). The tendency to avoid failure inhibits the student from attempting a task on which he is to be evaluated, especially when the probability of success is intermediate. If forced into achievement-oriented situations, individuals who are dominated by a tendency to avoid failure are likely to choose tasks with a very high or a very low chance of success. Doing so minimizes their anxiety about failure, for if the chance of success is very high they are almost sure not to fail, and when the chance for success is very low no one can blame them for failure. Failure, furthermore, reduces the attraction individuals feel toward peers (Ashmore, 1970; Blanchard, Adelman, & Cook, 1975).

Two ways for teachers to maintain student motivation in competitive situations are to (a) use competition only as an entertaining change of pace and (b) reformulate homogeneous competitive clusters each time competition is used so that students always face new competitors.

Maximizing the number of winners.   By arranging a class into small clusters of evenly matched students, teachers can provide a challenging and realistic competition among students and maximize the number of winners in the class at the same time. In a class of thirty, for example, there is only one winner if the class

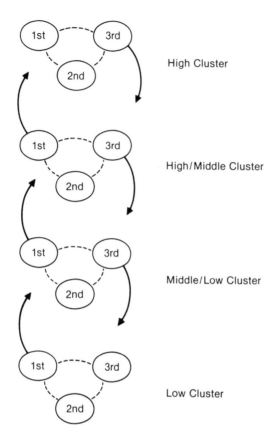

FIGURE 5.1 Bumping process

participates as a whole in a competition. If the class is divided into triads, there are ten winners in a class of thirty. This method increases the likelihood of any one student believing that he or she can win, especially when students are as-signed to homogeneous triads.

Even when students are placed in a triad with classmates who achieve at the same level, if a stable pattern of who wins and who loses develops, the perceived likelihood of winning will decrease drastically for the "losers." Teachers, there-fore, will wish to change the membership in each triad each time a competition is held. A procedure for doing so is called bumping (see Figure 5.1). Bumping involves (1) ranking the competitive triads from the highest (the three highest achievers are members) to the lowest (the three lowest achievers are members), (2) moving the winner in each triad up to the next highest triad, and (3) moving the loser down to the next lowest triad. In this way, students will always face new competitors and believe that they have a chance to win.

Ability to monitor progress of competitors.   Participants in an appropriate competition need to be able to audit and monitor the relative progress of competitors in order to know whether they are ahead or behind. In competition, the only way individuals can judge their progress is by comparing themselves with their competitors. In athletic events there is a scoreboard to keep players posted. Successful competition in schools requires the same sort of ongoing feedback. Such auditing or monitoring may facilitate performance on simple, unitary, nondivisible, overlearned tasks but may hinder performance on complex tasks (Bond & Titus, 1983).

Unimportance of who wins or loses   Competition is most appropriate when it is viewed not as a crucial test, but as an interlude, fun, a change of pace, as students collaborate to complete an assignment or master a body of knowledge. A group relay race is an example, as students race up and down the playground for the fun of it rather than to win at all costs. In the example at the beginning of this chapter, students engage in temporary competition while completing a cooperative unit on burning candles. If students can compete for fun and enjoyment, win or lose, competitive drills are an effective change of pace in the classroom as a low-key test of the success of cooperative learning groups in ensuring that all members have mastered the material being studied.

In an appropriate competition, it should be relatively unimportant whether one wins or loses. Winning cannot be a life-or-death matter if it is to be enjoyed. While competing, students should view their learning goal as being relatively unimportant so that they can accept either winning or losing. The focus should be on learning rather than winning. High levels of anxiety appear when winning becomes too important, along with all the destructive consequences of competition noted by the research. Healthy competition creates a relatively low level of anxiety by focusing on having fun. It should always be more fun to win than to not win, but in school winning is not an end in itself. Students should focus first on learning, second on having fun, and last on winning.

Clear boundaries and criteria.   In a competition, interaction among students is strictly controlled through the rules and procedures. Although the students are encouraged to share their progress, they are not expected to share ideas or solutions. Some talking may be necessary. In general, however, there is little discussion allowed except where it deals with challenging the correctness of each other's answers.

In order for competition to be constructive, the procedures, rules, and boundaries of the competition must be clear. Competitions need to have a clear beginning, a clear ending, clear criteria for selecting winners, and a clear set of rules and procedures that control interaction. The period of competition (when it starts and ends) must be clearly specified. This can be done in terms of (1) the time or number of attempts allowed to make the response (as in races where competitors are ranked on time taken to travel a certain distance or golf where competitors are ranked on number of strokes required) or (2) the response criteria that must be met for the contest to be concluded (games such as table tennis, where the first person to obtain 21 points wins).

Many competitions are poorly defined, with no clear starting line, no clear criteria for determining winners or losers, no clear finish line, vagueness about rules, and ambiguity about where and when competition does and does not exist. Most teachers do not structure specific competitive conditions except during examinations; at other times a diffuse and ambiguous competitive climate exists. This ambiguous competitive climate (where students are unsure of whether they are ahead or behind, unclear as to what the rules are, and unclear as to what they must do to win) has several destructive consequences. Students become insecure, hostile toward classmates, and fearful about being defeated. As a consequence, they may behave inappropriately and feel unhappy. Ambiguity ruins competition, because too much time is spent worrying about what is fair and unfair, what the procedures actually are, and whether or not one's responses are better than those of others.

Student Role Expectations

The basic role expectations for students within competitive learning situations are to expect to review previously learned material, to have an equal chance of winning, to enjoy the activity (win or lose), to monitor the progress of competitors, and to compare their abilities, skills, or knowledge with those of similar peers. In a competitive learning situation, students are to (1) interact in planned and informal ways to keep track of each other's progress, (2) look less to the teacher for judgment of progress and more to other students to compare their progress, (3) have a set of materials either individually or in common with a triad of students, according to the demands of the situation, (4) follow the rules (i.e., play fair), (5) have fun, and (6) be good winners and losers. Fair play is embodied in modesty in victory, in graciousness in defeat, and in that generosity of outlook that creates warm and lasting human relationships.

Evaluation System

Within competitive learning situations a norm-referenced evaluation system is used, such as grading on the normal curve and having students ranked from best to worst. In a competition, it is imperative that participants can be clearly ranked from best to worse in performance. When competition is based on a period of time, quantity or quality of the competitive response is used to rank competitors. If the contest ends when response criteria are met, ranking is based on time or the number of attempts required to reach criteria. Since in a competition rewards

are received only by one or a few of the participants, and the reward one receives depends on how highly one's response is ranked on a specified criterion, the criterion and the procedure for ranking must be clear, objective, and unbiased for competition to work.

Be content with your lot; one cannot be first in everything. —*Aesop*

No man lives without jostling and being jostled; in all ways he has to elbow himself through the world, giving and receiving offence. —*Thomas Carlyle*

You can't make the world all planned and soft. The strongest and best survive—that's the law of nature after all—always has been and always will be. —*Businessman in* Middletown, *Lynd and Lynd*

There's no gap so large as the gap between being "first" and being "second" —*Anonymous second-place finisher*

It's not whether you win or lose, it's how you play the game. —*Unknown*

The enjoyment of competing, win or lose, encourages competition; having to win each time discourages it. —*Anonymous competitor*

A good answer may not be good enough. It has to be better than someone else's —*R. Dreeben in* On What is Learned in School *(1968)*

ESTABLISHING A COMPETITIVE STRUCTURE

A science class has been working on a unit involving things that sink and float. The class was divided into cooperative learning groups, and the groups experimented with a variety of materials. One of the materials was clay. Each group was given the same weight of clay and instructed to build a clay boat. As the groups experimented with different designs, the teacher decided to have an entertaining change of pace by structuring a class competition to see which group could design and build the boat that would hold the most weight. Each cooperative group was told to build a boat and ensure that all group members understood the design. The group members were then assigned to competition triads consisting of members of three different groups who were at the same achievement level. Each member was given a new lump of clay and told to build a boat according to his or her group's design and explain its design to the other two competitors. The boats were then placed in water, and weights were placed inside each boat until it sank. The boat that supported the most weight before sinking won. The winning boat was worth 6 points, the second-place boat was awarded 4 points, and the last-place boat was awarded 2 points. After the competition students returned to their cooperative groups and added up their points for a total group score. The winning group was announced. The class then studied the winning design and determined why it was better than the others. Each group then built a replica of the winning boat.

The essence of a competitive goal structure is to give students individual goals and use a norm-referenced evaluation system in rewarding them. Assigning the individual goal of being the best speller in the class, giving a test, ranking students from best to worst on spelling, and distributing rewards accordingly would be an example. The teacher's role in using competition appropriately is explained in the following paragraphs. The procedures described are indebted to the Teams-Games-Tournament (TGT) procedure pioneered by David DeVries and Keith Edwards at Johns Hopkins University (DeVries & Edwards, 1974). Inspired by the implications of James Coleman's research on adolescents, DeVries and Edwards developed TGT as a classroom procedure combining cooperative learning, intergroup competition, and a game format. Their work at the Center for Social Organization of Schools at Johns Hopkins University in developing, evaluating, and implementing TGT is a landmark in the development of cooperative learning procedures. Their pioneering work was continued by one of David DeVries' doctoral students, Robert Slavin.

The teacher's role in conducting competitive lessons consists of the following sixteen steps.

Objectives

1. Specifying instructional objectives.   The academic objective needs to be specified at the correct level for each student and matched to the right level of instruction according to a conceptual or task analysis. Often the objective will be to review previously learned material.

Decisions

2. Assigning students to heterogeneous cooperative learning groups.   Students are assigned to cooperative learning groups of four members so that each group is a cross section of the class in academic performance (one high, one low, and two middle achievers) and various other individual characteristics such as sex and ethnic background. The groups should be balanced so that the average academic performance levels of all the groups are about equal. The cooperative learning group prepares its members to do well in the academic competitions. The groups periodically compete with each other to be the best group in the class. Cooperative groups are given time to study together so that students can help and encourage each other to learn, and group membership is held stable for a period of time so that group cohesion and commitment can be built. An intergroup competition takes place once a week or so as a change of pace. Most of the time inter-group cooperation is structured.

3. Planning the competition.   The competition is conducted as follows:

a. Students are assigned to competition triad so that each student is placed in compe-tition with two other students, each of whom represents a different cooperative learning group. In order to create equitable competition, each triad consists of students of comparable academic achievement (as determined by prior perform-ance).

b. The competition lasts for 30 to 50 minutes. At the end of a competition the students in each triad compare their scores to determine the top scorer. the middle scorer, and the low scorer. The ranks are converted into points, with a fixed number of points assigned to the top scorer (6 points), middle scorer (4 points), and the low scorer (2 points) in each triad. If two students tie for first place, each receives 5 points. If two students tie for second place, each receives 3 points. In a three-way tie, each student receives 4 points.

c. A cooperative learning group score is derived by adding the scores of all the individ-ual members. Group scores are then ranked and listed. Care should be taken to ensure that having fun is more important than winning.

4. Assigning students to competitive triads.   A class competition is structured so that each student competes as a representative of his or her cooperative learning group with students of equal aptitude from other groups. When students com-pete, they should be placed in homogeneous triads based on ability or previous achievement. Groups of three maximize the number of winners in the class (pairs tend to make the competition too personal). Rank the students in each coopera-tive learning group from highest to lowest on the basis of their previous achieve-ment. Given that only one student from a group can be in a competitive triad, assign the three highest achieving students in the class to Table 1, the next three to Table 2, and so on until the three lowest achievement students in the class are in the bottom triad. This system creates equal competition within each triad and makes it possible for students of all achievement levels to contribute maximally to their group scores if they do their best. Figure 5.2 illustrates the relationship between the cooperative learning groups and the competitive triads.

5. Preparing instructional materials.   Make a question sheet consisting of about thirty items, an answer sheet, a copy of the rules, and a set of cards numbered from 1 to 30. On each card write one question from the question sheet. The questions can be either recognition or recall questions. Each competitive triad should receive one set of cards and one answer sheet. An example of the cards and answer sheet are given in Table 5.2. The rules appear in Table 5.3.

6. Arranging the classroom.   The room should be arranged so that the triads are separated from each other and students within each triad sit close to each other.

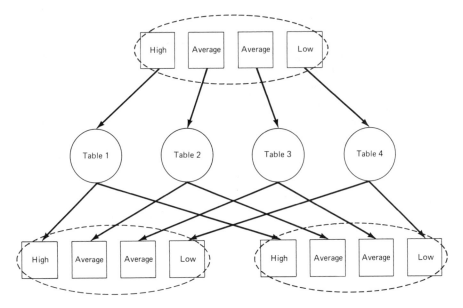

FIGURE 5.2 Assignment to tournament tables

Explaining the Task and Goal Structure

7. Explaining the academic task.   The task is to learn and demonstrate mastery of the assigned material.

8. Structuring negative goal interdependence.   Explain to students that their goal is to answer more questions correctly than the other two members of the triad in order to maximize the number of points they take back to their cooperative learning group so that their group can win by having more overall points than any other group in the class. Make sure the procedures, rules, criteria for winning, and the definition of what is and is not a correct answer are clearly understood by all students. Competition bogs down if there are disputes or misunderstandings over such matters.

9. Explaining criteria for success.   Within each triad, the student who answers the most questions correctly receives 6 points, the second place student receives 4 points, and the last place student receives 2 points to take back to his or her cooperative learning group. If two students tie for first place, each receives 5 points. If two students tie for second place, each receives 3 points. In a three-way tie, each student receives 4 points. In a cooperative learning group of four members, the group could have between 8 and 24 points total. The group that has the most points wins.

TABLE 5.2 Sample Game

Background of the game: The students in a seventh grade English class were studying sentences. In the game they were asked to identify the item as either a complete or an incomplete sentence. If the item was an incomplete sentence, the player had to tell why it was incomplete. A sentence was incomplete because either the verb or subject was missing.

We stopped for lunch. (B-4)	A clown and monkey rode at the head of the parade. (B-24)
Leaving the lake in the morning. (B-3)	Leaned out the window. (B-23)

Sentences Game II: Answer Sheet B

B-1	Complete sentence	B-13	Complete sentence
B-2	Complete sentence	B-14	Complete sentence
B-3	Incomplete sentence; no subject	B-15	Incomplete sentence; no subject
B-4	Complete sentence	B-16	Complete sentence
B-5	Incomplete sentence; no verb	B-17	Complete sentence
B-6	Incomplete sentence; no verb	B-18	Incomplete sentence; no verb
B-7	Complete sentence	B-19	Incomplete sentence; no subject
B-8	Complete sentence	B-20	Complete sentence
B-9	Incomplete sentence; no verb	B-21	Incomplete sentence; no verb
B-10	Incomplete sentence; no verb	B-22	Incomplete sentence; no subject
B-11	Incomplete sentence; no verb	B-23	Incomplete sentence; no subject
B-12	Incomplete sentence; no subject	B-24	Complete sentence

This game was developed by David DeVries, Keith Edwards, and Gail Fennessey in cooperation with Carol Hopkins, a teacher at Northern Parkway Junior High School, Baltimore, Md.

*10. **Specifying desired behaviors.*** Each student should try to win in his or her triad. They are to work alone answering each of their questions without consultation with other group members. If they need help or clarification, they are to ask the teacher. They should keep track of where they stand in the competition and make adjustments in their strategy accordingly. In addition, they should

a. Seek fun and enjoyment.
b. Win with humility and pleasure.
c. Lose with dignity.

TABLE 5.3 Rules of Play

I. To start the game shuffle the cards and place them face down on the table. Play is in a clockwise rotation.

II. To play, each player in turn takes the top card from the deck, reads it aloud, and does one of two things:

A. Says he does not know or is not sure of the answer and asks if another player wants to answer. If no one wants to answer, the card is placed on the bottom of the deck. If a player answers, he follows the following procedure.

B. Answers the question immediately and asks if anyone wants to challenge the answer. The player to his or her right has the first chance to challenge. If this player does not wish to challenge, then the next player to the right may challenge.

1. If there is no challenge, another player should check the answer:

a. If correct, the player keeps the card.

b. If incorrect, the player must place the card on the bottom of the deck.

2. If there is a challenge and the challenger decides not to answer, the answer is checked. If the original answer is wrong, the player must place the card on the bottom of the deck.

3. If there is a challenge and the challenger gives an answer, the answer is checked:

a. If the challenger is correct, he receives the card.

b. If the challenger is incorrect, and the original answer is correct, the challenger must give up one of the cards he has already won (if any) and place it on the bottom of the deck.

c. If both answers are incorrect, the card is placed on the bottom of the deck.

III. The game ends when there are no more cards in the deck. The player who has the most cards is the winner.

This game was developed by David DeVries, Keith Edwards, and Gail Fennessey in cooperation with Carol Hopkins.

d. Recognize and deal with inappropriate anxiety.

e. Monitor progress of competitors.

f. Form realistic perceptions of own skills.

Students need to know what behaviors are appropriate and desirable within a competitive learning situation.

Monitoring and Intervening

11. Monitoring students' behavior.   After explaining the rules, procedures, and expected behaviors to students, teachers must observe to see that they are being followed. Much of the teacher's time should be spent in observing students in order to see what problems they are having in completing the assignment and in working competitively. The teacher should move throughout the room, checking triads for understanding, answering questions, settling disputes over answers, and checking for the expected student behaviors. Some systematic and anecdotal record keeping will enhance the processing at the end of the lesson and is easily done by tallying on an observation sheet the number of times the teacher sees targeted desired behaviors and jotting down specific instances of appropriate behavior.

12. Providing task assistance.   In monitoring the triads, teachers will wish to clarify instructions, review important procedures and rules, and teach task-competitive skills as necessary. The teacher is the major resource for student learning and is also the judge and jury in settling disputes over which answer is correct. The major focus of the competitive triads should be on reviewing the previously learned material and not arguing over answers. The teacher's task assistance should focus attention on the learning and minimize the importance of winning. Make sure that rules are followed, no one cheats, and disputes are settled quickly.

13. Intervening to teach competitive skills.   Students will have experience in competing but will often lack the skills to compete appropriately. Students may take the competition too seriously or feel so anxious that they do not enjoy it. Intervene to encourage the fun of competing or to deemphasize the importance of winning when it seems necessary. It is important that students learn to compete appropriately for fun and enjoyment. It strengthens cooperative learning when students can review previously learned material in a gamelike situation.

14. Providing closure to the lesson.   At the end of the lesson, students should have adequately reviewed previously learned material so that they can easily contribute their learning to future collaborative efforts.

Evaluation and Reinforcement

15. Evaluating and reinforcing the quality and quantity of students' learning.   Within the competitive triads, students' performance needs to be evaluated by a norm-referenced procedure. Similarly, groups are then evaluated by a norm-referenced procedure.

16. Processing the competition.   It is important that competitions be discussed afterward to allow students to evaluate their skills, discuss their feelings, and realize how to behave even more appropriately next time. Processing may be done individually with students completing a questionnaire on their reactions and behavior, may be done in their competitive triads or cooperative learning groups, or

In a large city high school, a teacher had just finished chatting with two students and moved to the front of the class, the signal that class was about to begin. "You've spent the last few weeks doing projects that relate to the fifteenth, sixteenth, and seventeenth centuries," she began. "Now, we'll give you a chance to see what you know about some of the people you've met in your reading." She explained that they were going to play a game called *Contemporaries,* in which one student would name a famous person and describe that person's contribution to the times; the next student would then name a contemporary person and that person's contribution, and so on. Any student who was stuck without a name to contribute, or suggested a name that was challenged and found not to be contemporary, would drop out until a new game was started. Meanwhile, the game would continue until one student was the winner.

The teacher divided the class into groups of five, using a list that grouped students in such a way that each student in a cluster had a reasonable chance to win. The students jumped into the game with great enthusiasm and obvious enjoyment. Occasionally there was a burst of laughter when a name came up that was obviously not contemporary or when a challenged student was proven correct and the challenger had to drop out. Near the end of the period the teacher stopped the game and gave the winners from each group a chance to try their skill against each other, temporarily establishing a class champion. The last few minutes before the bell were spent discussing the several instances in which many in the class didn't realize that two famous people were contemporaries, and what it would take to be able to win next time. After class, the teacher jotted down a few notes about things she had noticed or overheard, observing especially where students seemed to have difficulty with the competition.

How appropriate is this instance of competition? Check it out with the summarized criteria.

may be done as a whole class. A combination of individual and small group processing is usually effective. During their monitoring, teachers may observe students engaging in inappropriate actions and plan to provide personal feedback later. Most feedback, however, should be positive. An open and frank discussion of the competition can defuse hurt feelings and ensure increased constructiveness of future competitions.

COMPETITIVE SKILLS

Students in Midwest Middle School are learning how to build paper airplanes as part of a physics unit. Different designs are built and demonstrated in order for students to learn the principles of flight. As an entertaining change of pace, the teacher decides to have a competition to see which cooperative group can design

the plane that flies the farthest, stays in the air the longest, is the most acrobatic, and is the most accurate. (Teachers who conduct such competitions may wish to add another category that brings elements of luck and humor into the competition.) The class then studies the winning designs and determines why the planes were so effective. Finally, each group has to build replicas of the winning designs.

Competition, when it is appropriate, is fun and adds spice to classroom life.* Competition involves much less interaction among students and less coordination of behavior than cooperation, and there are fewer skills essential to competing than to cooperating. Appropriate competition, however, does require several skills.

The first competitive skill is playing fair. Students must understand and obey the rules. Rules should be clarified before the competition begins so that students know what is and is not fair. In some competitions, for example, stu-

---

*The two authors once decided that they had a reasonable chance to win a footrace with their dad. At the time the two authors were four and five years old, and their father was twenty-seven. We decided that an old man of twenty-seven would not be very much competition! So we refused to come home for dinner, thinking he could never catch us. A short race and some swiftly administered physical aversive stimuli ended all motivation to race our father again in the future.

Teacher Role Checklist For Competitive Learning

1. What are the desired outcomes for the drill activity?

2. Is the classroom arranged so that students
   _____ Are clustered together, working on their own, but able to monitor the progress of their competitors?
   _____ Have access to each other only (a) if it is required by the nature of the competition or (b) to know whether they are ahead or behind the others?
   _____ Have an individual set of self-contained materials?

3. Have you effectively communicated to students that
   _____ The instructional goal is relative (to win more points for one's group than competitors win for theirs)?
   _____ Each student will be rewarded on the basis of how his or her work compares to the work of the other students in the competition triad?

4. Have you effectively communicated the expected patterns of student-student interaction? Do students know that they should
   _____ Interact only to check the progress of other students and to abide by the rules of the competition?
   _____ Work on the assignment by trying to do the task better, faster, and more completely than competitors?
   _____ Perceive teacher praise or support of a competitor's work as an indication that their own work is inferior and teacher criticism of a competitor's work as an indication that their own work is superior?
   _____ Ignore comments from other students?
   _____ Go to the teacher for all help and assistance needed?

5. Have you effectively communicated the expected pattern of teacher-student interaction? Do students know that the teacher
   _____ Wants each student to try to do better on the assignment than the other students and will evaluate students' work on the basis of how it compares with the work of other students?
   _____ Will interact with each triad of students to clarify rules and the task without giving one student more help than another, and often making clarifications to the entire class?
   _____ Will praise and support students working alone and trying to do better, faster, and more work than any other student in the triad or classroom?

dents are allowed to enhance their chances of winning by obstructing their opponents' progress (e.g., "sending" another player's ball away from the wicket in croquet), while in other competitions such disruption of opponents' progress would be declared unfair (e.g., cutting in too soon in a track race). If the rules are clear in the beginning, students' actions will usually be appropriate. If any student feels it is necessary to break the rules, the situation is probably inappropriate for competition (e.g., the student perceives that the goal is too important and the situation is too serious).

A second skill is being a good winner and a good loser. This means winning with humility, pleasure, and modesty, and being gracious when you lose. Any student should be able to win or lose gracefully. The third skill is enjoying the competition, win or lose. The purpose of competition is to have an enjoyable experience drilling on previously learned material. The fourth skill is monitoring the progress of competitors to know how one stands in the competition. Since winning is the goal of competition, the only way to know where one stands is to know where the others are. Teachers can promote the development and use of monitoring skills by

1. Making clear that monitoring is part of the competition and that students can watch each other's progress.
2. Setting up several methods of monitoring including charting students' progress on the board, checking periodically to bring everyone up to date, and modifying the triads in which students compete.

The fifth skill is *not* to overgeneralize the results of the competition. Winning does not make a student a more worthwhile person, and losing does not make a student less worthwhile. Being defeated in a spelling contest does not make a student a "loser." The results of any one competition provides very limited information about a student's personal worth. Clearly separating the results of competitions from one's view of oneself is an important competitive skill.

SUMMARY

To be most effective, individuals should be able to cooperate, compete, and work autonomously on their own appropriately (Johnson & Johnson, 1989a). Being able to compete for fun and enjoyment is an important competence. The major concern with the instructional use of competition is that students bring more to the competition than is intended by the teacher. Students may begin a competition with the attitude that they would "prefer to die" rather than be defeated. The anxiety produced in such students and the students around them is counterproductive. Competitions need to be kept light and fun, emphasizing review or drill, probably in a game format. Students should be homogeneously grouped so that they perceive themselves as having a chance to win, probably in threesomes to maximize the number of winners. The instructions, rules, procedures, and materials need to be clear and specific. The teacher needs to be the major resource for all students and the arbitrator of disputes. The major teacher role is to keep students focused on learning and not getting sidetracked by arguments or hurt feelings. Processing afterward is a vital part of teaching students to handle competition appropriately and enjoy it. Students need to learn how to win with enjoyment and lose with dignity. Students can be defeated, but are never "losers."

The importance of spreading an umbrella of cooperation over the class before competition is initiated cannot be overemphasized. Having students work together, get to know each other, cheer for shared successes, and develop collaborative skills is the best foundation for making competition appropriate. In one of our teacher-training sessions, a coach announced that he was not excited about cooperation. He preferred competition, believed in it, and liked to stress it with his teams. After several cooperative experiences we structured a competition involving vocabulary words, and the coach lost badly. After quiet reflection, he concluded, "I learned something about myself today. I have always hated to lose, but I found that I do not mind losing nearly as much when I lose to people I like." Building a strong cooperative learning environment may be the best way to provide a setting in which students can learn how to compete appropriately.

6

Creating Positive Interdependence

KEY TO COOPERATION: WE INSTEAD OF ME

United we stand, divided we fall.

Watchword of the American Revolution

William Manchester wrote several years ago in *Life* magazine about revisiting Sugar Loaf Hill in Okinawa, where thirty-four years before he had fought as a marine. He describes how he had been wounded and sent to a hospital and, in violation of orders, had escaped from the hospital to rejoin his unit at the front. Doing so meant almost certain death. "Why did I do it?" he wondered. The answer lies in the power of positive interdependence.

Positive interdependence is the perception that you are linked with others in a way so that you cannot succeed unless they do (and vice versa); that is, their work benefits you, and your work benefits them. It promotes a situation in which individuals work together in small groups to maximize the learning of all members. In such a situation, individuals have the following perceptions:

1. Group members are striving for *mutual benefit* so that all members of the group will gain. There is recognition that what helps other group members benefits you and what promotes your productivity benefits the other group members. Each member invests time and energy into helping groupmates; this investment pays dividends and capital gains when groupmates score high on tests and reciprocate the helping.

2. Group members share a *common fate* where they all gain or lose on the basis of their overall performance.

3. The performance of group members is *mutually caused.* Within a cooperative learning group, you are *responsible* for giving the help and assistance other members need to be productive and *obligated* to the other members for the support and assistance they gave to you. Each member is instrumental in the productivity of each other member. Your productivity, therefore, is perceived to be caused by (a) your own efforts and abilities and (b) the efforts and abilities of the other group members, and the performance of the other group members is perceived to be due partially to your encouragement and facilitation. The mutual responsibility and mutual obligation inherent in the mutual causation within cooperative learning groups result in a *mutual investment* by members in each other.

4. There is a *shared identity* based on group membership. Besides being a separate individual, you are a member of a team. The shared identity binds members together emotionally.

5. The *self-efficacy* of members is increased through the empowerment inherent in the joint efforts. Being part of a cooperative learning group increases students' confidence that if they exert effort, they will be successful. Cooperative groups empower their members to act by making them feel strong, capable, and committed. Being part of a team effort changes feelings of "I can't do it" to "We can do it." Success that is impossible for one person to achieve is attainable within a cooperative group. A student may believe, "I can't do algebra, it's too hard," until two other students say, "Stick with us; we'll get you through algebra with at least a B." The student then tends to believe, "We can do algebra."

6. There are *joint celebrations* based on (a) mutual respect and appreciation for the efforts of group members and (b) the group's success. Being part of a team effort results in feelings of (a) camaraderie, belonging, and pride and (b) success. Feelings of success are shared, and pride is taken in others' accomplishments as well as one's own.

BARRIERS TO POSITIVE INTERDEPENDENCE: THE DELUSION OF INDIVIDUALISM

The feelings and commitment that drove William Manchester to risk his life to help protect his comrades do not automatically appear when students are placed in learning groups. There are barriers to positive interdependence. Among many current high school and college students, their own pleasures and pains, successes and failures, occupy center stage in their lives (Conger, 1988; Seligman, 1988). Each person tends to focus on gratifying his or her own ends without concern for others. Over the past twenty years, self-interest has become more important than commitment to community or country. Young adults have turned away from careers of public service to careers of self-service. Many young adults have a *delusion of individualism,* believing that (1) they are separate and apart from all other individuals, and, therefore, (2) others' frustration, unhappiness, hunger, despair, and misery have no significant bearing on their own well-being. With the increase in the past two decades in adolescents' and youths' concern for personal well-being, there has been a corresponding diminished concern for the welfare of others (particularly the less advantaged) and of society itself (Astin, Green, & Korn, 1987; Astin, Green, Korn, & Schalit, 1986).

The self is a very poor site for finding meaning. Hope does not spring from competition. Meaning does not surface in individualistic efforts aimed at benefiting no one but yourself. Empowerment does not come from isolation. Purpose does not grow from egocentric focus on own material gain. Without involvement in interdependent efforts and the resulting concern for others, it is not possible to realize oneself except in the most superficial sense. Contributing to the well-being of others within an interdependent effort provides meaning and purpose to life.

POWER OF POSITIVE INTERDEPENDENCE

For an individual, piloting a Boeing 747 is impossible. For the three-person crew, it is straightforward. The crew, furthermore, does not work in isolation. Large numbers of mechanics, service personnel, cabin attendants, air traffic controllers, pilot educators (who keep crew members abreast of the latest developments and sharp in their responses to problem situations), and many others are necessary to the flying of the plane. From the demands of repairing a flat tire on a dark highway ("You hold the light while I . . .") to the complex requirements of flying a modern passenger jet, teamwork is the most frequent human response to the challenges of coping with otherwise impossible tasks.

Within the real world, positive interdependence is pervasive on many levels. Individuals join together into a group that is structured around a mutual goal. The group fits into the larger mosaic of groups working toward a larger goal. Those groups also form a mosaic working toward an even larger superordinate goal. Thus there are individuals who work within teams that work within departments that work within divisions that work within organizations that work within a societal economic system that works within the global economic system.

Life in the real world is characterized by layers of positive interdependence that stretch from the interpersonal to the international. Life in schools is dominated by competitive and individualistic activities that ignore the importance of positive interdependence. It is time for classrooms to become more realistic.

POSITIVE INTERDEPENDENCE IN THE CLASSROOM

When positive interdependence is carefully structured, you tend to see students

1. Putting their heads close together over their work.
2. Talking about the work.

3. Drilling each other on the material being learned.

4. Sharing answers and materials.

5. Encouraging each other to learn.

When positive interdependence is not carefully structured, you may see students

1. Leaving their group impulsively.

2. Talking about topics other than the work.

3. Doing their own work while ignoring other students.

4. Not sharing answers or materials.

5. Not checking to see if others have learned the material.

To implement cooperative learning, you need to understand the types of positive interdependence and have specific strategies for implementing each one. In doing so you should use the following general procedure:

1. *Structuring* positive goal interdependence within a lesson and supplementing it with a number of other types of positive interdependence.

2. *Informing* students of the types of positive interdependence present in the lesson and emphasizing that they "sink or swim together."

3. *Monitoring* students' actions to ensure that they truly believe that they are responsible for each other's learning as well as their own.

4. Having groups *process* the extent to which they really believed that they were responsible for each other's learning and success.

With modifying a few words, this sequence may be called STOP (structure, tell, observe, process).

TYPES OF POSITIVE INTERDEPENDENCE

Since at first most students (especially older ones) do not automatically care about their groupmates, positive interdependence must be consciously and clearly structured by the teacher. Cooperative efforts begin with the establishment of mutual goals, around which the actions of each group member are organized. To ensure that the group works productively and exerts considerable effort toward accomplishing the mutual goal, members with different resources are assigned roles and given a task that requires coordination of efforts. They are also given a team identity and a setting in which to work. To highlight the importance of the goal, the long-term implications of success are spelled out. Threats to team success are identified. An identity based on the importance of the goal is established. Finally, the rewards of success are made salient to induce members to join in the joint effort.

Positive Goal Interdependence 1: Learning Goals

The first step in structuring positive interdependence within a cooperative learning group is to set a mutual goal that establishes that members are responsible for each other's learning and success as well as their own. *Positive goal interdependence* exists when students perceive that they can achieve their learning goals only if all other members of their group also attain their goals. Members of a learning group have a mutual set of goals that they all are striving to accomplish. Success depends on all members reaching the goal. The goal might be that all group members understand how to do long division with remainders or that all group members be able to analyze the plot of *Hamlet*. All cooperative lessons need to include positive goal interdependence. Other types of positive interdependence support and supplement the effects of positive goal interdependence. Ways of structuring positive goal interdependence include the following:

1. Teachers explain that the group goal is to ensure that all members achieve a prescribed mastery level on the assigned material. To achieve this goal, each group member must have two responsibilities: (1) learn and (b) ensure that all other group members learn. Teachers may wish to say, "One answer from the three of you, everyone has to agree, and everyone has to be able to explain how to solve the problem or complete the assignment." Teachers may establish the prescribed mastery level as (a) individual levels of performance that each group member must achieve in order for the group as a whole to be successful (the group goal is for each member to demonstrate 90 percent mastery on a curriculum unit) or (b) improvement scores (the group goal is to ensure that all members do better this week than they did last week).

2. Teachers "enlarge the shadow of the future" in two ways:
   a. Teachers should show that the long-term benefits of cooperation outweigh the short-term benefits of taking advantage of the other group members or of not cooperating. Teachers may wish to demonstrate that sharing the work and helping each other learn is more productive and more fun than competing or working alone. The long-term vision must be more compelling than the temptation of short-term personal advantage.
   b. Teachers should highlight frequent interactions among group members and durable relationships among team members. The shadow of the future looms largest when interactions among students are frequent and durable. *Durability* promotes cooperative efforts because it makes interpersonal relationships long lasting. It ensures that students will not easily forget how they have treated, and been treated by, each other. *Frequency* promotes stability by making the consequences of today's actions more salient for tomorrow's work. When students realize they will work with each other frequently and for a long period of time, they see the need to be cooperative and supportive in current dealings with each other.

3. Teachers add the scores of all group members to determine an overall group score. This score is compared with the preset criterion of excellence. Teachers may wish to say, "The goal of each triad is to reach a total group score of 135 out of 150 potential correct answers." Since there are 50 questions on the test, each member

needs to get at least 45 correct on the test. To highlight the goal of maximizing the total group score, teachers may wish to keep a group progress chart. Total group scores may be plotted each day or each week. Students are then responsible for raising their own and their groupmates' performances in order to show progress on the group chart.

4. Teachers randomly choose the worksheet, report, or theme of one group member to be evaluated. Consequently, members are responsible for reading and correcting each other's work to ensure that it is 100 percent correct before the teacher selects one representative paper on which to evaluate the group. Variations include randomly selecting one member to demonstrate mastery of a concept, translate a sentence in a foreign language class, or take the test for the group. Since this is a procedure to ensure that each individual group member is accountable for learning the assigned material, it demonstrates that there is an intimate relationship between goal interdependence and individual accountability. *Individual accountability* is the measurement of whether or not each group member has achieved the group's goal. Individual accountability cannot exist unless goal interdependence has been previously established.

5. Teachers request one product (such as a report, theme, presentation, or answer sheet) from the group that is signed by all members. Signatures indicate that each member was active in creating the product, agrees with it, and can rationally defend its content. A variation on this procedure is to implement a rule that no group member receives credit for doing homework until all group members have handed in the homework assignment. Groups may be responsible for writing a newsletter or making a presentation, and no member receives credit unless all group members contribute an article to the newsletter or make part of the presentation. This procedure may be extended into intergroup cooperation by having the class produce a newspaper in which each group has contributed a part (which in turn must contain work by each individual member), or by having the class give a Renaissance Day in which each group must make a presentation (which in turn must include all members).

Students will contribute more energy and effort to meaningful goals than to trivial ones. Being responsible for others' learning as well as for one's own gives cooperative efforts a meaning that is not found in competitive and individualistic learning situations. In cooperative learning situations, the efforts of each group member contribute not only to their own success, but also to the success of groupmates. When there is meaning to what they do, ordinary people exert extraordinary effort. It is positive goal interdependence that gives meaning to the efforts of group members.

Positive Goal Interdependence 2: Outside Enemy Interdependence

The goal of a learning group may be to learn more than other groups in order to win a competition. *Positive outside enemy interdependence* exists when groups are placed in competition with each other. Group members then feel interdependent as they strive to beat the other groups. A procedure we like is having students compete with the score made by last year's class or the total class score made last week. A teacher might say, "Last year's class made a total score of 647 on this test. Can you do better? Sure you can." Such competition reduces the negative behavior that often accompanies competing against other groups in the same class.

Positive Goal Interdependence 3: Fantasy Interdependence

The goals that learning groups strive to achieve do not have to be real. *Positive fantasy interdependence* exists when students imagine that they are in an emergency situation (such as surviving a shipwreck) or must deal with problems (such as ending air pollution in the world) that are compelling but unreal. A teacher may say, "You are the world's leading scientists. Your challenge is to save the world by finding the answers to these difficult and mystifying equations!" We like to tell students that they are word detectives who must look for a certain word in a reading assignment and describe how it is used by the author. Students may also be character detectives who analyze a character in a story or play.

Positive Reward and Celebration Interdependence

In order for students to look forward to working in cooperative groups and enjoy doing so, they must feel that (1) their efforts are appreciated and (2) they are respected as individuals. Long-term commitment to achieve is largely based on feeling recognized and respected for what one is doing. Thus students' efforts to learn and promote each other's learning need to be (1) observed, (2) recognized, and (3) celebrated. The celebration of individual efforts and group success involves structuring reward interdependence (see Table 6.1).

TABLE 6.1 Comparison of Reward Practices

ERRORS	EFFECTIVE PRACTICES
Not knowing if students are helping each other	Constant monitoring of groups to make helping visible
Informing teachers	Swapping "good news" among group members
Only recognition from teacher is important	Recognition and respect from peers
Recognizing only the few class superstars	Recognizing almost everyone
Trivializing rewards by rewarding students for anything	Rewarding only completed valuable actions

Source: D. W. Johnson, R. Johnson & E. Holubec: *Circles of learning: Cooperation in the classroom.* (3rd ed.) Edina, MN. Interaction, 1990, p. 75. Reprinted with permission of authors.

Positive reward interdependence exists when each group member receives the same reward for completing the assignment. A joint reward is given for successful group work. Everyone is rewarded, or no one is rewarded. As an example of reward interdependence, every group member may receive 5 bonus points (or 15 extra recess minutes) when all group members get 90 percent correct on a test. The rewards should be attractive to students, inexpensive, and consistent with your philosophy of teaching. It is important that groups that do not reach the criteria do not receive the reward. The rewards, furthermore, should probably be removed as soon as the intrinsic motivation inherent in cooperative learning groups becomes apparent. You will know that this time has arrived when students pressure you to let them work in groups. Ways of structuring positive reward interdependence include the following:

1. Teachers give bonus points that are added to all members' academic scores when everyone in the group achieves up to criterion.
2. Teachers give nonacademic rewards (such as extra free time, extra recess time, stickers, stars, or food) when all group members reach criteria on an academic task.

3. Teachers give teacher praise (i.e., social rewards) for the group as a whole when all group members reach criteria.

4. Teachers give a single group grade for the combined efforts of group members. This method should be used cautiously until all students (and parents) are very familiar with cooperative learning.

5. Group members swap "good news" about each other's efforts to promote each other's learning and celebrate their joint success. Group members and teachers should

   a. Seek out valuable, completed actions by group members in completing assignments and helping groupmates complete assignments.

   b. Honor the actions with all sorts of positive recognition. In doing so, interpersonal recognition rather than formal evaluation should be emphasized. Supportive, encouraging, and caring interaction among team members is the key. There is nothing more motivating to students than having groupmates cheering them on and jointly celebrating their successes.

Positive Resource Interdependence

Positive resource interdependence exists when each member has only a portion of the information, resources, or materials necessary for the task to be completed and members' resources have to be combined in order for the group to achieve its goal. Thus the resources of each group member are needed if the task is to be completed. Ways of structuring positive resource interdependence include the following:

1. The teacher limiting the resources given to the group. Only one pencil, for example, may be given to a group of three students. Other resources that can be limited include textbooks, answer sheets, scissors, dictionaries, maps, typewriters, computers, and periodic charts of elements.

2. The teacher jigsawing materials so that each member has part of a set of materials. Materials that can be jigsawed include vocabulary words, lines of a poem, letters of a word, sentences of a paragraph to be sequenced, words for a sentence, pictures, definitions, puzzle pieces, problems, parts of directions, resource materials, lab equipment, parts of a map, art supplies, ingredients for cooking, and sections of a report. One social studies teacher gave each member of his cooperative learning groups a different social studies text and then gave assignments requiring students to share what each text had to say about the issue. Each member of a group may be given one sentence of a paragraph, and the group is given the task of sequencing the sentences. A group could be given the assignment of writing a biography of Abe Lincoln and information on Lincoln's childhood given to one member, information on Lincoln's early political career given to another, information on Lincoln as president given to a third, and information on Lincoln's assassination given to the fourth member. A different type of jigsaw is created when the assignment is to make a collage and one member has the paste, another has the scissors, and a third has the magazines.

3. The teacher giving students a writing assignment with the stipulation that each member must offer a sentence in each paragraph, contribute an article to a newsletter, write a paragraph or an essay, or do a chapter in a "book."

Positive Task Interdependence

Positive task interdependence exists when a division of labor is created so that the actions of one group member have to be completed if the next team member is to complete his or her responsibilities. Dividing an overall task into subunits that must be performed *in a set order* is an example of task interdependence. This "factory-line" model exists when one student is responsible for obtaining swamp water, another is responsible for making slides, another is responsible for viewing the slides through a microscope, and the fourth member is responsible for writing down the organisms found in the swamp water. Another example is a "chain reaction" in which a student named Bill learns a concept and then is responsible for teaching it to another student named Jane, and the test score received by Jane is given to Bill. While task interdependence is closely related to resource interdependence, it is used much less frequently because not very many academic tasks lend themselves to such a "lockstep" division of labor.

Positive Role Interdependence

Positive role interdependence exists when each member is assigned complementary and interconnected roles that specify responsibilities that the group needs in order to complete a joint task. Any of the skills discussed in Chapter 5 may be used. Usually the roles are rotated daily so that each student obtains considerable experience in each role. Some roles to get you started are these:

Reader: Reads the group's material out loud to the group, carefully and with expression, so that group members can understand and remember it.

Writer/recorder: Carefully records the best answers of the group on the worksheet or paper, edits what the group has written, gets the group members to check and sign the paper, then turns it in to the teacher.

Materials handler: Gets any materials or equipment needed by the group, keeps track of them, and puts them carefully away.

Encourager: Watches to make certain that everyone is participating, and invites reluctant or silent members to contribute. Sample statements: "Jane, what do you think?" "Robert, do you have anything to add?" "Nancy, help us out." "Juanita, what are your ideas on this?"

Checker: Checks on the comprehension or learning of group members by asking them to explain or summarize material learned or discussed. Sample statements: "Terry, why did we decide on this answer for number two?" "James, explain how we got this answer." "Anne, summarize for us what we've decided here."

Praiser: Helps members feel good about their contributions to the group by telling them how helpful they are. This is a good role to assign to help combat "put-

downs." Sample statements: "That's a good idea, Al." "Sharon, you're very helpful." "Karen, I like the way you've helped us." "Good job, John."

Prober: In a pleasant way, keeps the group from superficial answering by not allowing the members to agree too quickly. Agrees when satisfied that the group has
explored all the possibilities. Sample statements: "What other possibilities are
there for this problem or question?" "What else could we put here?" "Let's
double-check this answer."

Some other role possibilities include *noise monitor* (uses a nonverbal signal to remind group members to quiet down), *energizer* (energizes the group when it starts
lagging), *summarizer* (summarizes the material so that group members can check
it again), *observer* (keeps track of how well the team members are collaborating),
time keeper, and *paraphraser.* Come up with roles that fit the task and your students.

Identity Interdependence

Positive identity interdependence exists when the group establishes a mutual identity
through a name, flag, motto, or song. English teachers may wish to give poets'
names to groups (the Whitmans, Frosts, Cummingses, and Hugheses). Science
teachers can give famous scientists' names to groups. Teachers may let students
think of their own group names, make a flag for their group, establish a group
motto, or create some other symbol of their joint identity.

Environmental Interdependence

Environmental interdependence exists when group members are bound together by
the physical environment in some way. Examples include giving each group a
specific area to meet in, putting chairs or desks together, having group members
hold hands or put their arms around each other, requiring group members to
have their feet touching in a circle as they work, or placing a rope fence around
the group. A first-grade teacher we once worked with made circles on the floor
with masking tape and required all group members to be within the circle while
they worked together. Being stranded in the barn's haymow with your older
brother because he carelessly knocked over the ladder is another example of
environmental interdependence.

Final Point

Pull together. In the mountains you must depend on each other for survival.

Willi Unsoeld

Cooperative efforts begin when group members commit themselves to a mutual
purpose and coordinate and integrate their efforts to achieve it. What is true in

real life needs to be true of classroom life. In the classroom, the mutual purpose and coordinated actions spring from the positive interdependence structured by you, the teacher. By structuring positive interdependence you remind your students, *None of us is as smart as all of us!*

The more ways you structure positive interdependence within learning groups, the better. Never use one when two will do. Many students are highly competitive and will initially not believe that they really do have to help others learn. Given that every cooperative lesson must include mutual goals, the more ways positive interdependence is structured within a lesson, the clearer the message will be to students that they must be concerned about and take responsibility for both their own and other's learning. The real test of whether or not positive interdependence has been successfully structured is whether group members really care about each other's learning. If they do not care whether or not group-mates learn, then they do not really believe that they sink or swim together.

REDUCING PROBLEM BEHAVIORS

When students first start working in cooperative learning groups, they sometimes engage in unhelpful behaviors. Whenever inappropriate student behavior occurs, the teacher's first move should be toward strengthening the perceived interdependence within the learning situation. When you see a student not participating or not bringing work or materials, you may wish to increase positive interdependence by jigsawing materials, assigning the student a role that is essential to a group's success, or rewarding the group on the basis of their average performance (thus increasing the peer pressure on the student to participate).

When a student is talking about everything *but* the assignment, you may wish to give a reward that this student or group finds especially attractive and structure the task so that all members must work steadily and contribute in order for the group to succeed and attain the reward.

When you see a student working alone and ignoring the group discussion, you may wish to limit the resources in the group (if there is only one answer sheet or pencil in the group, the member will be unable to work independently) or jigsaw materials so that the student cannot do the work without the other members' information.

When you see a student refusing to let other members participate or bullying other members, you may wish to jigsaw resources, assign roles so that other group members have the most powerful roles, or reward the group on the basis of the lowest two scores by group members on a unit test.

POSITIVE INTERDEPENDENCE
AND INDIVIDUAL ACCOUNTABILITY

In cooperative situations, participants share responsibility for the joint outcome. Each group member takes personal responsibility for (a) contributing his or her

TABLE 6.2   Summary Table of Student Performances

STUDENT'S NAME _____ DATE _____

TEACHER'S NAME_____ CLASS _____

	OUTCOMES	POINTS	RATING
Cognitive	Mastery of assigned content (assignments, quizzes, reports, work units, homework)		
	Mastery of assigned skills (work units, use in problem-solving situations, homework)		
	Mastery of concepts and principles (group scores, reports, homework, observations)		
	Verbal ability 1. Communicates ideas and feelings effectively (observations, direct discussion.)		
	2. Participates actively in problem-solving groups		
	Writing ability (homework, reports)		
	Cooperative ability (observations, group products)		
	Competitive ability (observations, performances in competitions)		
	Ability to work independently (observations, performances in individualized activities)		
	Ability to apply knowledge and resources to the solution of problems (observations, group products)		
Affective	Has appreciation of subject area		
	Appreciates learning (receives enjoyment and satisfaction from learning)		
	Aware of and appreciates own abilities, achievements, talents, and resources		
	When appropriate, helps others, shares resources, expresses warmth & caring, trusts		
	Accepts and appreciates cultural, ethnic, and individual differences		
	Willing to meet the expectations of others when it is appropriate		
	Values free and open inquiry into all problems		

report
card

To Parent:

This is a report of work and progress.
Our schools wish to develop each pupil
to the limit of his capacity
that he may make the most of himself
and contribute the greatest good to society.
Citizenship, character, service, and loyalty—
knowledge, skills, attitudes, and appreciation
are our goals.
Home and school must work together.
We are here to serve you and yours.

Sincerely yours,

Superintendent

efforts to accomplish the group's goals and (b) helping other group members to do likewise. The greater the positive interdependence structured within a cooperative learning group, the more students will feel personally responsible for contributing their efforts to accomplish the group's goals. The shared responsibility adds the concept of *ought* to members' motivation—one ought to do one's share, contribute, and pull one's weight. The shared responsibility also makes each group member personally accountable to the other group members. Students will realize that if they fail to do their fair share of the work, other members will be disappointed, hurt, and upset.

POSITIVE INTERDEPENDENCE AND GIVING GRADES

Ideally, each student in your classes will participate in a variety of cooperative, competitive, and individualistic instructional activities over the grading period. When summative grades are to be given, the number of points each student received in all three types of goal structures are added up to summarize achievement. A criterion-referenced evaluation procedure will have to be used if the student is to receive a specific single grade: a norm-referenced evaluation procedure will undermine all cooperative and individualistic learning activities in the future.

Grades represent the most common reward given in most classrooms. Current grading systems, however, have created a tragedy in many schools in the United States. Almost every child comes to school optimistic about his or her chances for success. Most end up believing they are failures or losers. Ask first-grade students entering school how they are going to do academically. Most will respond, "I am going to do well." By the end of second grade, however, many are not so sure. By the end of elementary school, many students believe they are not intelligent and are poor students.

One cause of this tragedy is the evaluation and recognition systems used in our classrooms. Some students consistently receive recognition, and other students receive little or no recognition. There are winners and there are losers.

The situation is changed dramatically when high-, medium-, and low-achieving students are placed in a cooperative learning group. When the group succeeds, all members are recognized as having contributed to their joint success. Even low-ability students believe, *we* can succeed, *we* are successful. Being part of a cooperative learning group empowers each student by increasing his or her self-efficacy—the belief that if effort is exerted, success is possible. All students are recognized as contributing to the group's success. How to give grades to communicate to students that they "sink or swim together" is one of the most difficult aspects of structuring learning situations cooperatively. Here are a number of suggestions:

1. *Individual score plus bonus points based on all members reaching criterion:* Group members study together and ensure that all have mastered the assigned material.

Each then takes a test individually and is awarded that score. If all group members achieve over a preset criterion of excellence, each receives a bonus. An example is as follows:

CRITERIA FOR BONUS POINTS		GROUP	SCORES	TOTAL
100	15 points	Bill	100	110
90–99	10 points	Sally	90	100
80–89	5 points	Jane	95	105

2. *Individual score plus bonus points based on lowest score:* The group members prepare each other to take an exam. Members then receive bonus points on the basis of the lowest individual score in their group. An example is as follows:

CRITERIA FOR BONUS POINTS		GROUP	SCORES	TOTAL
71–75	1 point	Bill	100	103
76–80	2 points	Sally	98	101
81–85	3 points	Jane	84	87
86–90	4 points			
91–95	5 points			
96–100	6 points			

This procedure emphasizes encouraging, supporting, and assisting the low achievers in the group. The criterion for bonus points can be adjusted for each learning group, depending on the past performance of their lowest member.

3. *Individual score plus bonus based on improvement scores:* Members of a cooperative group prepare each other to take an exam. Each takes the exam individually and receives his or her individual grade. In addition, bonus points are awarded on the basis of whether members' percentage on the current test is higher than the average percentage on all past tests (i.e., their usual level of performance). Their percentage correct on past tests serves as their base score that they try to better. Every two tests or scores, the base score is updated. If a student scores within 4 points (above or below) his or her base score, all members of the group receive 1 bonus point. If they score 5 to 9 points above their base score, each group member receives 2 bonus points. Finally, if they score 10 or more points above their base score, or score 100 percent correct, each member receives 3 bonus points.

4. *Group score on a single product:* The group works to produce a single report, essay, presentation, worksheet, or exam. The product is evaluated, and all members receive the score awarded. When this method is used with worksheets, sets of problems, and examinations, group members are required to reach consensus on each question and be able to explain it to others. The discussion within the group enhances the learning considerably.

5. *Random selection of one member's paper to score:* Group members all complete

the work individually and then check each other's papers and certify that they are perfectly correct. Since each paper is certified by the whole group to be correct, it makes little difference which paper is graded. The teacher grades one paper chosen at random, and all group members receive the score.

6. *Average of academic scores plus collaborative skills performance score:* Group members work together to master the assigned material. They take an examination individually, and their scores are averaged. Concurrently, their work is observed, and the frequency of performance of specified collaborative skills (such as leadership or trust-building actions) is recorded. The group is given a collaborative skills performance score, which is added to their academic average to determine their overall mark.

SUMMARY

In revisiting Sugar Loaf Hill in Okinawa, William Manchester gained an important insight:

> I understand at last, why I jumped hospital that long-ago Sunday and, in violation of orders, returned to the front and almost certain death. It was an act of love. Those men on the line were my family, my home. They were closer to me than I can say, closer than any friends had been or ever would be. They were comrades; three of them had saved my life. They had never let me down, and I couldn't do it to them. I had to be with them, rather than let them die and me live with the knowledge that I might have saved them. Men, I now knew, do not fight for flag or country, for the Marine Corps or glory or any other abstraction. They fight for their friends.

Positive interdependence results in individuals striving together to achieve mutual goals, which, in turn, promotes caring and committed relationships. The more caring and committed the relationships, furthermore, the more interdependent individuals will perceive themselves to be and the more individuals will dedicate themselves to achieving the group's goals. Positive interdependence is the essence of cooperative learning. There are a number of ways of structuring positive interdependence. Teachers may structure positive goal interdependence, reward interdependence, resource interdependence, role interdependence, task interdependence, outside enemy interdependence, fantasy interdependence, identity interdependence, and environmental interdependence. The more types of positive interdependence teachers structure, the more effective cooperative learning will be. Many of the problems in student participation within learning groups may be prevented or resolved through the systematic use of positive interdependence. Grades are one of the ways in which students are given the message, "We sink or swim together."

After positive interdependence is carefully structured, teachers may wish to focus on teaching students the cooperative skills they need to function effectively within the learning groups. The next chapter focuses on this topic.

7

Student Acquisition of Collaborative Skills

INTRODUCTION

Once upon a time there were three students named Shadrach, Meshach, and Abednego. Shadrach was very concerned with being better than Meshach and Abednego. Whenever the teacher asked the three to work together, Shadrach would hide his own ideas and draw out the ideas of Meshach and Abednego. Shadrach would then secretly write his own report, taking pride that it was "better than" the group's report. This did not make Meshach and Abednego very happy. In fact, they began to refuse to work with Shadrach. Whenever the teacher said, "Would you three please work on this project together," Meshach and Abednego would say, "NO!" This did not make the teacher happy. Shadrach would just sit and smile and say, "I'm best!" After failing many times to get Shadrach to cooperate with Meshach and Abednego, the teacher sought the advice of two wise educators. They suggested that perhaps Shadrach had never learned the skills needed to cooperate. "Teach Shadrach to be cooperative," they suggested, "and his behavior will change." So the teacher did. And, not only did Shadrach's behavior change, but Meshach and Abednego also learned how to cooperate more successfully.

This story illustrates an important point in using goal structures in your classroom. You now know how to structure instruction so that cooperative, competitive, or individualistic behavior by students is appropriate, but it does not follow that students will *engage* in cooperative, competitive, or individualistic behavior. The students must have the appropriate skills in order to respond to the goal structure implemented by the teacher. With each type of goal structure comes a set of skills that each student needs to have mastered. Teachers often assume that students have the skills necessary to cooperate or compete with other students, or to work productively by themselves. This is often not the case, even when students are in high school or college. Family background and the nature of a student's peer groups influence the development of such skills. Many students come to school unable to work alone, to cooperate with others, or to compete successfully. To use all three types of goal structures successfully, teachers should deliberately teach the skills students need in order to engage in behavior appropriate to each type of goal structure, and they should make sure that students perceive the goal structures correctly (see Chapter 10). They should also establish classroom norms and climate that support the use of the skills.

TEACHING STUDENTS COLLABORATIVE SKILLS

Students who have never been taught how to work effectively with others cannot be expected to do so. Thus the first experience of many teachers who structure cooperative learning is that their students cannot collaborate with each other. Yet it is within cooperative situations, where there is a task to complete, that social skills become most relevant and should ideally be taught. All students need to become skillful in communicating, building and maintaining trust, providing leadership, and managing conflicts (Johnson, 1990; 1991; Johnson & F. Johnson, 1991). Teaching collaborative skills becomes an important prerequisite for academic learning, since achievement will improve as students become more effective in working with each other.

There are two reasons why collaborative skills are directly taught in classrooms where teachers are serious about using cooperative learning. The first is that interpersonal and small-group skills are the engine that powers cooperative learning groups. For cooperative learning groups to be productive, students must be able to engage in the needed collaborative skills. Without good leadership, effective communication, the building and maintenance of trust, and the constructive resolution of conflicts, cooperative learning groups will not maximize their productivity and effectiveness.

Second, collaborative skills in and of themselves are important instructional outcomes that relate to future career and life success. Most people realize that a college education or vocational training improves their career opportunities. Many people are less aware that interpersonal skills may be the most important set of skills to their employability, productivity, and career success. Employers typically value verbal-communication, responsibility, interpersonal, initiative, and decision-making skills. A question all employers have in mind when they interview a job applicant is: Can this person get along with other people? Having a high degree of technical competence is not enough to ensure a successful career. A person also has to have a high degree of interpersonal competence.

In 1982, for example, the Center for Public Resources published *Basic Skills in the U.S. Workforce,* a nationwide survey of businesses, labor unions, and educational institutions. The center found that 90 percent of the people fired from their jobs were fired for poor job attitudes, poor interpersonal relationships, and inappropriate behavior. Being fired for lack of basic and technical skills was infrequent. Even in high-tech careers, the ability to work effectively with other high-tech personnel is essential, and so is the ability to communicate and work with people from other professions to solve interdisciplinary problems.

In the real world of work, the heart of most jobs, especially the higher-paying, more interesting jobs, is getting others to cooperate, leading others, coping with complex problems of power and influence, and helping solve people's problems in working together. Millions of technical, professional, and managerial jobs today require much more than technical competence and professional expertise. They also require leadership. Employees are increasingly asked to get things done by influencing a large and diverse group of people (bosses, subordinates, peers, customers, and others), despite lacking much or any formal control over them, and despite their general lack of interest in cooperating. They are expected to motivate others to achieve goals, negotiate and mediate, get decisions implemented, exercise authority, and develop credibility. The interpersonal and small-group skills developed within cooperative efforts are important contributors to personal employability and career success.

In addition to career success, social skills are directly related to building and maintaining positive relationships and to psychological health. Maintaining a set of good friends your whole life long, being a caring parent, maintaining a loving relationship with your spouse, all directly relate to how interpersonally skilled you are. Quality of life as an adult largely depends on social skills. The more socially skilled a person is, furthermore, the healthier he or she tends to be psychologically. For these and many other reasons, it is important that students learn the interpersonal and small-group skills necessary to build and maintain cooperative relationships with others.

In this chapter we shall first discuss how students learn skills. We shall then discuss the skills a student needs in order to cooperate, compete, or function individualistically. Ensuring that students have the needed skills is an important first step in using goal structures in your classroom.*

HOW DO YOU TEACH SKILLS?

What is your role in teaching students skills? As the previous chapter indicates, one of the major reasons for monitoring students' behavior is to be able to identify the students who are having difficulties owing to missing or underdeveloped

---

*Students may at times overestimate their skill level and attempt behavior of which they are not really capable. Once the younger of the two authors decided that he had the skills needed to beat up the older of the two authors (he was at the young and foolish age of three). He proceeded to demonstrate his skills the first time the older of the two authors made a face at him. Besides being cruelly humiliated, the younger of the two authors has had to look at his brother making faces at him for the past fifty years without being able to do anything about it.

skills. Periodically you will want to review crucial skills with all your students. What are the steps you go through to ensure that students learn cooperative, competitive, and individualistic skills?

Step 1: Ask the students what skills they think they will need in order to cooperate (compete, work individually) successfully. To be motivated to learn a skill, the students must see the need for the skill. If students do not suggest the needed skills, you will, of course, have to. But it is important to help students understand why they need the skill.

Step 2: Help the students get a clear understanding of what the skill is, conceptually and behaviorally. In order to learn a skill, the student must have a conception of what the skill is and how the behaviors are executed. First, the behaviors have to be identified and placed in proper sequence and in close succession. It is often helpful to demonstrate the skill, describe it step by step, and then demonstrate it again. Therefore, you need to be able to describe and do the skills being taught. Pointing out good models in other students is also useful. You might ask your students to identify someone in the class who has mastered that particular skill and can be used as a model. (See Table 7.1 for an activity example.)

Step 3: Set up practice situations. Once the skill is properly understood, the behavioral patterns need to be practiced until they are firmly learned.

TABLE 7.1 Constructing a T-Chart

1. Write the name of the skill to be learned and practiced and draw a large T underneath.
2. Title the left side of the T "Looks Like" and the right side of the T "Sounds Like."
3. On the left side write a number of behaviors that operationalize the skill. On the right side write a number of phrases that operationalize the skill.
4. Have all students practice "Looks Like" and "Sounds Like" several times before the lesson is conducted.

ENCOURAGING PARTICIPATION

Looks Like	Sounds Like
Thumbs Up	"What is your idea?"
Smiles	"Good idea!"
Eye Contact	"Awesome!"
Pat on the Back	"That's interesting."

Source: D. W. Johnson, R. Johnson & E. Holubec: *Circles of learning: Cooperation in the classroom* (3rd ed). Edina, MN. Interaction, 1990. Reprinted with permission of the authors.

Step 4: Ensure that each student receives feedback on how well he is performing the skill. Receiving feedback on performance is necessary in order to correct errors, identify problems in learning the skill, identify progress in skill mastery, and compare actual performance with the desired standard of performance. Feedback may be the single most important factor affecting the acquisition of skills. The more immediate, specific, and descriptive (as opposed to evaluative) the feedback, the more it will help skill development (see Johnson, 1990, for a full discussion of feedback). The better the advance conceptualization or understanding of the skill, the more helpful the feedback will be concerning the enactment of the behaviors involved in the skill. Feedback is often quite interesting to students and increases their motivation to learn the skill. An important aspect of feedback is captured in rewarding students who successfully master the skill being taught. When students have been rewarded for skill mastery, they will tend to use the skills, and other students will imitate the behavior of those rewarded. It is not necessary to provide feedback for every student. Dividing the students into cooperative groups in which they give each other feedback on skill performance is often just as effective.

Step 5: Encourage students to persevere in practicing the skill. In learning skills, students will need to persevere. The process of learning most skills involves a period of slow beginning, followed by a period of rapid gain, followed by a plateau in which performance does not increase, followed by another spurt of learning, followed by another plateau, and so on. Plateaus are quite common in skill learning, and perseverance is necessary to keep one practicing until the next period of rapid gain begins.

After a series of classroom observations, anthropologist Jules Henry (1963) suggested that teachers encourage competition and criticism among students by modeling competitive behavior and rewarding it when it occurs—an observation that is consistent with existing research results (Bandura, Ross, & Ross, 1963). Because there is evidence that students are most likely to imitate the person with the greatest power and control over the distribution of rewards, the teacher's behavior will have a powerful influence on student behavior. In addition, a recent study by Masters (1972) indicates that if teachers offer an inequitable distribution of valued rewards to students, low-rewarded students are unlikely to be imitated. Thus, if a teacher models competitive behaviors and rewards students for engaging in competitive behaviors, the effect will be a great deal of competitive behavior on the part of most students.

Step 6: Set up situations in which the skills can be used successfully. Students need to experience success in skill development. It is their increasing sense of mastery that motivates further efforts to learn complex skills. If the skills are as necessary as the authors believe they are (and as research indicates), students will receive some reinforcement naturally as they begin to function more effectively within the goal structures.

Step 7: Require the skills to be used often enough to become integrated into the students' behavioral repertoires. A new skill must be integrated into a student's behavioral repertoire. It is at this stage that the performance of the skill becomes involuntary, automatic, and, finally, natural. After students have engaged in cooperative, competitive, and individualistic skills for a sufficiently long period, they will believe that the behavior is a natural response to the goal structure and will use the skills with little conscious awareness of doing so.

Step 8: Set classroom norms to support the use of the skills. Even if students master needed skills, they will not use them unless they believe that they are appropriate and supported. Johnson (1970) has a detailed discussion of how to establish classroom norms. Teacher modeling of the skills, the rewarding of students who appropriately engage in the skills, and the explicit statement of how you expect students to behave will influence the degree to which students engage in behavior appropriate to the goal structures.

Teacher Checklist for Student Skill Development

1. Do students believe the skill is needed and useful?
2. Do students understand what the skill is, what the behaviors are, what the sequence of behaviors is, and how it looks when it is all put together?
3. Have students had an opportunity to practice the skill?
4. Have students received feedback on how well they perform the skill? Was the feedback immediate, descriptive, and specific?
5. Have students persevered in practicing the skill?
6. Have students had the opportunity to use the skill successfully?
7. Have students used the skill frequently enough so that they have integrated the skill into their natural behavior?
8. Do the classroom norms support the use of the skill?

COOPERATIVE SKILLS

No skills are more important to a human being than the skills of cooperative interaction. Most human interaction is cooperative interaction. Cooperation is the most important and basic form of human interaction, and the skills of cooperating successfully are the most important skills anyone needs to master. There is no way to overstate this point. Competitive and individualistic behavior cannot take place unless persons are interacting within a broad cooperative framework. As stated previously, cooperation is the forest; competition and individualized effort are but trees.

Because almost all human behavior is cooperative, all interpersonal, group, and organizational skills can be identified as cooperative skills. It is impossible to list all such skills in this section, so we shall concentrate upon the more important and basic ones. Readers interested in a more thorough coverage of interpersonal and group skills are referred to Johnson (1990) and Johnson and F. Johnson (1991). The skills especially important for cooperation are communication skills, skills in building and maintaining trust, and controversy skills.

The Importance of Peer Tutoring

In most classrooms the resources of the students are seriously underutilized under a rigid competitive or individualistic goal structure in which the teacher is supposed to teach each student. The opportunities for students to teach other students are lost. Yet considerable research indicates that many students may learn better from their peers than from adults and that many students benefit greatly from teaching other students. Learning is apparently inhibited for some children when they are taught by what to them are giants and representatives of an alien adult world. Some children learn considerably better if they have the opportunity to learn from their peers. Communication may be more effective, amount of reinforcement may increase, and peer group encouragement may be more motivating when students teach each other. Although some students may be clumsy teachers at first, the research indicates that with practice and reinforcement for effective tutoring, most children can become rather good teachers.

1. Peer tutors are often effective in teaching children who do not respond well to adults.

2. Peer tutoring can develop a deep bond of friendship between the tutor and the person being helped, the result of which is very important for integrating slow learners into the group.

3. Peer tutoring takes pressure off the teacher, who can then teach a large group of students; at the same time, it allows the slow learners the individual attention they need.

4. The tutors benefit by learning to teach, a general skill that can be very useful in an adult society.

5. Peer tutoring happens spontaneously under cooperative conditions, so the teacher does not have to organize and manage it in a formal, continuing way.

COMMUNICATION SKILLS*

Communicating is the first step in cooperating. Unless people can communicate with each other, they cannot cooperate. Although it is very difficult to find a definition of communication with which everyone will agree, it is clear that *communication* is the exchange or sharing of thoughts and feelings through symbols that represent approximately the same conceptual experience for everyone involved. In emphasizing communication skills to students, it is possible to divide these skills into two categories, sending and receiving. Each student must be able to send messages that correctly represent her ideas, beliefs, feelings, opinions, reactions, needs, goals, interests, resources, and a host of other things; the skills needed to send these messages we will lump under "sending skills." Each student must also be able to receive messages accurately so that he can understand the other person's ideas, beliefs, feelings, and so on; the skills needed to receive these messages we will lump under "receiving skills." Through sending and receiving, two students can clarify their mutual goals, plan how they are going to proceed to accomplish their goals, provide relevant information and intuitions to each other, reason together, coordinate their behavior, share their resources, give help and assistance to each other, and spark each other's creativity. Thus it is upon sending and receiving skills that we shall focus in this section. What are important sending skills? The following are some of the most crucial (Johnson, 1973).

1. Clearly and unambiguously communicate your ideas and feelings. Clearly "own" your message by (a) using personal pronouns such as "I" and "my" and (b) letting others know what your thoughts and feelings are. Students "disown" their messages when they use expressions such as "most people," "some people," "our group," making it difficult to tell whether they really think and feel what they are saying or are simply repeating the thoughts and feelings of others.

2. Make your message complete and specific. Include clear statements of all necessary information that the receiver needs in order to comprehend the message. Being complete and specific seems obvious, but often people will not communicate the frame of reference they are using, the assumptions they are making, their intentions in communicating, or the leaps in thinking they are making. Thus, although listeners may hear the words, they will not comprehend the "meaning" of the message.

3. Make your verbal and nonverbal messages congruent with each other. Every face-to-face communication involves both verbal and nonverbal messages. Usually these messages are congruent, so by smiling and expressing warmth nonverbally, a person can be saying that she has appreciated your help. Communication problems arise when a person's verbal and nonverbal messages are contradictory; if

---

*For a more complete discussion of communication and a series of exercises to increase communication skills, see Johnson (1990) and Johnson and F. Johnson (1990). Many of the misunderstandings between the authors when they were young stemmed from poor communication. Because the younger author didn't talk at all until about age four and then not so well, the older author needed to communicate in a more or less nonverbal manner.

a person says, "Here is some information that may be of help to you" with a sneer and in a mocking tone of voice, the meaning you receive is confused by the two different messages being simultaneously sent.

4. Ask for feedback concerning the way in which your messages are being received. In order to communicate effectively, you must be aware of how the receiver is interpreting and processing your messages. The only way to be sure is to seek feedback continually as to what meanings the receiver is attaching to your messages.

Being skilled in sending messages is only half of what is needed to communicate effectively; one must also have receiving skills. Receiving skills include providing feedback concerning the reception of another person's message; this feedback facilitates clarification and continued discussion. The major purpose for providing such feedback is to communicate one's desire to understand completely the ideas and feelings of the sender. The major barrier to effective communication is the tendency most people have to judge, evaluate, approve, or disapprove of the messages they are receiving. For instance, the receiver may respond nonverbally or openly with, "I think you're wrong," "I don't like what you said," "I think you're right," or "That is the greatest (or worst) idea I have ever heard!" Such evaluative receiving will make the sender defensive and cautious, thereby decreasing the openness of the communication. Thus it is highly important for the receiver to indicate that he wants to understand the sender and will not evaluate the sender's messages until full understanding is reached. The specific receiving skills are paraphrasing, perception checking for feelings, and negotiating for meaning.

General Guidelines for Paraphrasing

1. Restate the sender's expressed ideas and feelings in your own words rather than mimicking or parroting her exact words.

2. Preface paraphrased remarks with, "You think . . . ," "Your position is . . . ," "It seems to you that . . . ," "You feel that . . . ," and so on.

3. Avoid any indication of approval or disapproval.

4. Make your nonverbal messages congruent with your verbal paraphrasing; look attentive, interested, and open to the sender's ideas and feelings, and show that you are concentrating upon what the sender is trying to communicate.

5. State as accurately as possible what you heard the sender say and describe the feelings and attitudes involved.

6. Do not add to or subtract from the sender's message.

7. Put yourself in the sender's shoes, and try to understand what she is feeling and what the message means.

5. Paraphrase accurately and nonevaluatively the content of the message and the feelings of the sender. The most basic and important skill involved in receiving messages is paraphrasing. To paraphrase is to restate the words of the sender, and it should be done in a way that indicates an understanding of the sender's frame of reference. The basic rule to follow in paraphrasing is: You can speak up for yourself only after you have first restated the ideas and feelings of the sender accurately and to the sender's satisfaction.

6. Describe what you perceive to be the sender's feelings. Sometimes it is difficult to paraphrase the feelings of the sender if they are not described in words in the message. Thus a second receiving skill is the perception check for the sender's feelings. This check is made simply by describing what you perceive to be the sender's feelings. This description should tentatively identify the sender's feelings without expressing approval or disapproval and without attempting to interpret or explain the causes of the feelings. It is simply saying, "Here is what I understand your feelings to be. Am I accurate?"

7. State your interpretation of the sender's message, and negotiate with the sender until there is agreement on the message's meaning. Often the words contained in a message do not carry the actual meaning. A person may ask, "Is it safe to drive this fast?" and mean, "Please slow down." A person may say, "That's a good suggestion," and mean, "I will ignore what you are saying and get rid of you by giving a superficial response." Sometimes paraphrasing the content of a message will do little to communicate your understanding of the message. In such a case, you negotiate the meaning of the message. You may wish to preface your response to the sender with, "What I think you mean is . . ." If you are accurate, you then continue the discussion; if you are inaccurate, the sender restates the message until you can state what the essential meaning of the message is. Keep in mind that it is the process that is important in negotiating meaning, not the actual phrasing you use. After the process becomes natural, a variety of introductory phrases will be used. Be tolerant of others who are using the same phrases over and over as they are developing this skill.

The sending and receiving skills described here seem very simple to most people. Yet they are very difficult to master fully and are indispensable when interacting with others. You should practice them consciously until they are as automatic as saying good morning.

Another element that has a great influence upon both communication and cooperation is the trust level within a relationship. It is to this issue that we now turn.

BUILDING AND MAINTAINING A TRUSTING CLIMATE

Why is trust important? Trust is a necessary condition for stable cooperation and effective communication. The higher the trust, the more stable the cooperation and the more effective the communication. Students will more openly express their thoughts, feelings, reactions, opinions, information, and ideas when the trust level is high. When the trust level is low, students will be evasive, dishonest, and inconsiderate in their communications. Students will more honestly and frequently declare their cooperative intentions and make contributions to a cooperative effort when they believe they are dealing with highly trustworthy individuals. Cooperation rests upon everyone's sharing resources, giving and receiving help, dividing the work, and contributing to the accomplishment of mutual goals. Such behaviors will occur when there is trust that all are contributing to the group's progress and are using their openness and resources for group rather than personal gain. The development and maintenance of trust are discussed at length in Johnson (1990); if possible, you should review the chapters on trust, self-disclosure, and acceptance before going ahead with this chapter.

What is trust? Making a choice to *trust* another person requires the perception that the choice can lead to gains or losses, that whether you will gain or lose depends upon the behavior of the other person, that the loss will be greater than the gain, and that the person will likely behave so that you will gain rather than lose. Sounds complicated, doesn't it? There is nothing simple about trust; it is a complex concept and difficult to explain. Examples may help.

Trust is lending your older brother your bicycle; you may either gain his

appreciation or lose your bike—which one happens depends upon him. You will suffer more if your bike is wrecked than you will gain by his appreciation, and you really expect him to take care of your bike! (Sad experience has led the younger of the two authors to recommend that you never lend your bike to your older brother.) For another example, consider this situation: A student is in a small group that is supposed to complete a report on the play *Macbeth*. The student begins to contribute to the discussion knowing that she will gain if she contributes good ideas that others accept and will lose if her ideas are laughed at and belittled. Whether she gains or loses depends upon the behavior of the other members of her group. She knows she will feel more hurt if she is laughed at than satisfaction if her ideas are appreciated. Her expectation is that the other group members will consider her ideas and accept them. The issue of trust is expressed in the question every student asks: "If I openly express myself, will what I say be held against me?"

When student groups work on problem-solving tasks, what are the crucial elements of trust? Student cooperation requires openness and sharing, which are determined by the expression of acceptance, support, and cooperative intentions. *Openness* is the sharing of information, ideas, thoughts, feelings, and reactions to the issue the group is pursuing. *Sharing* is the offering of one's materials and resources to others in order to help them move the group toward goal accomplishment. *Acceptance* is the communication of high regard for another person and his contributions and behavior. *Support* is the communicating to another person that you recognize his strengths and believe he has the capabilities needed to productively manage the situation he is in. *Cooperative intentions* are the expectation that you are going to behave cooperatively and that everyone else will also. From these definitions, *trusting behavior* may be defined as openness and sharing, and *trustworthy behavior* may be defined as expressing acceptance, support, and cooperative intentions. In assessing a student's trustworthy behavior, it is important to remember that accepting and supporting the contributions of other group members does not mean that one will agree with everything they have to say. A person can express acceptance and support the openness and sharing of others while at the same time expressing different ideas and opposing points of view. This is an important point in building and maintaining trust.

What is the teacher's role in initiating and encouraging trust among students during periods of cooperative activities? The following are some suggestions:

1. Encourage students to contribute openly their information, ideas, thoughts, feelings, intuitions, hunches, and reactions to the group's discussion and work.
2. Encourage students to share materials and resources.
3. Ensure that the students have the skills to express acceptance, support, and desire to cooperate.
4. Encourage students to express cooperative intentions, acceptance, and support toward each other during their cooperative interactions.

5. Point out rejecting and nonsupportive behaviors that shut off future cooperation, such as silence, ridicule, and superficial acknowledgment of an idea.

6. Periodically, have groups that are cooperating fill out the questionnaire on trusting and trustworthy behavior and discuss the results to see how their cooperation could be improved in the future.

Productive cooperation will exist within a group when members are both trusting and trustworthy; nonproductive cooperation will take place when group members are distrustful and untrustworthy. It is also possible for members of a group to be trusting but not trustworthy or to be trustworthy but not trusting. This pattern is represented as follows:

	High Acceptance and Support	Low Acceptance and Support
High Openness and Sharing	Trusting and trustworthy	Trusting, but untrustworthy
Low Openness and Sharing	Distrustful, but trustworthy	Distrustful and untrustworthy

EXAMINATION OF TRUST BEHAVIOR

In order to help you assess the level of trust within groups of students working cooperatively, a questionnaire is provided. This questionnaire may be reproduced and given to classes old enough to read or be used as a guide to interview students who cannot read at the necessary level. The procedure for using the questionnaire is as follows:

1. Have the students complete the questionnaire.
2. Have the students score the questionnaire.
3. Have the students discuss in their cooperative groups the way in which each member completed the questionnaire. Group members are to share their impressions of each other's trusting and trustworthy behavior. If such a discussion cannot take place, the students are to discuss the level of trust in the group indicated by such a lack of openness and feedback.
4. Instruct the students as to how they can skillfully build and maintain trust in their cooperative groups.

Remember that trust is appropriate only when individuals are cooperating. When they are competing, other skills are appropriate. The emphasis, therefore, should be placed on trust within a specific cooperative situation, not upon trust relationships in a wide variety of situations. The questionnaire is given in the next section. It is followed by instructions on scoring.

Your Behavior

Following are a series of questions about your behavior in the cooperative situation you have now completed (or are involved with). Answer each question as honestly as you can. There are no right or wrong answers. It is important for each student to describe his or her behavior as accurately as possible.

1. I offer facts, give my opinions and ideas, provide suggestions and relevant information to help the group discussion.

    Never   Seldom   Frequently   Always

2. I express my willingness to cooperate with other group members and my expectations that they also will be cooperative.

    Never   Seldom   Frequently   Always

3. I am open and candid in my dealings with the entire group.

    Never   Seldom   Frequently   Always

4. I give support to group members who are on the spot and struggling to express themselves intellectually or emotionally.

    Never   Seldom   Frequently   Always

5. I keep my thoughts, ideas, feelings, and reactions to myself during group discussions.

    Never   Seldom   Frequently   Always

6. I evaluate the contributions of other group members in terms of whether their contributions are useful to me and whether the other group members are right or wrong.

    Never   Seldom   Frequently   Always

7. I take risks in expressing new ideas and my current feelings during a group discussion.

    Never   Seldom   Frequently   Always

8. I communicate to other group members that I am aware of, and appreciate, their abilities, talents, capabilities, skills, and resources.

    Never   Seldom   Frequently   Always

9. I offer help and assistance to anyone in the group in order to bring up the performance of everyone.

    Never   Seldom   Frequently   Always

10. I accept and support the openness of other group members, supporting them for taking risks and encouraging individuality in group members.

    Never   Seldom   Frequently   Always

11. I share any materials, books, sources of information, or other resources I have with

the other group members in order to promote the success of all members and the group as a whole.

Never   Seldom   Frequently   Always

12. I often paraphrase or summarize what other members have said before I respond or comment.

Never   Seldom   Frequently   Always

13. I level with other group members.

Never   Seldom   Frequently   Always

14. I warmly encourage all members to participate, giving them recognition for their contributions, demonstrating acceptance of and openness to their ideas, and generally being friendly and responsive to them.

Never   Seldom   Frequently   Always

To score this questionnaire, count "Never" as 1, "Seldom" as 2, "Frequently" as 3, and "Always" as 4. ✓Reverse the scoring on questions 5 and 6. Then add the scores in the following way:

Openness and Sharing	*Acceptance and Support*
1. _____	2. _____
3. _____	4. _____
✓5. _____	✓6. _____
7. _____	8. _____
9. _____	10. _____
11. _____	12. _____
13. _____	14. _____
Total _____	Total _____

If a student has a score of 21 or more, classify him as trusting or trustworthy, whichever the case might be. If a student has a score of less than 21, classify him as distrustful or untrustworthy, whichever the case might be.

Tutoring Skills

In order to provide help and assistance to fellow cooperators, a student needs to learn

1. How to recognize that he or she needs help.

2. How to ask others for help.

3. How to search for others who may need assistance.

4. How to provide instruction, feedback, and reinforcement for other students.

Such skills can be easily learned through a series of role-playing situations developed by the teacher.

LEADERSHIP SKILLS

Perhaps Benjamin Franklin became a renowned leader because he was able to vary his behavior systematically from situation to situation so as to provide the appropriate leadership actions at the appropriate time. There is currently a consensus among social scientists that leadership skills and competencies are not inherited from one's ancestors, that they do not magically appear when a person is assigned to a leadership position, and that the same set of competencies will not provide adequate leadership in every situation. Different situations require different approaches to leadership.

Groups have at least two basic objectives: to complete a task and to maintain effective collaborative relationships among the members. The *distributed-actions* theory of leadership emphasizes that certain functions need to be filled if a group is to meet these two objectives. It defines *leadership* as the performance of acts that help the group to complete its task successfully and maintain effective working relationships among its members. For a group to complete its task successfully, group members must obtain, organize, and use information to make a decision. In doing so they require certain task-leadership actions. Members have to contribute, ask for, summarize, and coordinate the information. They have to structure and give direction to the group's efforts and provide the energy to motivate decision making. For any group to be successful, such task-leadership actions have to be provided.

But it does no good to complete a task if the manner of doing so alienates several group members. If a number of group members refuse to come to the next meeting, the group has not been successful. Thus members must pay attention to maintaining good working relationships while working on the task. The task must be completed in a way that increases the ability of group members to work together effectively in the future. For these things to happen, certain maintenance-leadership actions are needed. Members have to encourage one another to participate. They have to relieve tension when it gets too high, facilitate communication among themselves, and evaluate the emotional climate of the group. They have to discuss how the group's work can be improved, and they have to listen carefully and respectfully to one another. These leadership actions are necessary for the maintenance of friendly relationships among members and indeed, for the success of the group.

The distributed-actions theory of leadership includes two basic ideas: (1) any member of a group may become a leader by taking actions that help the group complete its task and maintain effective collaborative relationships; (2) any leadership function may be fulfilled by different members performing a variety of relevant behaviors. Leadership, therefore, is specific to a particular group in a particular situation. Under specific circumstances any given behavior may or may not serve a group function. Under one set of conditions a particular behavior may be helpful; under another set it may impair the effectiveness of the group. For example, when a group is trying to define a problem, suggesting a possible solution may not be helpful; however, when the group is offering various solutions to a defined problem, suggesting a possible solution may indeed be helpful.

From the perspective of this theory, leadership is a learned set of skills that anyone with certain minimal requirements can acquire. Responsible group membership and leadership both depend on flexible behavior, the ability to diagnose what behaviors are needed at a particular time in order for the group to function most efficiently, and the ability to fulfill these behaviors or to get other members to fulfill them. A skilled member or leader, therefore, has to have diagnostic skills in order to be aware that a given function is needed in the group and must be sufficiently adaptive to provide the diverse types of behaviors needed for different conditions. In addition, an effective group member or leader must be able to utilize the abilities of other group members in providing the actions needed by the group.

For at least three reasons, it is usually considered necessary for the behaviors that fulfill group functions to be distributed among group members. First, if members do not participate, then their ideas, skills, and information are not being contributed. This hurts the group's effectiveness. The second reason is that members are committed to what they help build. Members who participate become more committed to the group and what the group has done. Members who remain silent tend not to care about the group and its effectiveness. The more members feel they have influenced the group and contributed to its work, the more committed they will be to the group. The third reason is that active members often become worried or annoyed about the silent members and view them as unconcerned about task completion. Unequal patterns of participation can create maintenance problems within the group.

Sometimes actions within a group not only help it to operate but serve the individual as well. Such individually oriented behavior sometimes involves issues or personal identity (Who am I in this group? Where do I fit in?); personal goals and needs (What do I want from this group? Are the group's goals consistent with my personal goals?); power and control (Who will control what we do? How much power and influence do I have?); and intimacy (How close will we get to each other? How much can I trust the other group members?).

The distributed-actions theory of leadership is one of the most concrete and direct approaches available for improving a person's leadership skills and for improving the effectiveness of a group. People can be taught the diagnostic skills and behaviors that help a group accomplish its task and maintain effective collaborative relationships among its members. There is, however, some criticism of the approach. Members can take so many different actions to help in task achievement and group maintenance that specific ones are hard to pin down. What constitutes leadership then depends on the view of the person who is listing the leadership behaviors.

UTILIZING CREATIVE CONTROVERSY

Have you learned lessons only of
those who admired you, and were tender
with you, and stood aside for you?

Have you not learned great lessons
from those who braced themselves
against you, and disputed the passage
with you?

Walt Whitman, Leaves of Grass

Involved participation in cooperative groups will inevitably produce conflicts among ideas, opinions, conclusions, theories, and information of members. Such controversies are an important aspect of cooperative learning. *Controversy* exists when one person's ideas, information, conclusions, theories, and opinions are incompatible with those of another, and the two seek to reach an agreement. When teachers structure an academic controversy, they assign students to cooperative groups of four, divide the group into two pairs, and assign a "pro" position to one pair and a "con" position to another pair. Teachers carefully establish (1) positive goal interdependence by stating that the goal of the controversy is to write a group report that represents the best thinking of all members, (2) positive resource interdependence by dividing the materials into pro and con positions, and (3) individual accountability by announcing that a test will be given to each student on both positions. Teachers then require the pairs of students to do the following things (Johnson & Johnson, 1991):

1. Prepare the best case for their assigned position.
2. Present and advocate their assigned position to the opposing pair.
3. Refute the opposing pair's position and reasoning while rebutting attacks on their own position and reasoning.
4. Reverse perspectives by presenting the opposing position as sincerely and forcefully as they can.
5. Reach a decision based on a synthesis of the best ideas and thinking from both sides.

In effect, students are required to rehearse orally the relevant information; advocate a position; teach their knowledge to peers; analyze, critically evaluate, and rebut information; reason both deductively and inductively; and synthesize and integrate information into factual and judgmental conclusions that are summarized into a joint position to which all sides can agree. Controversy enhances individual achievement, higher-level reasoning, and long-term retention, as well as the quality of relationships among group members. In order to function effectively within a cooperative learning group, students will have to have the skills required for promoting and managing controversies constructively. These skills are as follows:

1. Define controversies as problem-solving situations in which differences need to be clarified, rather than as "win-lose" conflicts in which one person's ideas have to dominate. Destructive controversies are characterized by an orientation on the part of students to "win" at the expense of other group members whose ideas are defeated. In a "win-lose" situation, every action is seen in terms of who is going to dominate whom. Such a competitive orientation within a cooperative situation will seriously undermine cooperation. When controversy is approached from a problem-solving point of view, students tend to recognize the legitimacy of each other's ideas and contributions and search for a solution accommodating the needs of all group members.

2. Be critical of ideas, not persons. Ideas are discussed, not personalities, and nothing personal is meant in disagreement. It is possible to express disagreement without personally rejecting, and students should be encouraged to do so. This is an important skill for cooperators to learn.

3. Appropriately pace the differentiation phase (bringing out differences) and the integration phase (putting the different ideas together) of the problem-solving process. First, all different points of view are brought out and explored. Second, creative syntheses to arrive at the best solution are sought. It is a serious mistake to look for ways to integrate ideas before all the differences have been explored. The potential for integration is never greater than the adequacy of the differentiation already achieved.

Many of the controversy skills are promoted by inquiry learning situations. There is a strong relationship between inquiry teaching and cooperation; inquiry tasks are problem-solving situations, and a cooperative goal structure is generally the most appropriate one to use. The question-asking strategies, brainstorming of alternatives, open discussion of ideas, and other aspects of inquiry teaching will all help in resolving controversies. Other suggestions for inquiry teaching are these:

1. Initiate controversy in order to increase student interest and motivation. Sharpening up students' ideas, opening up new possibilities, and deepening the level of analysis and insight can all be accomplished by teachers when they initiate controversies.

2. Reward the posing of alternatives (which will increase controversy) by students.

3. Reward students for changing their minds when confronted with evidence (this is an important behavior for teachers to model).

4. Encourage students to consider alternatives from different points of view (the story of the three blind men and an elephant is always a good example of the value of perspective taking).

4. Take the point of view or perspective of other students so that you understand what they are saying from their frame of reference. This procedure, sometimes called role reversal, is a skill that everyone must master. It is the ability to understand how a situation appears to other students and how they are reacting cognitively and emotionally to the situation. It is crucial for integrating different perspectives into a more complete and higher-quality solution to the problem being worked upon. The opposite of such perspective taking, *egocentrism,* is the inability to take another person's perspective.

In addition to promoting constructive controversy within cooperative learning groups, there are other conflict procedures and skills that teachers will wish students to develop. Much of teachers' time is spent dealing with conflict among students, between students and staff, between staff and parents, or even among staff members. Conflicts are inevitable whenever committed people work together to achieve mutual goals. Conflicts are constructively managed through a five-step procedure (Johnson & Johnson, 1987). The first step is creating a cooperative context. In order for long-term mutual interests to be recognized and valued, individuals have to perceive their interdependence and be invested in each other's well being. The second step is structuring academic controversies. In or-

der to maximize student achievement, critical thinking, and higher-level reasoning, students need to engage in intellectual conflicts. Within structured controversies, students work with a learning partner in examining an academic issue, preparing a pro or con position, advocating their position to an opposing pair, criticizing the opposing position, reversing perspectives, and synthesizing the best arguments on both sides to derive a conclusion. The use of academic controversy is a very powerful instructional procedure that will move cooperative learning groups to new heights of productivity and higher-level learning.

The third step is teaching students how to negotiate, and the fourth step is teaching students how to mediate. Students may be taught the basic steps and skills of negotiating an agreement with an opponent. They may then be trained as mediators to help their classmates successfully negotiate resolutions to their conflicts. Students first try to negotiate their conflicts and, if negotiation fails, ask a peer mediator for help. Finally, when mediation fails, the teacher or principal arbitrates the conflict (step 5). This is a last resort because it typically involves deciding who is right and wrong, leaving at least one student angry toward the arbitrator. The procedures for using this five-step process of utilizing constructive conflict to improve instruction may be found in *Creative Conflict* by Johnson and Johnson (1987).

USING BONUS POINTS TO TEACH SOCIAL SKILLS

Many teachers may want to use a structured program to teach students the interpersonal and small-group skills they need to cooperate effectively with classmates. Such a program will provide students with the opportunity to help their groups earn bonus points using targeted cooperative skills. These points can be accumulated for academic credit or for special rewards such as free time or minutes listening to one's own choice of music. The procedure for doing so is as follows:

1. Identify, define, and teach a social skill you want students to use in working cooperatively with each other. This skill becomes a target for mastery.
2. Use group points and group rewards to increase the use of the cooperative skill:
   a. Each time a student engages in the targeted skill, the student's group receives a point.
   b. Points may only be awarded for positive behavior.
   c. Points are added and never taken away. All points are permanently earned.
3. Summarize total points daily. Emphasize daily progress toward the goal. Use a visual display such as a graph or chart.
4. Develop an observational system that samples each group an equal amount of time. In addition, utilize student observers to record the frequency of students using the targeted skills.

5. Set a reasonable number of points for earning the reward. Rewards are both social and tangible. The social reward is having the teacher say, "That shows thought"; "I like the way you explained it"; "That's a good way of putting it"; "Remarkably well done." The tangible reward is the points earned, which may be traded in for free time, computer time, library time, time to play a game, extra recess time, and any other activity that students value.

6. In addition to group points, class points may be awarded. The teacher, for example, might say, "Eighteen people are ready to begin and help the class earn a reward," or, "I noticed twelve people worked the last 25 minutes." Class points may be recorded with a number line, beans in a jar, or checks on the chalk board.

7. In addition to social skills, potential target behaviors include following directions, completing assigned tasks, handing in homework, behaving appropriately in out-of-class settings such as lunch or assemblies, or helping substitute teachers.

Processing Checklist

_____ 1. Teacher selects two or three skills to observe for.

_____ 2. Teacher appoints observers and prepares observation form.

_____ 3. Teacher observes and intervenes when necessary.

_____ 4. Student observers assess how well collaborative skills have been performed.

_____ 5. Groups process by using student observers as a source of feedback.

_____ 6. Whole class processes, summarizing the feedback from each group and the teacher's observation.

_____ 7. Group members set goals for performing collaborative skills in the next group session.

SUMMARY

If the potential of cooperative learning is to be realized, students must have the prerequisite interpersonal and small-group skills and be motivated to use them. These skills need to be taught just as systematically as math and social studies. Doing so involves communicating to students the need for the social skills, defining and modeling the skills, having students practice the skills over and over again, processing how effectively the students are performing the skills, and ensuring that students persevere until the skills are fully integrated into the students' behavioral repertoire. Doing so will not only increase student achievement, but will also increase students' future employability, career success, quality of relationships, and psychological health.

Nothing we learn is more important than the skills required to work cooperatively with other people. Most human interaction is cooperative. Without some skill in cooperating effectively, it is difficult (if not impossible) to maintain a marriage, hold a job, or be part of a community, society, and world. In this chapter we have only discussed a few of the interpersonal and small-group skills needed for effective cooperation. For a more thorough and extensive coverage of these skills see *Reaching Out* (Johnson, 1990), *Joining Together* (Johnson & F. Johnson, 1991), *Human Relations and Your Career* (Johnson, 1991), *Circles of Learning* (Johnson, Johnson, Holubec, 1990), and *Creative Conflict* (Johnson & Johnson, 1987).

'90

8

Cooperative Informal and Base Groups

EMPOWERING STUDENTS THROUGH COOPERATIVE LEARNING

The most important aspect of school life is empowering individuals by organizing them into cooperative teams. Such empowerment begins in the classroom. Students often feel helpless and discouraged. Giving them cooperative learning partners provides hope and opportunity. Cooperative learning groups empower their members to act by making them feel strong, capable, and committed. It is social support from and accountability to valued peers that motivate committed efforts to achieve and succeed. If classrooms are to be places where students care about each other and are committed to each other's success in academic endeavors, a cooperative structure must exist. A cooperative structure consists of the integrated use of three types of cooperative learning groups.

TYPES OF COOPERATIVE LEARNING GROUPS

The best answer to the question 'What is the most effective method of teaching?' is that it depends on the goal, the student, the content, and the teacher. But the next best answer is "Students teaching other students." There is a wealth of evidence that peer teaching is extremely effective for a wide range of goals, content, and students of different levels and personalities.

McKeachie, Pintrich, Lin, & Smith (1986, p. 63)

Cooperative learning may be incorporated into classroom life through the use of formal learning groups, informal learning groups, and base groups. *Formal learning groups* are more structured and stay together until the task is done (e.g., a triad that ensures all members master the information assigned about the Revolutionary War). *Informal learning groups* are short-term and less structured (check the person next to you to see if he understood). *Base groups* are long-term groups whose role is primarily one of peer support and long-term accountability. We have discussed the use of formal cooperative learning groups and the five essential components that make cooperation work. Positive interdependence and the teaching of social skills have been covered in some depth. Once a teacher understands how to use the five essential components to structure lessons cooperatively, the other two types of cooperative learning groups need to be added to the classroom. This chapter, therefore, first covers informal cooperative learning groups and then discusses base groups.

INFORMAL COOPERATIVE LEARNING GROUPS

Lecturing, or direct teaching, is an essential aspect of classroom instruction. It is now the most common teacher behavior in elementary and secondary schools as well as colleges and universities. Even in training programs in business and industry, lecturing dominates. Though lecturing, or direct teaching, has traditionally been conducted within competitive and individualistic structures, lectures can be made cooperative through the use of informal cooperative learning groups.

Informal cooperative learning groups are temporary, ad hoc groups that last for only one discussion or one class period. Their purposes are to focus student attention on the material to be learned, set a mood conducive to learning, help organize in advance the material to be covered in a class session, ensure that students cognitively process the material being taught, and provide closure to an instructional session. Informal cooperative learning groups also ensure that misconceptions, incorrect understanding, and gaps in understanding are identified and corrected, that the discussion and elaboration that promote retention and transfer take place, and that learning experiences are personalized. They may be used at any time but are especially useful during a lecture or direct teaching before the students' eyes begin to glaze over (some estimates of the length of time that people can attend to a lecture are around 12 to 15 minutes; students then need to process what they are hearing, or their minds drift away). During direct teaching the instructional challenge for the teacher is to ensure that students do the intellectual work of organizing material, explaining it, summarizing it, and integrating it into existing conceptual networks. This may be achieved by having students do the advance organizing, cognitively process what they are learning, and provide closure to the lesson. Breaking up lectures with short cooperative processing times will give you slightly less lecture time but will enhance what is learned and build relationships among the students in your class. It will help counter what is proclaimed as the main problem of lectures: "The information passes from the notes of the professor to the notes of the student without passing through the mind of either one."

The following procedure may help to plan a lecture that keeps students actively engaged intellectually. It entails having *focused discussions* before and after a lecture (i.e., bookends) and interspersing *turn-to-your-partner* discussions throughout the lecture.

1. Focused discussion 1: Plan your lecture around a series of questions that the lecture answers. Prepare the questions on an overhead transparency or write them on the board so that students can see them. Have students discuss the questions in pairs. The discussion task is aimed at promoting *advance organizing* of what the students know about the topic to be presented and establishing *expectations* about what the lecture will cover.

2. Turn-to-your-partner discussions: Divide the lecture into 10- to 15-minute segments. This is about the length of time an adult can concentrate on a lecture. Plan a short discussion task to be given to pairs of students after each segment. The task needs to be short enough that students can complete it within three or four minutes. Its purpose is to ensure that students are actively thinking about the material being presented. The discussion task may be to

a. Summarize the answer to the question being discussed.
b. Give a reaction to the theory, concepts, or information being presented.
c. Elaborate the material being presented (relate it to past learning so that it gets integrated into existing conceptual frameworks).
d. Predict what is going to be presented next.
e. Attempt to resolve the conceptual conflict the presentation has aroused.
f. Hypothesize answers to the question being posed.

Each discussion task should have four components: *formulate* an answer to the question being asked, *share* your answer with your partner, *listen* carefully to his or her answer, and *create* a new answer that is superior to each member's initial formulation through the processes of association, building on each other's thoughts, and synthesizing. Students will need to gain some experience with this procedure to become skilled in doing it within a short period of time.

3. Focused discussion 2: Prepare an ending discussion task to summarize what students have learned from the lecture. The discussion should result in students integrating what they have just learned into existing conceptual frameworks. The task may also point students toward what the homework will cover or what will be presented in the next class session. This provides closure to the lecture.

Once such preparation has been completed, the lecture may be given by

1. Having students choose partners. The nearest person will do. You may wish to require different seating arrangements each class period so that students will meet and interact with a number of other students in the class.

2. Giving the pairs the cooperative assignment of completing the initial (advance organizer) task. Give them only four or five minutes to do so.

3. Delivering the first segment of the lecture. Then give the pairs a discussion task. Give them only three or four minutes to complete it. Use the *formulate/share/listen/create* procedure. Randomly choose two or three students to give 30-second summaries of their discussions. It is important that students be randomly called on to share their answers after each discussion task. Such *individual accountability* ensures that the pairs take the tasks seriously and check each other to ensure that both are prepared to answer.

4. Delivering the second segment of the lecture and then giving a second discussion task. Repeat this sequence until the lecture is completed.

5. Giving students the ending focused discussion task to provide closure to the lecture. Give students five or six minutes to summarize and discuss the material covered in the lecture.

6. Processing the procedure with students regularly to help them increase their skill and speed in completing short discussion tasks. Processing questions may include, (a) "How well prepared were you to complete the discussion tasks?" and (b) "How could you come even better prepared tomorrow?"

The informal cooperative learning group is not only effective for getting students actively involved in understanding what they are learning, it also provides time for you to gather your wits, reorganize your notes, take a deep breath,

and move around the class listening to what students are saying. Listening to student discussions can give you direction and insight into how the concepts you are teaching are being grasped by your students (who, unfortunately, do not have graduate degrees in the topic you are presenting).

ENEMIES OF THE LECTURE

1. *Students who are preoccupied with what happened during the previous hour or with what happened on the way to class.* In order for lectures to succeed you must focus student attention on the subject area and topic you are dealing with in class.

2. *Emotional moods that block learning and cognitive processing of information.* Students who are angry or frustrated about something are *not* open to new learning. In order for lectures to work, you must set a constructive learning mood.

3. *Students who go to sleep or who turn on a tape recorder while they write lettes or read comic books.* In order for lectures to work, you must focus students' attention on the material being presented and ensure that they cognitively process the information and integrate it with what they already know.

4. *Students who do not understand the lecture and mechanically write down what the instructor says.* Such students often learn material incorrectly and incompletely because of lack of understanding. In order to make lectures work there has to be some means of checking the accuracy and completeness of students' understanding of the material being presented.

5. *Students who are isolated and alienated and believe that no one cares about them as persons or about their academic progress.* In order to make lectures work students have to believe that there are other people in the class who will provide help and assistance because they care about them as people and about the quality of their learning.

6. *Entertaining and clear lectures that misrepresent the complexity of the material being presented.* While entertaining and impressing students is nice, it often does not help students understand and think critically about complex material. To make lectures work students must think critically and use higher-level reasoning in cognitively processing course content. One of our colleagues, whom we now team teach with regularly using cooperative learning procedures, is a magnificent lecturer. His explanation of the simplex algorithm for solving linear programming problems is so clear and straightforward that the students go away with the view that it is very simple. Later when they try to solve a problem on their own, they find that they don't have a clue as to how to begin. Our colleague used to blame himself for not explaining well enough. Sometimes he blamed the students. Now he puts small groups of students to work on a simple linear programming problem, circulates and checks the progress of each group and student, provides help where he feels it is appropriate, and only gives his brilliant lectures when the students understand the problem and are ready to hear his proposed solution. Both he and the students are much happier with their increased understanding.

The use of cooperative learning strategies will overcome these enemies by focusing students' attention on academic material, setting a productive learning mood, ensuring that students engage intellectually in the material, keeping students' attention focused on the content, ensuring that misconceptions, incorrect understanding, and gaps in understanding are corrected, providing an opportunity for discussion and elaboration that promote retention and transfer, and making learning experiences personal and immediate.

BASE GROUPS: WHAT ARE THEY?

Jim stands at the school door. "In this school," he thinks, "no one really knows me, no one cares about me, and no one will miss me when I am gone." Jim is a student *at risk* for academic failure, interpersonal isolation, psychological maladjustment, and social incompetence. There are many such students at risk, students who feel alone in the school, outside of its purposes, connected to no faculty member, and liked by few if any of their classmates. Many of these students drop out of school. They are not missed by anyone, nor are they grieved for.

Schools can only influence students who are physically present. Children and youth must attend school if they are to achieve valuable knowledge, form constructive peer relationships, and develop personally and socially in healthy ways. Attending school, however, comes primarily from the heart, not the head. It is caring and committed relationships that keep students in school. Students must believe that they belong. They must believe that their friends are in school. Students' membership in the school must be promoted through social bonding and attachment to teachers and classmates. If attachment is weak or absent, students can act without regard for the feelings of others. Without attachment it is easy to say, "I do not care," and to believe that others "do not care about me." It is then a short step to not coming to school at all.

Caring and committed relationships cannot be created from memos and announcements over the loudspeaker that "in this school you are required to like each other." Caring and committed relationships evolve from working together to get the job done. It is out of being part of a joint effort to accomplish something worthwhile that friendships evolve. There must be a meaningful job to do. The efforts of others must contribute to your success, and your efforts must benefit others as well as yourself. At-risk students must exert mental and physical effort to learn if they are to commit themselves to gaining an education. They must realize that schooling requires hard work but is worth it because it (a) contributes to others' success as well as their own and (b) prepares them to succeed later in life. Schools are the practice field for later careers and informed citizenship in a community, society, and world. Students must be willing to follow the adages of "Teamwork!" and "You have to sweat on the practice field before you can perform on the playing field." Unless students participate, exert effort, and succeed in the activities school offers, it is unlikely that commitment to achieve academically can be sustained. To provide all students with the long-term caring and committed relationships with classmates required to motivate them to achieve in school, teachers will wish to utilize cooperative base groups.

Base groups are long-term, heterogeneous cooperative learning groups with stable membership whose primary responsibilities are to (a) provide support, encouragement, and assistance in completing assignments and (b) hold each other accountable for striving to learn. More specifically, base groups

1. Are heterogeneous in membership so that they represent a cross section of the school population in terms of gender, ability, and ethnic and cultural background.
2. Last for the duration of the class (a semester or year) and preferably for several years. When students know that they will spend several years within the same cooperative base group, they become committed to find ways to motivate and encourage their groupmates. Problems in working with each other cannot be ignored or waited out.
3. Meet regularly.
4. Personalize the work required and the learning experiences.

Base groups have two major purposes:

1. To provide each other with the support, encouragement, and assistance needed to complete assignments and make good academic progress. This support includes letting absent group members know what went on in class, interacting informally every day within and between classes, discussing assignments, and helping each other with homework.
2. To hold each other accountable for striving to make academic progress.

WHY USE COOPERATIVE BASE GROUPS?

There are many reasons why cooperative base groups should be used in schools. One of the major outcomes of cooperative learning is that students who "work together to get the job done" develop positive relationships with each other. The longer the group is together, the more positive and personal the relationships among members become. The caring and committed relationships built within base groups are essential for motivating long-term efforts to achieve and for healthy social, cognitive, and physical development. The development of academically oriented values depends on long-term caring relationships.

The Necessities of Life

There are certain basics in life that all children need in order to develop in healthy ways. One set of necessities involves good nutrition, adequate sleep, and appropriate clothing and shelter. Another set involves caring and committed relationships. All children need to know that there are people in the world who love you, are committed to you, will provide you with help and assistance when it is needed, and will put your needs ahead of their own. Schools need to ensure that every student is involved in long-term caring and committed relationships with peers. One way to do so is through cooperative base groups.

Need for Long-term Permanent Relationships

Most relationships in schools are, at best, shipboard romances. When most teachers face their classes and when most classmates look at each other in September, they implicitly say, "I will care about you for one year." Students know that next year, they will have a different teacher and, to a large extent, different classmates. Relationships are temporary because in most schools it is assumed that "any classmate will do" and "any teacher will do." Classmates and teachers are perceived to be replaceable parts in the education machine. Thus, when it is time to assign first-graders to second-grade classrooms, little attempt is made to keep intact classes together. It is assumed that a student's classmates are basically irrelevant to the educational process. Similarly, first-graders are assigned to second-grade classrooms with the assumption that it really does not matter who the second-grade teacher is, as "any second grade teacher will do." While there are some advantages to changing classmates and teachers, it creates fragmented, temporary relationships.

It is important that some of the relationships built within school are permanent. School has to be more than a series of shipboard romances. Receiving social support and being held accountable for appropriate behavior by peers who care about you and have a long-term commitment to your success and well-being constitute an important aspect of growing up and progressing through school. It increases achievement and promotes psychological health. In permanent relationships there is increased opportunity to transmit achievement-oriented values. Learning for your caring and committed groupmates is a powerful motivator. Thus permanent cooperative base groups may be formed to create the caring and committed relationships that improve attendance, personalize the school experience, increase achievement, and improve the quality of life within the classroom.

"I Couldn't Let My Group Down!": Motivation Comes from the Heart, Not the Head

Schools are not successful unless each student is working hard to do the best with what he or she has got. Not everyone has a 130 IQ or complex talents. But every student can work hard to maximize his or her achievements, conceptual understanding of the material being studied, level of reasoning, and creativity. Numerous students, however, spend very little time studying, even those students who are graduating and getting good grades. They often avoid hard subjects like math, science, and foreign languages and simply coast along, doing far less than they are capable of doing. Some students (perhaps over 50 percent in some schools) choose to do almost no schoolwork at all.

In order to increase the effort students commit to learning and achievement, they must be involved in caring and committed relationships within which (a) they are held accountable for exerting considerable effort to learn and (b) they are given the help, assistance, encouragement, and recognition they need to sustain their efforts to achieve. Long-term, hard, persistent efforts to achieve come from the heart, not from the head. When faced with the choice to watch television or do their homework, the decision may be based more on emotional than intellectual grounds. There may be no more powerful motivator than students realizing that they have to turn off the television and do their schoolwork because "their group is counting on them." Many a student who couldn't care less what a teacher thinks will say, "I did my homework because I couldn't face my group and tell them I didn't do it. I couldn't let my group down."

Changing Students' Attitudes About Schoolwork

There are many students who do not value schoolwork, do not aspire to do well in school, do not plan to take the more difficult courses, and do not plan to go on to college. One of the responsibilities of the school staff is to change the attitudes of these students so that they value school, education, and working hard to learn. In doing so, there are several general principles, supported by research (see Johnson & F. Johnson, 1987), to guide your efforts:

1. Attitudes are changed in groups, not individual by individual. Focus your efforts on having students within small groups persuade each other to value education.
2. Attitudes are changed as a result of small group discussions that lead to public commitment to work harder in school and take education more seriously. Attitudes are rarely modified by information or preaching.
3. Messages from individuals who care about, and are committed to, the student are taken more seriously than messages from indifferent others. Build committed and caring relationships between academically oriented and nonacademically oriented students.
4. Appeals to value education should be personally tailored to the student. General messages are not nearly as effective as personal messages. The individuals best able to construct an effective personal appeal are peers who know the student well.
5. Plan for the long term, not sudden conversions. Internalization of academic values will take years of persuasion by caring and committed peers.
6. Support from caring and committed peers is essential to modifying attitudes and behaviors and maintaining the new attitudes and behaviors. Remember, "You can't do it alone. You need help from your friends."

Students may be best encouraged to value education, work hard in school, take the valuable but difficult courses (such as math, science, and foreign languages), and aspire to go to college by placing them in permanent base groups that provide members with help and encouragement and hold members accountable for working hard in school. The base group provides a setting in which academic values may be encouraged and the necessary caring and committed relationships may be developed.

USING BASE GROUPS EFFECTIVELY

Sam was a low-achieving fourth-grade student who was receiving services for the learning disabled. Early in the year, before his teacher began using cooperative learning groups, Sam was failing social studies, health, and language arts. The teacher had to monitor Sam constantly just to get him to stay on task. He paid little attention to classroom discussions and seldom completed assignments. Once part of a long-term cooperative learning group, however, Sam changed. With the help and encouragement of his group, he completed many assignments during class and brought back homework consistently. Soon he earned a B in health and a C in language arts, and his social studies average went up markedly. By mid-February, he was passing every subject, and he was able to maintain his grades for the rest of the year. From a dejected, isolated child at the beginning of the year, Sam became a cheerful, confident child whose achievement had improved dramatically by the end of the year. Sam is a good example of the power of base groups.

There are several key ingredients in using base groups effectively:

1. Frequently use formal cooperative learning groups for instructional purposes until the five essential components are understood and some expertise in using cooperative learning groups is gained.
2. Make base groups slightly larger than formal cooperative learning groups (base groups may have four or five members rather than two or three).
3. Do not assign students to base groups the first day of class. Wait for a few days until you get to know the students somewhat.
4. Schedule frequent meetings of base groups.
5. Plan an important agenda for each meeting. The agendas for base groups can include the following:
   a. *Academic support tasks,* such as checking to see what assignments each member has and what help she needs to complete them. Members can give each other advice on how to take tests and "survive" in school. Members can prepare each other to take tests and go over the missed questions afterward. Members can share their areas of expertise (such as art or computers) with each other. Above all, members monitor each other's academic progress and make sure all members are achieving.
   b. *Routine tasks* such as taking role or collecting field trip slips.

c. *Personal support tasks,* such as listening sympathetically when a member has problems with parents or friends, having general discussions about life, giving each other advice about relationships, and helping each other solve nonacademic problems. Teachers may increase the likelihood of personal support by conducting trust-building exercises with the base groups.

6. Expect some base groups to have relationship problems. Not all base groups cohere right away. Be ready to help unskillful members integrate themselves into their groups. Periodically you may wish to structure a base group meeting to process the relationships among members or give the group hypothetical problems to solve (such as, "What if one member of your group did 90 percent of the talking? What are three strategies to help them listen as well as contribute?"). Persistence and patience are good teacher qualities with poorly functioning base groups.

BASE GROUP PROCEDURES

Base groups may be used in elementary schools, secondary schools, and college classes.

Elementary Base Groups

At the beginning of the academic year, students should be assigned to base groups. Some attention should be paid to building a group identity and some group cohesion. The first week the base groups meet, for example, base groups can pick a name, design a flag, or choose a motto. If a teacher in the school has the proper expertise, the groups will benefit from participating in an age-appropriate "challenge course" involving ropes and obstacles. This type of physical challenge that the groups complete together builds cohesion quickly.

During the year, elementary base groups meet twice each day, first thing in the morning and last thing in the afternoon. At the beginning of each day members meet in their base groups to

1. Congratulate each other for coming to school on time with all their books and materials and check to see that none of their group is under undue stress. The two questions to discuss are "Are we all prepared for the day?" and "How are you today?"

2. Check to see if members have completed their homework or need help and assistance in doing so. The questions to discuss are "Did you do your homework?" and "Is there anything you did not understand?" If there is not time to help each other during the base group meeting, an appointment is made to meet again during free time or lunch. Periodically, the base groups may be given a checklist of academic skills and assess which ones each member needs to practice more.

3. Review what members have read and done since the evening before. Members should be able to give a brief, terse, succinct summary of what they have read, thought about, and done. They may come to class with resources they have found and want to share, or copies of work they have completed and wish to distribute to their base group members.

4. Get to know each other better and provide positive feedback by discussing such questions as "What do you like about each other?", "What do you like about yourself?", and "What is the best thing that has happened to you this week?"

At the end of the day members meet in their base groups to see that everyone is taking his homework home, understands the assignments to be completed, and has the help and assistance he needs to do his work (during the evening students can confer on the telephone or even study together at one house). In addition, base groups may wish to discuss what members have learned during the day and check to see if all members plan to have some fun and do something interesting that evening.

In elementary schools, base groups should stay together for at least a year, and ideally, for six years. If each year base groups are promoted to the same classroom, the base group that begins in the first grade could thus stay together for six years.

Secondary Base Groups

If all members of the same elementary school base groups attend the same junior high school, the group can be continued. If not, base groups should be formed at the beginning of the academic year. An initial emphasis should be placed on building group identity and cohesion. At this age level also, a physical activity such as an obstacle course can be used to create cohesion quickly.

In junior high and high schools, class schedules should be arranged so that members of base groups are assigned to as many of the same classes as possible. Members will then spend much of the day together. In essence, the computer is programmed to assign base groups to classes (whenever possible) rather than individuals.

Each week base groups formally meet at least twice (perhaps first thing on Monday and last thing on Friday) to discuss the academic progress of each member, provide help and assistance to each other, and hold each member accountable for completing assignments and progressing satisfactorily through the academic program. The meeting on Monday morning refocuses the students on school, provides any emotional support required after the weekend, reestablishes personal contact among base group members, and helps students set their academic goals for the week (what is still to be done on assignments that are due, and so forth). The meeting on Friday afternoon helps students review the week, set academic goals for the weekend (what schoolwork has to be done before Monday), and share weekend plans and hopes. Tasks similar to those used in the elementary school base group meetings could be given. Members should carefully review each other's assignments and ensure that members have the help and assistance needed. In addition, they should hold each other accountable for committing serious effort to succeed in school.

College Base Groups

Two years ago a student in the social psychology of education course gave one of the authors the following feedback. The student stated that this was his last quarter of course work for his doctorate. After taking 120 quarter hours of courses, he stated that this was the first class in which he really got to know other students. The procedure for his doing so was the base group.

College and university life can be lonely. Many students arrive on campus without a clear support group. Students can attend class without ever talking to other students. In such impersonal settings, it is important to use base groups.

There are two ways base groups may be used in the college level. The first is to organize all students within base groups and have them function as part of college life. These base groups stay together for at least a year and preferably for four years. The second is to have a base group in each class. These base groups stay together only for the duration of the course.

The larger or more impersonal the class, and the more complex the subject matter, the more important it is to have base groups. The members of base groups should exchange phone numbers and information about schedules as they may wish to meet outside of class. The base group's functions in support of its members include the following:

1. It gives assistance, support, and encouragement for mastering the course content and skills, and it provides feedback on how well the content and skills are being learned.

2. It gives assistance, support, and encouragement for thinking critically about the course content, explaining precisely what one learns, engaging in intellectual controversy, getting the work done on time, and applying what is learned to one's own life.

3. It provides a set of interpersonal relationships to personalize the course and an arena for trying out the cooperative learning procedures and skills emphasized within the course.

4. It provides a structure for managing course evaluation.

Members have three major responsibilities:

1. To master and appropriately implement the theories, concepts, and body of knowledge (as well as skills) emphasized in the course.

2. To ensure that all members of your base group master and appropriately implement the theories, concepts, and body of knowledge (as well as skills) emphasized in the course.

3. To ensure that all members of the class master and appropriately implement the theories, concepts, and body of knowledge (as well as skills) emphasized in the course. In other words, if the group is successful, members should find another group to help until all members of the class are successful.

At the beginning of each session, class members meet in their base groups for the following purposes:

1. To congratulate each other for living through the time since the last class session and check to see that none of their group is under undue stress.

2. To check whether members have completed their homework or need help and assistance in doing so.

3. To review what members have read and done since the last class session. Members should be able to give a brief, terse, succinct summary of what they have read, thought about, and done. They may come to class with resources they have found and want to share, or copies of work they have completed and wish to distribute to their base group members.

Base groups are available to support individual group members. If a group member arrives late, or must leave early on occasion, the group can provide information about what that student missed. In addition, group members may assist one another in writing the required papers for the class. The assignments may be discussed in the base groups, papers may be planned, reviewed, and edited in base groups, and any questions regarding the course assignments and class sessions may be first addressed in the base group.

There is no way to overemphasize how important base groups can be. In the early 1970s, for example, a graduate student in social psychology of education suffered a psychological breakdown and was hospitalized for most of the quarter in a locked psychiatric ward of a local hospital. Two years later, she came to visit one of the authors and thank him for his course. She stated that it was the only course she had completed during that very difficult year. The other members of her base group had obtained permission from her psychiatrist to visit her weekly in the hospital. They spent two hours a week with her, going over her assignments, helping her write her papers, giving her the tests, and ensuring that she completed the course. She got a B.

TURNOVER OF MEMBERSHIP

When considering using base groups, teachers may wonder about how to manage turnover. In many schools there is considerable student turnover during the year. While teachers cannot prevent the parent(s) of students from moving, they can ease the students' transitions from school to school by having a structured "hello" and a structured "goodbye."

When a new student arrives, he or she should have immediate support. Instead of wandering the halls for two or three weeks to find someone to relate to, a new student could be immediately assigned to a base group. The base group should have some skill in welcoming a new member. One teacher has her base groups practice welcoming a new member. Each member role-plays arriving as a new student (to give some insight into how it feels), and the other three members role-play welcoming the new member. The teacher then brainstorms ideas from the whole class as to how the welcoming can be best done.

When students move away, the worse thing that can happen is for the students to believe that in the old school no one knew them, no one cared, and no one will miss them now they are gone. A structured goodbye in a base group will prevent such feelings. One teacher reported the following procedure. Members of a base group gave a student who was leaving four self-addressed, stamped envelopes. "We want to hear from you after you get to your new school," they said. "We especially want to know how you are doing in math. We have worked hard on math with you. We want to know how well you do in your new school."

BASE GROUPS AND DROPPING OUT OF SCHOOL

In many school districts, large numbers of students drop out. Base groups provide a means of both discouraging and combating dropping out of school. Base groups provide a set of personal and supportive relationships that may prevent many students from dropping out of school. Dropping out often results from being alienated from the school and the other students. In some cases the school is not sure for weeks whether a student is skipping school, sick, or dropping out. Any student who believes that "in this school, no one knows me, no one cares about me, no one would miss me when I'm gone" is at risk of dropping out.

Base groups also provide a means of combating students' dropping out of school. A principal (or teacher) may approach a base group and say, "Roger thinks he is dropping out of school. Here are three passes. Go find Roger and bring him back. We're not going to lose him without a fight." Being confronted with a group of peers who care enough to fight to keep one in school has a powerful impact on a student's motivation to continue.

THE SEVEN-MINUTE ADVISEE/BASE GROUP

In many secondary schools it will seem difficult to implement base groups. Two opportunities are homerooms and advisor/advisee groups. Teachers may divide their homeroom students into base groups and then plan an important agenda for them to follow each day.

In a school we work with, all students are assigned an adviser. The teacher then meets once a week with all of her advisees. The meeting lasts for seven minutes. Though at first this seemed like an impossible time limitation, here is the procedure one teacher derived: First, the teacher divided the nine advisees into three base groups of three members each. The rule was set that all students are expected to be in their base group when the bell rings so that no time is lost in getting started. The base groups are then given four tasks:

1. A quick *self-disclosure task* such as, "What is the most exciting thing you did over Christmas break?" "What is the worst thing that happened to you last weekend?" "What is your biggest fear?" "What is your favorite ice cream?"
2. Any *administrative task* (such as lunch count) is conducted.
3. A quick *academic task* such as, "You have midterms coming up. As a group, write out three pieces of advice for taking tests. I will type up the suggestions from each group and hand them out next week."
4. Members wish each other good luck for the day.

SMALL SCHOOLS

Cooperative learning groups and cooperative base groups are the major means by which (a) the impersonality and anonymity of large schools are diminished and (b) students of very different abilities and backgrounds can each reach their potential by working together. The next step is to create "small schools" within large schools. Large schools may be divided into small schools of 90 to 120 students. Doing so helps to foster enduring relationships among students and between staff and students. The small school becomes a community within which everyone knows everyone else well. Instruction becomes personalized. Building a sense of belonging to a select group is consciously sought to boost the desire to learn. The cluster becomes an extended family where achievement is important, and so is caring for one another. Individual efforts of students contribute to the well-being of others and to the group, class, and cluster as a whole. The purposes for learning are to benefit oneself and to benefit others.

Students need permanent relationships with teachers as well as with each other. An interdisciplinary team of three to six teachers may be assigned to a cluster and work with it not for a semester or even a year, but for three years or more. It takes time for teachers to get to know and care for individual students. The routines derived to manage classroom life and discipline problems may be continued for years instead of having to be created anew each year. When teachers know that they will spend several years with the same students, they become committed to finding ways to motivate and encourage the students. Problems cannot be ignored or waited out. The quality of help and assistance teachers can provide increases every year they work with a student.

Having a team of teachers work together with the same students for a number of years, furthermore, builds a collegial support group that increases the quality of relationships among teachers. It also allows for the development of flexible patterns of organizing and scheduling instruction according to the demands of the topics studied and students' interests and readiness. As a result, instruction becomes personal.

The importance of a supportive environment where students care about other students cannot be overstated. In Norway groups of twenty-five students stay together with the same teacher for six years. The results are so encouraging that the period will soon be extended to nine years. At twenty-two high schools in the Federal Republic of Germany, groups of ninety students and three teachers stay together for six years–fifth through tenth grade. Although the minority, poverty, single-parent family percentages are the same as in other schools, the results are staggering—a fraction of the dropout rate of other high schools (1% versus 14%); more than twice as many students who score sufficiently well on the high-school exit exams to be admitted to a four-year college (60% versus 27%); and practically no truancy, teacher absenteeism, or discipline problems. The teachers and students take responsibility not only for academic development, but also for personal and social development. Cooperative learning at hundreds of schools in the United States is reaching students who are alienated and isolated and who feel that no one cares about them as human beings or about their learning. Students' achievement and social skills are improving, and students and teachers are having more fun.

SUMMARY

Whenever a learning task is assigned, a clear cooperative, competitive, or individualistic goal structure should be given, so that students know how to behave appropriately. While all three goal structures are important and should be used, the dominant goal structure in any class should be cooperative. Any lesson in any subject area may be taught cooperatively to students of any age. All it takes is a teacher who is skilled in translating the old competitive and individualistic lessons into cooperative ones. In order to be cooperative, a lesson must include positive interdependence, face-to-face promotive interaction among students, individual accountability, the use of interpersonal and small group skills, and the processing of how well the learning groups functioned. These elements must be included in all three types of cooperative learning groups: formal, informal, and base groups. Within *formal cooperative learning groups* the teacher's role in structuring learning situations cooperatively involves clearly specifying the objectives for the lesson, placing students in learning groups and providing appropriate materials, clearly explaining the cooperative goal structure and the learning task, monitoring students as they work, and evaluating students' performance.

Informal cooperative learning groups are temporary, ad hoc groups that last for only one discussion or one class period. They are used to focus student attention on the material to be learned, set a mood conducive to learning, help organize in advance the material to be covered in a class session, ensure that students stay intellectually active and cognitively process the material being taught, and provide closure to an instructional session. They also ensure that misconceptions, incorrect understanding, and gaps in understanding are identified and corrected, that the discussion and elaboration that promote retention and transfer take place, and that learning experiences are personalized. Informal cooperative learning groups are especially helpful to defeat the enemies of the lecture.

Base cooperative learning groups are long-term, heterogeneous cooperative learning groups with stable membership whose primary responsibilities are to (a) provide support, encouragement, and assistance in completing assignments and (b) hold each other accountable for striving to learn. Caring and committed relationships are a necessity for healthy cognitive and social development. Long-term permanent relationships are keys to academic achievement and psychological health. Motivation to achieve springs from caring and committed relationships. Attitudes toward education are heavily influenced by peers who are part of one's support groups. Base groups provide the permanent and long-term relationships that ensure that students will exert considerable effort to learn, develop in healthy ways, and develop constructive friendships.

The larger the school and the more complex and difficult the subject matter, the more important it is to have base groups. Learning for your groupmates is a powerful motivator. Receiving social support and being held accountable for appropriate behavior by peers who care about you and have a long-term commitment to your success and well-being are important aspects of growing up and progressing through school.

When used in combination, these formal, informal, and base cooperative learning groups provide an overall structure to classroom life. Of the three, it is the use of formal cooperative learning groups that provides the basis for teachers to gain the expertise in using cooperative learning procedures. Adding the other two enriches the lives of students and their learning and extends the cooperative experience and effects.

9

Approaches to Cooperative Learning

CONCEPTUAL AND DIRECT APPROACHES TO COOPERATIVE LEARNING

Practically everyone knows how to run a VCR. You tune the TV to the appropriate channel, turn on the VCR, insert the tape, and press "play." When the VCR breaks, very few of us know how to repair it. Most of the things we use, we use as technicians. We can follow the instructions (step 1, step 2, step 3), but we really do not understand how the thing works, we cannot adapt and modify it to our unique circumstances, and we cannot repair it when it breaks. A few of us are engineers in the sense that we have the conceptual knowledge required to modify and adapt the things we use and repair them when they break. In training teachers to use cooperative learning, some teachers have been trained to use cooperative learning like a technician (step 1, step 2, step 3), and some teachers have been trained in a conceptual understanding of cooperative learning that allows them to gain real expertise in adapting it to their specific teaching circumstances.

A carefully crafted approach to cooperative learning requires a combination of clear conceptual understanding of the essential components of cooperative learning, concrete examples of lessons and strategies, and continued implementation in classrooms and schools. While a combination of both is necessary, approaches to implementing cooperative learning may be placed on a continuum with conceptual applications at one end and direct applications at the other. *Conceptual applications* are based on an interaction among theory, research, and practice. Teachers are taught a general conceptual model of cooperative learning (based on the essential elements of positive interdependence, face-to-face interaction, individual accountability, social skills, and group processing) that they use to tailor cooperative learning specifically for their circumstances, students, and needs. In essence, teachers are taught an *expert system* of how to implement cooperative learning that they use to create a unique adaptation to their specific circumstances, students, and needs. The resulting expertise is based on a metacognitive understanding of cooperative learning. Conceptual applications may be contrasted with *direct applications* that consist of packaged lessons, curricula, and strategies that are used in a lockstep prescribed manner.

There are two types of approaches to cooperative learning: the conceptual or essential elements approach and the direct approach. The direct approach may be divided into three subcategories: strategy, curriculum package, and lesson approaches.

CONCEPTUAL/ESSENTIAL COMPONENTS APPROACH

Expertise comes from applying what one knows to a specific situation to arrive at a unique adaptation. Conceptual understanding is a prerequisite to expertise. An example is given by Aesop in his story about the crow and the pitcher. In a spell of dry weather, when the birds could find very little to drink, a thirsty crow found a pitcher with a little water in it. But the pitcher was high and had a narrow neck, and no matter how he tried, the crow could not reach the water. The poor thing felt as if he must die of thirst. Then an idea came to him. Picking up some small pebbles, he dropped them into the pitcher one by one. With each pebble the water rose a little higher until at last it was near enough so he could drink.

This book takes a conceptual approach to cooperative learning. The essential components approach requires teachers to learn both a conceptual understanding of cooperative learning and the skills to use that understanding to apply (and even create) strategies and teach cooperative lessons. Teachers gear cooperative learning to their specific students. Teachers are trained to implement the essential elements of cooperative learning. Once understood, the essential elements allow teachers to think metacognitively about cooperative learning and create any number of strategies and lessons. In the training, specific lessons are demonstrated and a variety of strategies are taught within the context of the essential components of cooperative learning. The goal of the conceptual approach is to develop teachers' expertise in a system of cooperative learning based on validated theory that they can use in the following ways:

1. Taking any lesson in any subject area and structuring it cooperatively.
2. Practicing and practicing the use of cooperative learning until it is at a routine/integrated level of use, and implementing cooperative learning at least 60 percent of the time in their classrooms.
3. Describing precisely what they are doing and why they are doing it in order to

(a) communicate to others the nature of cooperative learning and (b) teach them how to implement cooperative learning in their classrooms and settings.

4. Applying the principles of cooperation to other settings, such as colleagial relationships and faculty meetings.

The conceptual approach assumes that each teacher faces a complex and unique combination of circumstances, students, and needs, and, therefore, cooperative learning needs to be adapted and refined to fit each teacher's situation uniquely.

The conceptual approach is used in all technological arts and crafts. An engineer designing a bridge, for example, applies validated theory to the unique problems imposed by the need for a bridge of a certain length, to carry specific loads, from a bank of one unique geological character to a bank of another unique geological character, in an area with specific winds, temperatures, and susceptibility to earthquakes. Teachers engage in the same process by (a) learning a conceptualization of essential components of cooperative learning and (b) applying that conceptual model to their unique teaching situation, circumstances, students, and instructional needs.

Expertise depends on conceptually understanding the essential elements of cooperative learning and implementing them with real fidelity. Teachers gain expertise in using cooperative learning through a process of *progressive refinement.* Once the essential components of cooperation are understood, teachers

1. Plan and teach a cooperative lesson.
2. Assess the strengths and weaknesses of the lesson.
3. Reflect on how to teach the next lesson better (thus clarifying the teacher's conceptual understanding).
4. Plan and teach a second cooperative lesson with the modifications suggested by the feedback received about the first.

The strengths and weaknesses of the second lesson are then assessed, modifications are made in understanding and implementing, and a third lesson is taught. This process of progressive refinement in using cooperative learning should continue throughout the teacher's career.

DIRECT APPROACHES

Teachers may be trained in cooperative learning by being taught how to conduct a specific cooperative learning lesson, how to use a specific cooperative learning curriculum, or how to use a specific cooperative learning strategy. The direct approaches assume that teachers need only to know the steps involved in using cooperative learning.

The *strategy approach* trains teachers to apply specific cooperative learning strategies, such as arranging reading assignments like a jigsaw puzzle or having students work together to complete a group project. Examples of the strategy approach include the following:

1. *Teams-Games-Tournament* (TGT) is a combination of intragroup cooperation, intergroup competition, and instructional games (DeVries & Edwards, 1974). It begins with the teacher directly teaching a lesson. Students then meet in cooperative learning teams of four or five members (a mixture of high, medium, and low achievers) to complete a set of worksheets on the lesson. Students then play academic games as representatives of their teams. Who competes with whom is modified each week to ensure that students compete with classmates who achieve at a similar level. The highest scoring teams are publicly recognized in a weekly class newsletter. Grades are given on the basis of individual performance. Elements of TGT are discussed in Chapter 5. Its development was a pioneering contribution by David DeVries and Keith Edwards, who worked at the Center for Social Organization of Schools at Johns Hopkins University. Their work was continued by one of David DeVries' doctoral students, Robert Slavin.

2. *Student Teams-Achievement Divisions* (STAD) (Slavin, 1980) is a modification of TGT. It also stresses intergroup competition to learn predetermined facts. The

material to be learned is directly taught by the teacher or an audiovisual presentation. Students review the material in four-member teams (one high, one low, and two about average in ability), usually using worksheets or flashcards. Instead of playing academic games, students take a weekly quiz, and their scores contribute to a team score. Students' scores are based on the degree to which their performance has improved over their past averages. Teams receive recognition for the sum of the improvement scores of the team members. Teams with the highest exam or improvement scores are recognized each week in a class newsletter or other public forum. Grades are given on the basis of individual performance on the quizzes.

3. *Jigsaw* (Aronson et al., 1978) is a combination of cooperative and individualistic learning. Students learn in cooperative groups, but they take individual tests and are given individual grades. Resource interdependence is high, but an individualistic reward structure is used. Students are placed in five- to seven-member cooperative groups (heterogeneous in terms of ability, ethnic background, and sex). The curriculum materials to be studied or used are designed or rewritten so that each group member has only one unique section that is comprehensible without reference to the other sections. In studying the life of Sojourner Truth (a black abolitionist and women's rights activist), for example, each student is given material on a segment of Truth's life and, therefore, group members cannot learn her total life unless all members teach their parts. A group leader is appointed by the teacher and trained to model productive behavior and keep the group on task. Expert groups are used—students meet with the members of other teams who are learning the same topic to exchange information and master the material they will present to their teams. Students then return to their own teams and teach teammates what they have learned. Each group member is responsible for learning the whole unit. Students take a quiz on the unit and are given an individual grade based on their performance. Numerous variations of the jigsaw procedure have been developed.

4. *Group Investigation* is aimed at placing students in cooperative learning groups and giving them control over what they learn (Sharan & Hertz-Lazarowitz, 1980). In group investigation, students democratically take an active part in planning what they will study and how. They form cooperative groups according to common interests in a topic. All group members help plan how to research their topic. Then they divide the work among themselves, and each group member carries out his or her part of the investigation. Finally, the group synthesizes and summarizes its work and presents these findings to the class.

5. *Co-op Co-op* (Kagan, 1985) is aimed at giving students control over what and how they learn through the use of cooperative groups. It is very similar to group investigation and consists of ten steps. A class discussion is held to stimulate student curiosity. Students are assigned to heterogeneous (ability, ethnicity, sex) cooperative learning groups. Team-building exercises are conducted. Students divide the learning unit into topics so that each team is responsible for one aspect of the unit. Within the group, members decide how to divide their topic

into minitopics so that each group member does part. Working individualistically by themselves, students prepare their minitopics to present to the group. The groups then synthesize the minitopics into a group presentation. Group presentations are made to the whole class. Evaluation is made at three levels—team members evaluate individual minitopic presentations, classmates evaluate team presentations, and the teacher evaluates individual minitopic papers or projects.

6. *Think-Pair-Share*, developed by Frank Lyman at the University of Maryland, consists of having students listen while the teacher poses a question, take time in which to think of a response, then pair with a neighbor and discuss their responses, and share their responses with the whole group or class.

The *curriculum package approach* trains teachers to use a curriculum package within which lessons are structured cooperatively. As with all curriculums, the packages tend to be subject-area and grade-level specific. Dozens of curriculum packages that include instructions for using cooperative learning groups with the lessons are being published. A few examples of the curriculum package approach are as follows:

1. *Sunburst Integrated Co-op Learning Geometry Course* is a combination of a geometry curriculum, an interactive computer program, and cooperative learning groups. The curriculum takes a discovery or guided inquiry approach that enables students to investigate geometric relationships instead of the traditional method of having the teacher present the material to the class. Students are assigned to four-person cooperative learning groups that often divide into two pairs while they work at the computer. Students interact with the computer by gathering data and make generalizations or conjectures to convert them to theorems. After working in groups of two at the computer, the students reconvene in

their groups of four to discuss their findings. The cooperative groups nurture and facilitate mathematical exploration and problem solving, encourage critical thinking and sharing of ideas, and bolster mathematical confidence. In cooperative groups students formulate conjectures in their own words and from their own experiences. They then write proofs of their conjectures in paragraph or narrative form.

2. *Cooperative Integrated Reading and Composition* (CIRC) is a combination of cooperative interaction and an individualistic reward structure (Stevens, Madden, Slavin, & Farnish, 1987). It consists of a set of curriculum materials to supplement basal readers and ensure that cooperative learning is applied to reading, writing, spelling, and language mechanics. The class is divided into two reading groups of eight to fifteen members; one group focuses on phonic decoding and comprehension skills (code/meaning) and the other focuses on comprehension and inference skills (meaning). Students are assigned to a pair within the reading group and are then combined with a pair from the other reading group. Assignments are given to the groups of four which they complete either as pairs or as a whole group. Students' scores on all quizzes, compositions, and book reports contribute to a team score that results in certificates. Students are graded individualistically on their own work.

3. *Team-Assisted Individualization* (TAI) is basically not cooperative learning at all. It is a highly individualized math curriculum for grades 3 to 6 in which students work individualistically to complete their math assignments (Slavin, 1985). The emphasis is on self-instructional (programmed learning) curriculum materials that are completed individualistically. While students are assigned to four- or five-member teams, team members do not work together. They check each other's answers, administer tests, and provide help if a member requests it. Because the curriculum units are designed to be self-explanatory and because team members are usually working at quite different levels, cooperative interaction is held to a minimum. Team scores are computed weekly, and team members are given certificates on the basis of how much work each member completed. Students are graded strictly on their own individual work.

When teachers are trained in how to use cooperative learning from the *lesson approach*, they are given a specific lesson structured cooperatively (such as an English lesson on punctuation, a math lesson on long division, or a science lesson on what sinks and what floats) and exposed to demonstrations as to how the lesson is taught. Teachers are then expected to go back to their classrooms and conduct the lesson.

COOPERATIVE ACTIVITIES, SUPPORT SYSTEMS, AND GAMES

There are cooperative activities related to cooperative learning that may be used in the classroom.

1. Teachers can use *group-building activities* like "favorite sports and hobbies," "pets I wish I had," and "team juggling."

2. Teachers can use emotional *support groups* within the classroom.

   a. One cooperative support system is known as *Tribes* (Gibbs, 1986). A tribe is a heterogeneous group of five or six children who have regular group meetings throughout each day throughout the school year. The activities that the tribes engage in are (i) sharing personal concerns, feelings, and positive regard for one another and (ii) planning, problem solving, and maintaining an environment of positive support for all members.

   b. A *class meeting* can be held to discuss and solve class discipline problems and to provide support for students to act in more constructive ways (Glasser, 1969). Through the use of cooperative learning and class meetings, students (i) feel like they are involved in relationships with peers who care about and assist each other, (ii) are able to influence the people they are involved with, and (iii) enjoy learning (Glasser, 1986). It is through belonging, power, and fun that students are motivated to work up to their potential and to maintain interest in learning.

3. Another teaching strategy is *cooperative games*. We are a playful species. We start playing games in early childhood and keep playing them until we die. Games are fun and, we are told, help prepare us for real life. Chess is encouraged in war colleges to sharpen strategy skills useful in battle. Soccer and hockey are encouraged to ready players for the rough-and-tumble teamwork of business. Most games, however, ignore an important fact: in real life, most situations are such that both sides gain by cooperating. Games can be structured cooperatively. Two tennis players can see how many times they can hit the ball back and forth across the net rather than who wins over the other. A family that goes bowling can count the total number of pins they can knock down as a family rather than competing against each other. Terry Orlick (1981) and others have compiled descriptions of dozens and dozens of cooperative games.

The use of group-building activities, support groups, and cooperative games can significantly enhance the effectiveness of cooperative learning.

EMPOWERING STAFF THROUGH COOPERATIVE TEAMS

I never got very far until I stopped imagining I had to do everything myself.

F. W. Woolworth

Business and industry leaders are rediscovering a basic truth that has escaped educators for the past thirty years (Johnson, Johnson, & Holubec, 1988; Kouzes & Posner, 1987). They have rediscovered that long-term, persistent, committed effort to achieve is powered by caring and committed personal relationships (not tangible rewards or intellectual rationales). When asked about their success, the chief executives of the companies that have the best track records in North America state that they have been successful because they care about their people, not just as employees, but as human beings and as friends. Not only is their personal caring apparent to employees, but the chief executives are able to create teams in which members care about each other on a personal as well as professional level. The successful chief executives create a "family" within which members care deeply about each other and the mutual vision they are striving to actualize. It is genuine acts of caring that draw people together and move them forward.

It is time for educators to discover the same "truth." Within schools, the leadership to create caring and committed personal relationships that ensure long-term, persistent, committed efforts to achieve should be provided by the following actions (Johnson & Johnson, 1989b; Kouzes & Posner, 1987):

1. Challenging the status quo of competitive and individualistic efforts.
2. Inspiring a shared mutual vision of what the person, class, and school could and should be.
3. Empowering individuals through teamwork. Success comes from a "we" not "me" school and classroom organizational structure.
4. Leading by example by using cooperative procedures, joining in cooperative efforts, and taking risks to increase one's learning and competence.
5. Encouraging the "heart" of students and staff to persist by recognizing their efforts and celebrating their successes.

A cooperative school structure begins in the classroom. Teachers typically cannot promote isolation and competition among students all day and be collaborative with colleagues. What is promoted in the instructional situation tends to dominate relationships among staff members. Teachers who spend up to six hours a day telling students, "Do not copy," "I want to see what you can do, not your neighbor," and "Let's see who is best and who the winner is" will in turn tend to approach their colleagues with the attitudes of "Don't copy from me," and "Who is the winner in implementing this new teaching strategy." The cooperative context that is necessary for teachers to work cooperatively with their colleagues begins in the classroom.

What is good for students is even better for staff. The second level in promoting a consistent and coherent organizational structure is having cooperative teams dominate staff efforts. All staff members should be involved in groups that meet regularly and work on meaningful tasks. It is social support from and accountability to valued peers that motivate committed efforts to succeed. Empowering staff members through cooperative teamwork is done through collegial support groups, through task forces, and through ad hoc decision-making groups.

Collegial support groups are used to increase teachers' instructional expertise and success. A collegial support group consists of two to five teachers who have the goal of improving each other's professional competence and ensuring each other's professional growth. This goal is achieved through frequent professional discussions, coplanning lessons, and coteaching or making reciprocal observations of each other's use of cooperative learning. Teachers will not become proficient in using cooperative learning procedures by attending a workshop or from reading this book. Teachers become proficient and competent from *doing*. Expertise in cooperative learning is reached when teachers routinely structure lessons cooperatively without conscious planning or thought. To gain this expertise, teachers must use cooperative learning for several years while receiving in-classroom help and assistance. In order to ensure such an (a) sustained use of cooperative learning strategies and (b) support system, teachers must belong to a professional support group that provides continuous, immediate, in-class assistance in perfecting teachers' competencies. Accordingly, teachers and other staff members must be structured into collegial support groups aimed at teaching each other how to use cooperative learning strategies effectively. Membership is voluntary and inclusive. The administrator or leader approaches teachers he or she believes are interested, invites them to participate, networks them together, provides them with resources, and reinforces their efforts. Membership is inclu-

port groups the leader must recognize that it is personal commitment, not authority, that energizes change efforts by teachers. Participation in the collegial support groups is aimed at increasing teachers' belief that they are engaged in a joint venture ("We are doing it!"), public commitment to peers to increase their instructional expertise ("I will try!"), peer accountability ("They are counting on me!"), sense of social support ("They will help and assist me!"), sense of safety ("The risk is challenging but not excessive!"), and self-efficacy ("If I exert the effort, I will be successful!").

Task forces are used to plan and implement solutions to schoolwide issues and problems such as curriculum adoptions and lunchroom management. There are schoolwide issues and problems that require assessment, analysis, and planning before a recommendation may be formulated. Task groups are small problem-solving groups that define a problem, gather data about the causes and extent of the problem, consider a variety of alternative solutions, conclude which solution will be most effective, and make a presentation recommending it to the faculty as a whole. Thus teachers need to be trained in identifying problems, analyzing problems, hypothesizing major causes, verifying the existence of problems, identifying potential solutions, deciding on a recommendation, and presenting that recommendation persuasively to the whole staff. For example, Sam Jones was running through the announcements at a faculty meeting.

> There is increasing concern about the amount of littering taking place in the lunchroom, hallways, and school grounds. The problem has increased dramatically this year. I have asked Jane, Jim, Joan, and Jeremy to serve as a task force to consider the problem and make a recommendation to the faculty as to how it may be solved. Please give them any assistance they ask for. As soon as they have a recommendation ready, we will discuss the issue in a faculty meeting and decide what to do.

There are school issues that call for assessment and planning. Curriculum adoptions, in-service education, bus schedules, playground supervision, reduction of drug use by students, assurance of appropriate behavior in hallways and lunchrooms, school-parent communications, and many other issues that require considered planning and action by the school staff. The leader organizes a faculty task group, gives it its charge and a schedule, and then provides the resources required for the group to function. The group then brings a recommendation to the faculty. Membership is not strictly voluntary, since teachers are asked to serve.

Ad hoc decision-making groups are used during staff meetings to involve all staff members in important school decisions. During faculty meetings the school staff will be asked to make decisions about school policy and what recommendations should be adopted to solve schoolwide problems. The most effective way of making such decisions is to implement a small-group/large-group procedure involving ad hoc decision-making groups in which staff members listen to the recommendation, are assigned to small cooperative groups (usually three members), meet in the small groups and consider whether to accept or reject the recommendation and why, decide, and report their decision and rationale to the entire faculty. After all of the small groups have reported, a facultywide discussion is held, and a school decision is made. Such a procedure maximizes the participation and involvement of all staff members in the school's decision making. For example, Mary Field stood up, faced her staff, and said:

> We have just heard the recommendation of the task force on littering in the lunchroom, hallways, and school grounds. There are twenty-seven staff members in attendance. I am going to count off by nine to make groups of three. Each triad is to decide whether to accept or reject the recommendation of the task force and state their rationale for doing so. You are to come to consensus within the triad. Everyone should agree with the decision and be able to explain the rationale. I will randomly pick one teacher from each triad to explain their triad's rationale and decision. We will then discuss the recommendation briefly and take a vote of the entire faculty to decide whether or not to accept the task force's recommendation.

The third level is to implement administrative collegial support groups, task forces, and ad hoc decision-making groups within the district. The superintendent should structure the administrative staff in the same way that teachers structure the classroom and principals structure the school.

How to structure and use these three types of cooperative teams may be found in *Leading the Cooperative School* by Johnson and Johnson (1989a). By making the organizational structure of the school congruent, with cooperative learning dominating the classroom and colleagial support groups dominating the school, both the achievement of students and the productivity of the staff are improved. It also creates a school-based decision-making procedure that enhances staff commitment to achieving the goals of the school.

What cooperative learning achieves in the classroom foretells what is needed within the school. For schools to be effective, interaction among staff members must be structured as cooperatively as student-student interaction. To maximize the productivity of schools, there must be some congruence among classroom, school, and district organizational structure. If the classroom and the school are structured competitively, it will be difficult to promote teacher-teacher cooperation. If the classroom and the district are structured competitively, it will be difficult to structure cooperation among principals. A consistent and coherent organizational structure is established when teachers use cooperative learning in the classroom, administrators structure their faculty cooperatively, and the superintendent structures the administrators cooperatively. The support and assistance necessary for teachers to promote each other's success may then be sustained.

LONG-TERM PERSPECTIVE

The importance of structuring cooperation throughout all levels of the school district becomes most apparent when a realistic time perspective is taken for learning from colleagues. The process of gaining expertise in teaching is not different from gaining expertise in any other field. It takes at least one lifetime. Professional growth is a complex, time-consuming, and difficult process that places both cognitive and emotional demands on teachers. A support system is needed to encourage and assist teachers in a long-term, multiyear effort to improve continually their professional competence. With only a moderately difficult teaching strategy, for example, teachers may require from 20 to 30 hours of instruction in its theory, 15 to 20 demonstrations using it with different students and subjects, and an additional 10 to 15 coaching sessions to attain higher-level skills (Shalaway, 1985). For a more difficult teaching strategy, several years of training and support may be needed to ensure that teachers master it. Your commitment to implementing cooperative learning, and gaining expertise in using cooperative learning, needs to extend throughout your career.

SUMMARY

While the conceptual and direct approaches to cooperative learning are not contradictory, there are differences for the transfer of training from the workshop to the classroom and for the long-term implementation and survival of cooperative learning. Conceptual applications are theory-based, while direct applications are materials- and procedures-based. The conceptual approach promotes research that tests theory that generalizes to many different situations. Direct approaches promote evaluation studies that are in essence case studies demonstrating how well the curriculum or strategy was implemented in a specific instance, but the results do not generalize to other situations and implementations. Conceptual approaches are dynamic in that they are changed and modified on the basis of new research and refinements of the theory. Direct approaches are static in that they remain fixed no matter how the knowledge about cooperative learning changes.

The conceptual approach trains teachers to be engineers who adapt cooperative learning to their needs. Direct approaches train teachers to be technicians who use the cooperative learning curriculum or strategy without understanding how it works. As engineers, teachers can solve problems in implementation and adapt cooperative learning to their specific circumstances, students, and needs. As technicians they cannot. The development of expertise in using cooperative learning depends on conceptually understanding it. The conceptual approach promotes personal commitment by teachers to cooperative learning as they adapt it to their situation. The direct approach does not.

When teachers gain expertise in cooperative learning through conceptual understanding, they become independent of outside experts and can generate new lessons and strategies as the need arises. They can also transfer their use of cooperative learning to create more cooperative colleagial relationships, staff meetings, relationships with parents, and committees. They become important figures in the staff development process as they train their colleagues to use cooperative learning. Teachers trained in the direct approaches stay dependent on outside experts, cannot generate new lessons or strategies on their own, cannot transfer cooperation from the classroom to the school, and cannot train their peers (except in a direct way). Finally, the conceptual approach requires ongoing support and assistance in gaining expertise in cooperative learning. Direct approaches do not.

Direct approaches have value within the context of a long-term implementation of a training program emphasizing conceptual understanding of the essential elements of well-structured cooperative lessons. Without the conceptual context, direct approaches are, in the long run, inadequate at best and counterproductive at worst. Simply presenting a theoretical framework, on the other hand, is also inadequate. A carefully crafted training program requires a combination of a clear conceptual understanding of the essential elements of cooperative learning, concrete examples of lessons and strategies, and continued implementation in classrooms and schools.

10

Teacher Concerns

INTRODUCTION

In this book the authors have tried to build a bridge between the social-psychological knowledge of goal structures and the practices of teachers in real classrooms with real students. The first part of the book builds a foundation for teacher effectiveness by presenting the rationale for using goal structures. The rest of the book spells out how to put that knowledge into practice. The theory of goal structures becomes a teaching process of goal structuring, monitoring, and evaluating. The next step is for you, the reader, to extend the ideas in this book to your situation, modify them where it is needed to fit your classroom, and put them into practice. The reward for doing so is that teaching will be more enjoyable, more productive, and easier.

In our work with teachers to put these ideas to use in their classrooms, several teacher concerns have been expressed. This chapter presents some of these concerns and our joint attempts to solve them from what we have learned. Perhaps you will have some of these concerns as you implement the material in this book in your teaching. If so, you should find this final information helpful.

CLASSROOM MANAGEMENT

The major concerns of many teachers are classroom management, classroom control, and classroom discipline. Teachers are continually told by administrators, colleagues, parents, teacher educators, and the man on the street in subtle and

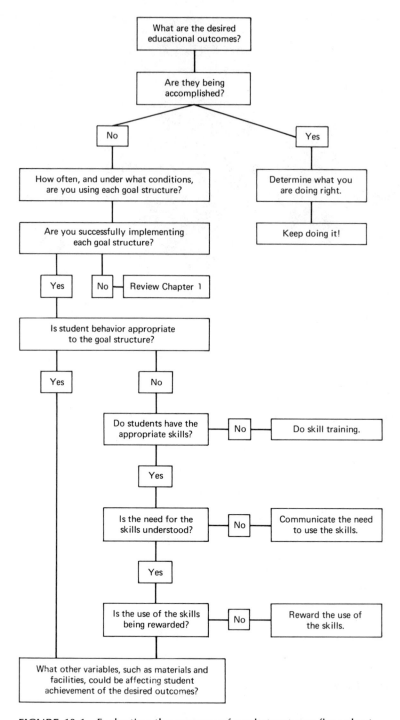

FIGURE 10.1 Evaluating the success of goal structures flow chart

not so subtle ways that classroom control is the most important part of teaching. It isn't! Certainly, any time you have twenty-five to forty people together in a room there are going to be some coordination and organizational problems to be solved. Managing the classroom is just an initial step toward the more important goals that relate to cognitive and affective learning. The cause of most discipline problems is the inappropriate use of competitive and individualized goal structures and the underuse of the cooperative goal structure. *The skillful use of the three goal structures will reduce the causes of discipline problems and ensure that they are not compounded through further aggravation.* Is it hard to believe this statement? We believe we can safely make it. Consider the effects of the appropriate use of cooperation on (1) disruptive, nonresponsive, unmotivated students, (2) depressed, shy, isolated, disliked students, and (3) student-student conflict.

Within most traditional classrooms there are students who are resistant to teacher influence, unmotivated to learn what is being taught, nonresponsive to the usual rewards teachers have to offer for appropriate behavior, and inappropriately aggressive, hostile, obstructive, irritating, and disobedient. Controlling and disciplining these students is a major problem for most teachers. Yet the results of research on cooperation show a way to minimize such problems! *The appropriate use of cooperation will reduce inappropriate, nonresponsive, and obstructive behavior by students.* In a cooperative situation students work together to achieve mutual goals and, therefore, are susceptible to influence from each other. Considerable research demonstrates that cooperators do exert influence on and accept influence from each other. This mutual influence results in more peer encouragement for achievement and a climate more oriented toward academic involvement. Instead of approval and support for learning coming from the teacher, it comes from peers. Instead of a student's demonstrating independence from adults by disobeying the teacher, a student demonstrates concern for her peers by helping the group achieve. A student who couldn't care less what grade the teacher assigns her work will care a great deal about how her peers view the quality of her effort. Hostility toward authority will not be expressed when working cooperatively with one's peers. Unmotivated, nonresponsive, obstructive students can be substantially helped by placing them in cooperative relationships in which there will be positive peer influences. The effectiveness of communication among cooperators, the level of trust built in cooperative groups, the peer tutoring that is available in cooperative learning situations, the student preference for, involvement in, and liking of cooperative experiences—all will contribute to positive peer influence in cooperative situations. Even if you had time to work individually with every student, you could not have as much influence on the student's behavior as do the student's peers. Cooperative groupings will reduce your discipline problems, and the cooperative situation is far different from the one in which you are expected to motivate, counsel, and discipline every student with whom you come into contact.

Most traditional classrooms have students who are isolated because of their shyness, depression, or negative self-attitudes, or because for one reason or another students have taken a dislike to them. Teachers are often at a loss as to how to help such students, how to integrate them more fully into classroom life. The research on cooperation provides an answer. *The appropriate use of cooperation will reduce isolation of shy, depressed, disliked, fearful students.* Cooperation requires interaction among students, thus reducing the isolation of all. Cooperative interaction results in positive interpersonal relationships characterized by mutual liking, positive attitudes toward each other, mutual concern, friendliness, and attentiveness; it also promotes positive self-attitudes and success experiences, which come about from contributing to group efforts and the utilization of one's resources by the group. As will be discussed later, even when students dislike each other intensely, view each other in negative ways, or want to avoid contact with each other, cooperation in achieving several mutually desired goals produces mutual liking and appreciation. You may help reduce isolation (and student shyness, depression, fear of rejection, and negative self-attitudes) when you encourage cooperation among students.

A major problem for teachers is the mediating role they are required to play in conflicts among students. Student-student conflicts can cause innumerable headaches for teachers. Teachers are rarely given specific training in conflict management or in the procedures for resolving conflicts. *The appropriate use of goal structures, however, will reduce conflict among students and promote constructive management of the conflicts that do arise.* There are two basic principles to remember in dealing with student-student conflicts: (1) the overuse and inappropriate use of competition produces conflicts among students; and (2) cooperative experiences reduce conflict among students. There is considerable research support for these statements. Thus teachers who have students who are regularly in conflict (and who doesn't?) may reduce the likelihood of future conflict by having the students cooperate on a series of projects and thus avoid inappropriate competition.

Of special interest to schools and classroom teachers is the problem of reducing student prejudice toward groups and individuals who are in some way different from the middle-class white majority. Ethnic groups, the lower socioeconomic groups, physically and mentally handicapped persons, and even the aged are discriminated against because of their "difference." Such prejudices create a great deal of student-student conflict in heterogeneous schools. Many teachers throughout the United States are required to mediate student-student conflicts based upon ethnic and cultural differences. *The appropriate use of cooperation among students can reduce substantially the amount of interethnic and intercultural conflict in the classroom and the school.* Considerable research demonstrates that such conflict will disappear after several weeks of cooperation among students from different backgrounds. Students in a cooperative relationship are, in general, accepting of each other. Since a heterogeneous group will problem-solve better than a homogeneous group, differences among students become appreciated, valued, and utilized for goal accomplishment. In a cooperative setting, students learn to value differences, as they are useful in a division of labor and in problem solving and facilitate the productivity of the group.

One factor that encourages more appropriate behavior among students is setting the goal structure for a lesson that clarifies how students are expected to interact with each other and with the teacher. In each goal structure it is important to list a specific set of expected behaviors, then monitor to see that they are there. Many teachers have a chart on the classroom wall that proclaims that when students are working cooperatively they should

1. Stay with their group and not wander around the room.
2. Use quiet voices.
3. Make sure every group member shares ideas.
4. Listen with real care to what other group members are saying.

It goes on to list whatever skills the teacher feels are important to stress.

Another strategy employed in the cooperative setting where interpersonal behaviors are vital is to assign roles to group members so that they know exactly what they are responsible for on that task. Assigning a student the role of voice monitor to keep voices quiet in the group may be important on some activities or with some groups. That student should have a nonverbal signal or sign to use whenever the group gets too loud. The responsibility for appropriate behavior in a cooperative group should lie primarily with the group.

RETURN TO THE MYTH OF THE LAZY STUDENT

Many teachers we have worked with are concerned with the "lazy" student in a cooperating group, who lets the others do all the work but shares in the benefits. With cooperation comes increased commitment and involvement that eliminate the possibility of parasites. Yet, if you occasionally have an unmotivated student in your classroom, here are some things you may try. First, you may ask the group to discuss the issue with the student and see why he is not contributing his share to the group's work. The group may be able to find a way to facilitate increased contributions by the student. Second, you may take the student aside and ask about the situation, seeking to determine his perception of the situation and what he thinks he can do about it. Problem-solving the alternative ways in which more commitment or involvement can be obtained is always a helpful process. Third, you can relax and let the group deal with the student in its own way and in its own time. This is often a very valuable learning experience for all students involved, and being too quick to intervene in such situations can seriously interfere with the education of your students. Fourth, you can present a skills lesson on problem solving such a situation in order to be sure that the students have the skills they need to deal with the "lazy" student constructively.

An unobtrusive way of highlighting the situation is to change the method by which the group score is calculated. One effective method that several researchers have used is to average the scores of the lowest members of the group. When all students are doing the same thing (such as completing a set of math problems), such a procedure can be used. It will motivate the group members to tutor the poorer students in the group, thereby resolving any problems with commitment and involvement in the learning tasks.

The major message that has to be given to a group when there is the possibility of an unmotivated member is that "hitchhiking" is dangerous in this class. The strategies discussed earlier for structuring individual accountability are effective in conveying this message. Whenever the teacher announces that he or she is going to enter a number of groups during the session and select one student to explain or defend the group's answer and does so, the students will want all their group members to know the material. This kind of oral exam not only gives a message to the hitchhiker, but also gives a message to the group that it is dangerous to *allow* hitchhiking in your group on this task.

THE SOCIALLY ISOLATED STUDENT

When a student in your class seems isolated and alienated, a number of strategies can help integrate the student into constructive relationships with other students:

1. *Ensuring constructive groupmates.* Select the other members of the learning group carefully to include supportive and encouraging classmates. Often the key to promoting constructive relationships within the classroom involves capitalizing on opportunities to "matchmake."

2. *Structuring resource interdependence.* Arrange materials into a jigsaw that requires participation by all members to ensure the participation of the socially isolated student.

3. *Structuring role interdependence.* Assign roles that the isolated student can successfully fulfill, such as *reader, recorder, observer,* or *encourager,* to ensure constructive participation in the group.

4. *Pretraining in collaborative skills.* Before introducing a collaborative skill to the class, teach the skill to the isolated student. Later, when the skill is being practiced by the group, the isolated student is an expert.

THE HIGH ACHIEVERS

There are some concerns about the high achievers in a heterogeneous, cooperative learning group. Will they be challenged? Will they end up doing all the work? Will they be slowed down? The research does not indicate any loss of achievement by bright students working in heterogeneous cooperative groups compared with bright students working competitively or individualistically. In fact, in a number of studies, bright students did better in heterogeneous, cooperative groups than they did alone. This is especially evident when you look not only at basic achievement but also at retention (they tend to remember the material longer) and strategies (they're more likely to have a strategy for doing the problem as well as the answer) when they work cooperatively. Bright students may work through the material more slowly and in more depth than when they work alone, but there is no evidence of achievement decline. At the same time, a host of other positive outcomes results when bright students work in heterogeneous, cooperative settings. They, along with their peers, have more positive attitudes about the learning situation, are more motivated, and tend to feel better about themselves. They practice and perfect collaborative skills such as leadership skills and conflict-resolution skills. Perhaps even more importantly, they are accepted by their peers and are seen as resources rather than as competitors to be feared and stereotyped.

It is important that bright students be included in the heterogeneous, cooperative groups, talk through the material, celebrate the group success, make friends, and perfect their cooperative skills. There are also a number of ways to challenge the academically high-achieving students in heterogeneous, cooperative groups. Some suggestions for doing so are as follows:

1. Structuring role interdependence. Some of the roles that promote high achievement are explaining how answers are derived, relating the material being learned to previously learned materials, and integrating the material into existing conceptual frameworks. The role of observing requires skills in tabulating and explaining data as well as giving groupmates feedback. These skills are often challenging to high-achieving students.

2. Adapting lesson requirements. While assigning a high-achieving student to a heterogeneous cooperative learning group, you will need to consider the appropriate criteria for success and be able to adapt the lesson to meet these criteria. Ways this can be done include the following:

a. Using different criteria for success for each group member.

b. Varying the amount each group member is expected to master.

c. Giving group members different lists, words, and problems, and then using the average percentage correct as the group's score.

d. Using improvement scores.

3. Ensuring constructive groupmates. In order to promote the cognitive processes most conducive to high-quality learning, it may be helpful to consider carefully who should collaborate with high-achieving students. Although it is sometimes productive to have several high-achieving students work together, usually it is more productive to match high achievers with middle- and low-achieving students, who will push for explanations and elaboration of the material being learned. Highly creative students (who may not be high academic achievers) and highly interpersonally skilled students who are middle achievers may be good matches for high-achieving students and may encourage them to think divergently and relate to others skillfully.

4. Rewarding interpersonal skills development. High-achieving students may be accustomed to experiencing success on individual academic tasks with relatively little effort. The ability to collaborate effectively with other students cannot be taken for granted. The evaluation of how effectively they interact within cooperative learning groups often provides new challenges to high-achieving students.

5. Giving bonus points for enriching the learning of others. Efforts made by high-achieving students (as well as middle and low achievers) to enrich the learning of other members of their group may qualify for bonus points. These provide an incentive for high achievers to broaden their study of a topic in order to bring in material not included in the texts and course handouts.

6. Creating clear positive interdependence. Some high achievers will see little benefit in helping other students learn. They may be inappropriately competitive or lack the empathy necessary for collaborating with low-achieving classmates. By ensuring that the positive interdependence is clear teachers can promote perceptions of mutuality and responsibility for others that will benefit high achievers considerably.

THE LOW ACHIEVERS

Integrating low achievers into heterogeneous cooperative learning groups can increase their achievement. Some suggestions that may be helpful include the following:

1. Assigning roles. Assigning specific responsibilities to low achievers ensures their participation in cooperative learning groups and reduces their anxiety about collaborating with middle- and high-achieving classmates. Examples of appropriate roles are summarizing group conclusions, checking to make sure every member can explain how to derive an answer, and praising other group members for participation.

2. Training in collaborative skills. Similar to the socially isolated student, low achievers can be given pretraining in collaborative skills so that they become the experts in the group.

3. Adapting lesson requirements. Just as the requirements of a lesson can be adapted for high achievers, requirements can also be adapted for low achievers.

4. Enhancing self-esteem and motivation through higher achievement. Low-achieving students tend to achieve higher when they are members of heterogeneous cooperative learning groups. Their higher achievement can be highlighted to enhance their self-esteem and achievement motivation. Encouragement to learn from valued peers can, in turn, promote even higher achievement.

THE DISRUPTIVE STUDENT

Disruptive students, who particularly need to increase their interpersonal skills and ability to collaborate with peers, will benefit from being placed in heterogeneous learning groups. Some suggestions for helping them work together include the following:

1. Ensuring constructive groupmates. The other group members can be carefully chosen to include classmates who may be able to control and encourage the disruptive student.

2. Pretraining groupmates in procedures for controlling the disruptive student. Once groups are formed, the teacher (with the help of the special education teacher, social worker, or counselor) can train the group members in procedures tailored for reducing the disruptive behavior of the target student. Such pretraining provides a variety of strategies for groupmates to try when the student becomes disruptive and reduces the anxiety and frustration of the groupmates.

3. Intervening to teach collaborative skills. When the disruptive student creates difficulties, the teacher may intervene to help the group members find ways to influence the disruptive student to behave more constructively. This intervention usually includes helping the group develop a plan of action, establishing clear expectations for the behavior of all group members, and taking appropriate action if the disruptive student violates the expectations. Specific training in collaborative skills becomes part of the plan of action dealing with violations of group expectations of appropriate behavior.

4. Coaching the disruptive student in collaborative skills. A special-education teacher, social worker, or counselor can train the disruptive student individually in specific collaborative skills and coach the student to use these skills in cooperative learning groups. The coaching includes meeting with the disruptive student immediately before a group session to review the collaborative skills and then observing him or her to count the frequency of the desired behaviors. The disruptive student's behavior is then reviewed during the meeting before the next group session.

5. *Varying the size of the group.* Sometimes disruptive students work better in pairs, where they can receive constant attention and interaction. Other times it may take several strong students to exert enough peer pressure to control the disruptive student's behavior.

6. *Regrouping.* As a last resort, when all else has failed, groups can be reconstituted so that the disruptive student is placed with another set of peers. Especially disruptive students might be passed around so that all members of the class work with the student the same amount of time.

CONFLICT AMONG GROUP MEMBERS

Sometimes students who are unaccustomed to collaborating are assigned to work together, and various types of conflicts can break out. Power struggles over who is to dominate the group, division between male and female members, competition among members, and other types of conflicts can occur. Teachers may wish to implement the following when intragroup conflicts occur:

1. *Reviewing the critical elements of cooperative learning groups.* The teacher may wish to review the positive interdependence, individual accountability, and expected behaviors that are essential aspects of cooperative learning groups. Reminding students of the critical elements often helps students refocus and collaborate more effectively.

2. *Structuring role interdependence.* Giving each member a specific role can avoid or solve many conflicts.

3. *Increasing processing.* Having one member observe the group work and then having the group discuss the results often generates the problem solving necessary to resolve the conflict.

INDIVIDUALIZED INSTRUCTION AND STUDENT INTERACTION

Many teachers ask the authors why it is not possible to individualize instruction and still have students interacting and helping each other. Like many key words in education, *individualize* is being stretched to include so many different practices that it is growing less and less useful as a descriptor. Critics of education often state that teachers never change their behavior; they just change the words describing their behavior. The original intent of individualizing instruction was to help students develop individual goals in order to work toward goal accomplishment in their own way and at their own pace, in a manner and sequence suited to them personally. Such a procedure (though useful in promoting mastery of facts and noncomplex skills) is not intended to encourage interaction between students. Requests by students for help from other students disrupt and interrupt goal accomplishment in an individualistic goal structure. It is also difficult for a student to be of assistance when his style of working is much different from that of another student, and when both are working on different, individualized goals. If you want to have students helping each other, interacting in positive ways, and sharing materials and resources, it is better to move to a cooperative goal structure rather than to stretch individualizing to cover all learning situations. If you are concerned about this issue, it may be helpful to review the discussion in Chapter 4 on when to use individualized goal structures.

COMPETITION AND MOTIVATION

Inappropriate competition does not increase motivation—it kills it. This point was discussed in Chapter 5. Yet many teachers remain unconvinced. Perhaps the most powerful statement on the subject was made by John Atkinson, the foremost psychologist in the area of achievement motivation (Atkinson & Raynor, 1974, p. xi):

> Achievement is a we thing, not a me thing, always the product of many heads and hands no matter how it may appear to one involved in the effort and enjoyment of it or to a casual observer.

Motivation to achieve is based not upon competition with others but upon the belief that there is a reasonable chance to accomplish a desired goal. The research clearly demonstrates that cooperation is much more facilitative of motivated effort and achievement than is competition.

Nothing else can be said on this issue.

STUDENTS WHO MUST ALWAYS WIN

What can be done with "life-or-death" competitors who approach all competition with taut muscles and high anxiety and miss the enjoyment and fun in the situation? Some students become so concerned with always winning (or never losing) that they can't learn to compete for fun and to enjoy the situation, win or lose. Especially when such competitive attitudes carry over to individualistic and cooperative situations, the inappropriate behaviors of the student are evident.* Some suggestions for helping such a student are as follows:

---

*For several years, the two authors competed inappropriately at Christmas by trying to determine who got the most presents. This not only ruined Christmas for the two of us but gave the rest of the family headaches. The behavior stopped when the rest of the family started giving the two authors aches in certain places whenever such a competition began!

A good answer may not be good enough. It has to be better than someone else's. —*R. Dreeben,* On What Is Learned in School, (1968)

First, find a good model in another student and put him in some low-key, friendly competitive situations with the overcompetitive student. Then reward fun and involvement rather than winning, while pointing out that taking competition too seriously takes the enjoyment out of it. A second approach is to reinforce cooperation whenever the overcompetitive student engages in it. A third possible approach is to ask the student to build a plan for reducing her competitiveness; you may provide any counseling she needs for constructing and implementing such a plan.

Math Tournament

One teacher constructed a math tournament among students in the following manner. Students were divided into clusters of four students. A series of weekly quiz questions was placed in a jar in the center of the table. The first student would draw a question from the jar and try to solve it. The other three students would then evaluate her answer and determine whether it was right or wrong. The second student would then draw a question from the jar, and so on, until all the quiz questions had been answered. The winner was the student who had answered the most questions correctly, and the other students were ranked second, third, and last. Winners across groups were compared to see who had the best performance in the class. This same procedure can be used in any type of class.

APPROPRIATENESS OF A GOAL STRUCTURE FOR A STUDENT

Many teachers have asked us whether certain students wouldn't do better if the teacher always used the same goal structure rather than varying goal structures according to desired outcomes of instruction. Certain students may have a predisposition and preference to compete, cooperate, or work individually. Yet a person who is going to function effectively in society must have the skills to do all three. It is not a question of matching the goal structure and the student; it is a question of the responsibility of the school (this means the teacher) to socialize students into the skills they need in order to be productive members of society.

GOAL STRUCTURES AND YOUR CLASSROOM

"Your ideas on goal structures sound good for _____ [insert your favorite target], but they won't work in my classroom [insert a description of your classroom]!" We have heard this statement often in the past four years. If you are doubtful that the ideas in this book can really be used in your classroom, stop and consider again. The research reviewed in Chapter 2 was conducted with all age groups in a variety of situations, from marble rolling to university-level examinations in psychology. *The material in this book is appropriate for any teaching situation,* whether it is a preschool program or a graduate school, a mathematics or a social studies class, vocational education or liberal arts. Any teacher who wishes to promote higher achievement, more positive attitudes, and broader educational outcomes should consider goal structuring as part of her instructional program.

In this book we have emphasized that cooperation should be used primarily with problem-solving activities. In many classrooms the majority of time is spent on basic skills, which some teachers assume cannot be taught in cooperative ways. Yet several research studies demonstrate clearly that performance (for all group members) on math problems is higher in a cooperative group than when students work individualistically or in competition with each other. Math and other basic skills involve learning concepts that are best done under cooperative conditions. Thus, even if you teach basic skills, you will want to use all three goal structures appropriately.

[9]Two are better than one, because they have a good reward for their toil. [10]For if they fall, one will lift up his fellow; but woe to him who is alone when he falls and has not another to lift him up. [11]Again, if two lie together, they are warm; but how can one be warm alone? [12]And though a man might prevail against one who is alone, two will withstand him. A threefold cord is not quickly broken. —*Ecclesiastes 4:9–13*

IMPLEMENTATION OF COOPERATIVE LEARNING: AN ATTITUDE OF EXPERIMENTATING, FINE-TUNING, AND OVERCOMING ROADBLOCKS

Implementing cooperative learning depends on adopting an attitude of experimentation, the fine-tuning of cooperative learning procedures to integrate them into the teacher's style and situation, and the overcoming of roadblocks to implementation. Without experimentation, fine-tuning, and overcoming roadblocks, no new teaching practice can be implemented.

An Attitude of Experimentation

In order to implement cooperative learning procedures, the teacher must first try out the new instructional strategy. Such experimentation involves the risk of failure, for the first few times cooperative learning is used the results may be less than ideal. Teachers who lack an attitude of experimentation will then think, "That did not go so well—cooperative learning does not work." Teachers who have an attitude of experimentation, however, will think, "That did not work so well—what can I change to improve my implementation of cooperative learning?" An attitude of experimentation means that teachers will

1. Believe that teaching is a continuous process of developing more effective procedures through modifying old procedures and integrating new ones into one's standard practices. The continuous improvement of teaching becomes both a personal and professional commitment.

2. Accept barriers and problems as a natural aspect of modifying teaching procedures (as opposed to believing they are proof that the new procedures will not work). Innovating always carries the risk of failure and of meeting problems and roadblocks. In highly innovative organizations there is a very high failure rate because new things are constantly being tried out.

3. View problems and roadblocks as signs that adjustments are needed in the implementation (as opposed to defeat or failure). Problems and roadblocks are viewed as temporary barriers rather than as permanent obstacles. Learning from one's mistakes is a talent found in teachers who continuously improve their teaching competence.

Fine-Tuning

One of the most important findings of the research on innovation in schools from the 1950s, 1960s, and 1970s is that curriculum packages are quickly adopted in schools and then quickly discontinued. Lasting implementation seems to require that teachers "reinvent" the teaching practice for themselves. Teachers may reinvent cooperative learning by adapting it to their style, personality, students, and school, and by "fine-tuning" the procedures for using cooperative learning until there is a good fit between them and the rest of their teaching. Different teachers, for example, structure positive interdependence differently (some through bonus points, some through divisions of labor, some through jigsawing materials, and some through group grades). The procedures selected for creating positive interdependence have to be compatible with a teacher's teaching philosophy and methods. The teachers who are most likely to make cooperative learning a part of their daily teaching are those who make it their own.

Roadblocks

A *roadblock* is a hurdle that causes temporary difficulties in reaching a goal. A roadblock can be external (such as a student being unwilling to share knowledge with classmates), or internal (such as teachers being uncomfortable if they do not implement cooperative learning perfectly the first time they try it).

One of the most common roadblocks is a natural resistance to change on the part of oneself, one's colleagues, students, and parents. Change almost always creates anxiety. The status quo, even with all its problems, often seems safer and preferable to the unknown consequences of changing current procedures and practices.

Other roadblocks to implementing cooperative learning successfully include the following:

1. The teacher not implementing cooperation clearly and specifically enough.
2. The students not having the collaborative skills needed.
3. Colleagues, administrators, parents, and students not understanding the power and importance of cooperative learning.

There are always roadblocks to change and growth. Teachers, therefore, should not be surprised by the appearance of roadblocks as they experiment with and fine-tune cooperative learning, because roadblocks are an inevitable part of the progress. The guidelines for overcoming roadblocks are as follows:

1. Find one or two colleagues who are supportive of you or of cooperative learning, schedule a time to meet, and then discuss with them the roadblock and how you plan to overcome it. Problem solving is almost always more effective when more than one person is involved.
2. Follow the six-point procedure outlined in the following list:

Procedure for Overcoming Roadblocks

1. Describe the roadblock/problem to your colleagues using a narrative style. Be as descriptive and specific as possible. Your colleagues should be silent—listening and taking notes.

2. Your colleagues ask questions to clarify details or to ask for more information about the situation. This is a fact-finding segment.

3. You and your colleagues brainstorm at least two or three possible solutions each (with three people there should be six or more possible solutions). Because brainstorming requires *no evaluation,* you should not comment on their suggestions, and especially you should avoid "Yes, but . . . " This is a divergent thinking segment.

4. With your colleagues, select the three possible solutions that have the most realistic chance of working. The top three should then be placed in rank order from most useful (1) to least useful (3). Try to achieve consensus on the ranking.

5. Implement the three suggested solutions. Then report back to your colleagues as to how well they worked. At this point you should all either celebrate your success or else repeat the procedure to find three new possible solutions.

6. Be sure to thank your colleagues for their help and assistance.

COOPERATION AMONG TEACHERS

Cooperation among students will be easier to establish and maintain if there is cooperation among school personnel. Many schools are scarred by competition among teachers. In these schools, teachers feel insecure, isolated, cold, reserved, defensive, and competitive in their relationships with fellow teachers and administrators. Feelings of hostility, guardedness, and alienation toward the rest of the school staff create anxiety in teachers, which in turn decreases their effectiveness in the classroom. The teachers act as though they never need help from their colleagues. A fiction is maintained that a "professional and highly trained teacher" has already achieved sufficient competence and skill to handle all classroom situations alone. The actual result, however, is that innovative and creative teaching is stifled by insecurity, anxiety, and competitiveness. And the environment is depressing and discouraging.

One of the most constructive contributions you can make to your school is to encourage cooperation among teachers and the use of the cooperative goal structure in the classroom. How do you encourage teacher cooperation? The process is the same as for implementing cooperation among students. Establish cooperative goals that all involved teachers wish to accomplish and that require interdependence and interaction among the teachers. Sufficient trust and openness must be present for teachers to feel free to visit one another's classrooms and ask one another for help or suggestions. Providing feedback about each other's teaching and providing help to increase teaching skills are equally important. Teachers must have the basic communication, trust-building, and controversy skills discussed in Chapter 6. Team teaching, coordinating all social studies curricula, establishing support groups in which teachers provide help and assistance to each other, coordinating the teaching of difficult students—all are examples of cooperative interaction among teachers. However you do it, implementing department- and schoolwide cooperation among teachers will immensely increase your enjoyment of teaching and of working in your school, and it will encourage cooperation among students within your classroom.

SUMMARY

There are without a doubt more teacher concerns than those we have discussed in this chapter, and after mastering the material in this book, you may be just as able to discuss the concerns of teachers and to provide answers to them as we are. How would you rate your teaching effectiveness now? How would you rate your ability to use successfully and appropriately the cooperative, competitive, and individualized goal structures? Through continued use of the three goal structures, you know you have improved your teaching, made it more enjoyable, and made teaching easier for yourself.

"a threefold cord is not quickly broken"

Ecclesiastes 4:13

11

Epilogue

In retrospect, a few points need to be stressed. Although we have discussed thoroughly all three goal structures, cooperation is what this book is about. It is the context in which both competition for fun and individualistically working on one's own take place. Cooperation gives meaning to the knowledge and skills gained in the other two goal structures, because it is within cooperative activities that such knowledge and skills are used to create alternatives and solve problems. This statement is as true of society as a whole as it is of instruction in schools. Cooperation is the "air" of society, which we constantly breathe; it is completely necessary to us but relatively unnoticed. We notice changes in the air, a whiff of perfume or a blanket of smog, but these are the rare instances. Like the perfume, the times we are locked (or licked) in competition and the things we achieve "on our own" stand out and are remembered because they are different from the majority of our efforts, which are cooperative. Just as the parochial myth that "smog is what most air is like, and we need to learn to live with it" can grow in the minds of those who live in a large city, so egocentric myths like "it's a survival-of-the-fittest society" have grown and have been nourished by those who ignore the many cooperative aspects of their lives, while concentrating on those aspects that are perceived as competitive. In American society (and schools) we share a common language, we drive on the appropriate side of the street, we take turns going out doors, we raise families, we seek friendship, we share the maintenance of life through an intricate division of labor. This is not to say that the skills of competition and individualization are unimportant. They are important, but only within the larger context of cooperation with others, and a person needs to know when to compete or work individualistically and when to cooperate. Unfortunately, instruction in schools at present seems to stress competition or perhaps individualization without much attention to the skills needed to facilitate effective cooperation. To encourage a positive and effective learning environment and to promote the achievement and socialization outcomes of schools, we must realize that cooperation is the forest—competition and individualization are but trees.

As the authors look back on the aspects of our growing up together that we shared with the reader in the preface and in various parts of this book, we realize that we may have misled you. The competition between us was a rather small part of the time we spent together. What made the instances of competition bearable was the constant supportive cooperation within our family, and later with our friends and our own families.

Without cooperation and the skills that it requires, life in a society or a school would be impossible.

References

ARONSON, E., BLANEY, N., STEPHAN, C., SIKES, J., & SNAPP, M. (1978). *The jigsaw classroom*. Beverly Hills, CA: Sage.

ASHMORE, R. (1970). Solving the problems of prejudice. In B. E. Collins (Ed.), *Social psychology*. Reading, MA: Addison-Wesley.

ASTIN, A., GREEN, K., & KORN, W. (1987). *The American freshman: Twenty year trends*. Los Angeles: University of California at Los Angeles, Higher Education Research Institute.

ASTIN, A., GREEN, K., KORN, W., & SCHALIT, M. (1986). *The American freshman: National norms for fall, 1986*. Los Angeles: University of California at Los Angeles, Higher Education Research Institute.

ATKINSON, J. (1965). The mainsprings of achievement-oriented activity. In J. D. Krumholtz (Ed.), *Learning and the educational process* (pp. 25–66). Chicago: Rand McNally & Co.

ATKINSON, J., & RAYNOR, J. (1974). *Motivation and achievement*. Washington, DC: Winston & Sons.

BANDURA, A., ROSS, D., & ROSS, S. (1963). Imitation of film-mediated aggressive models. *Journal of Abnormal and Social Psychology, 66*, 3–11.

BIGELOW, R. (1972). The evolution of cooperation, aggression, and self-control. In J. Cole and D. Jenson (Eds.), *Nebraska Symposium on Motivation* (pp. 1–110). Lincoln: University of Nebraska Press.

BLANCHARD, F., ADELMAN, L., & COOK, S. (1975). The effect of group success and failure upon interpersonal attraction in cooperating interracial groups. *Journal of Personality and Social Psychology, 32*, 519–530.

BOND, C., & TITUS, L. (1983). Social facilitation: A meta-analysis of 241 studies. *Psychological Bulletin, 94*, 265–292.

BRONFRENBRENNER, U. (1970). *Two worlds of childhood*. New York: Russell Sage.

CAMPBELL, J. (1965). *The children's crusader: Colonel Francis W. Parker*. Unpublished doctoral dissertation, Teachers College, Columbia University, New York.

COHEN, E. (1986). *Designing groupwork*. New York: Teachers College Press.

COLEMAN, J. (1959). Academic achievement and the structure of competition. *Harvard Educational Review, 29*, 339–351.

COLEMAN, J. (1961). *The adolescent society*. New York: Macmillan.

COLEMAN, J. (1972). The children have outgrown the schools. *Psychology Today, 5*, 72–75.

COLLINS, B. (1970). *Social psychology*. Reading, MA: Addison-Wesley.

CONGER, J. (1988). Hostages to fortune: Youth, values and the public interest. *American Psychologist, 36*, 1475–1484.

COOK, S. (1969). *Motives in a conceptual analysis of attitude-related behavior*. Paper presented at the Nebraska Symposium on Motivation, Lincoln, NE.

COTTRELL, N., WACK, D., SEKERAK, G., & RITTLE, R. (1968). Social facilitation of dominant responses by the presence of an audience and the mere presence of other. *Journal of Personality and Social Psychology, 9*, 245–250.

COUSINS, N. (1979). *Anatomy of an illness as perceived by the patient: Reflections on healing and regeneration*. New York: W. W. Norton.

CROCKENBERG, S., BRYANT, B., & WILCE, L. (1974, September). *The effects of cooperatively structured learning environments on intrapersonal behavior*. Paper presented at the annual meeting of the APA, New Orleans, LA.

DEUTSCH, M. (1949). A theory of cooperation and competition. *Human Relations, 2*, 129–152.

DEUTSCH, M. (1962). Cooperation and trust: Some theoretical notes. In M. Jones (Ed.), *Nebraska Symposium on Motivation.* Lincoln: University of Nebraska Press, 275–320.

DEVRIES, D., & EDWARDS, K. (1973). Learning games and student teams: Their effects on classroom process. *American Journal of Educational Research, 10,* 307–318.

DEVRIES, D., & EDWARDS, K. (1974, April). *Cooperation in the classroom: Towards a theory of alternative reward-task classroom structures.* Paper presented at the annual meeting of the American Educational Research Association, Chicago, IL.

DEVRIES, D., MUSE, D., & WELLS, E. (1971). The effects on students of working in cooperative groups: An exploratory study. Center Report No. 120, Center for Social Orgnization of Schools, Johns Hopkins University.

DEVRIES, D., SLAVIN, R., FENNESSEY, G., EDWARDS, K., & LOMBARDO, M. (1980). *Teams-games-tournament: The team learning approach.* Englewood Cliffs, NJ: Educational Technology Publications.

DIAMOND, J. (1989, May). The great leap forward. *Discover, 10,* 50–60.

DREEBEN, R. (1968). *On what is learned in school.* Reading, MA: Addison-Wesley.

FARB, P. (1963). *Ecology.* New York: Time, Inc.

GIBBS, J. (1986). *Tribes.* Santa Rosa, CA: Center Source Publications.

GLASSER, W. (1969). *Schools without failure.* New York: Harper & Row.

GLASSER, W. (1986). *Control theory in the classroom.* New York: Harper & Row.

GREEN, D. (1977). The immediate processing of sentences. *Quarterly Journal of Experimental Psychology, 29,* 135–146.

HALISCH, F., & HECKHAUSEN, H. (1977). Search for feedback information and effort regulation during task performance. *Journal of Personality and Social Psychology, 35,* 724–733.

HARTUP, W., GLAZER, J. & CHARLESWORTH, R. (1967). Peer reinforcement and sociometric status. *Child Development, 38,* 1017–1024.

HENRY, J. (1963). *Culture against man.* New York: Random House.

HILL, G. (1982). Group versus individual performance: Are N + one heads better than one? *Psychological Bulletin, 91,* 517–539.

HOLT, J. (1964). *How children fail.* New York: Dell.

HUNT, P., & HILLERY, J. (1973). Social facilitation in a coaction setting: An examination of the effects over learning trials. *Journal of Experimental Social Psychology, 9,* 563–571.

HURLOCK, E. (1927). Use of group rivalry as an incentive. *Journal of Abnormal and Social Psychology, 22,* 278–290.

ILLICH, I. (1971). *Deschooling society.* New York: Harrow.

JACKSON, P. (1968). *Life in classrooms.* New York: Holt, Rinehart & Winston.

JOHNSON, D. W. (1970). *The social psychology of education.* New York: Holt, Rinehart & Winston.

JOHNSON, D. W. (1973). *Student attitudes toward cooperation and competition in a midwestern school district.* Unpublished manuscript, University of Minnesota, Minneapolis.

JOHNSON, D. W. (1979). *Educational psychology.* Englewood Cliffs, NJ: Prentice-Hall.

JOHNSON, D. W. (1980). Group processes: Influences of student-student interactions on school outcomes. In J. McMillan (Ed.), *Social psychology of school learning.* New York: Academic Press.

JOHNSON, D. W. (1987, 1991). *Human relations and your career: A guide to interpersonal skills* (2nd & 3rd eds.). Englewood Cliffs, NJ: Prentice-Hall.

JOHNSON, D. W. (1990). *Reaching out: Interpersonal effectivenss and self-actualization* (4th ed.). Englewood Cliffs, NJ: Prentice-Hall.

JOHNSON, D. W., & JOHNSON, F. (1987, 1991). *Joining together: Group theory and group skills* (3rd & 4th eds.). Englewood Cliffs, NJ: Prentice-Hall.

JOHNSON, D. W., & JOHNSON, R. (1974). Instructional structure: Cooperative, competitive, or individualistic. *Review of Educational Research, 44,* 213–240.

JOHNSON, D. W., & JOHNSON, R. (1975, 1987). *Learning together and alone: Cooperation, competition, and individualization* (1st & 2nd eds.). Englewood Cliffs, NJ: Prentice-Hall.

JOHNSON, D. W., & JOHNSON, R. (1978). Cooperative, competitive, and individualistic learning. *Journal of Research and Development in Education, 12,* 3–15.

JOHNSON, D. W., & JOHNSON, R. (1979). Conflict in the classroom: Controversy and learning. *Review of Educational Research, 49,* 51–70.

JOHNSON, D. W., & JOHNSON, R. (1983a). The socialization and achievement crisis: Are cooperative learning experiences the solution? In L. Bickman (Ed.), *Applied Social Psychology Annual 4,* 119–164. Beverly Hills, CA: Sage.

JOHNSON, D. W., & JOHNSON, R. (1983b). Social interdependence and perceived academic and personal support in the classroom. *Journal of Social Psychology, 120,* 77–82.

JOHNSON, D. W., & JOHNSON, R. (1986). Motivational processes in cooperative, competitive, and individualistic learning situations. In C. Ames and R. Ames (Eds.), *Attitudes and attitude change in special education: Its theory and practice* (pp. 249–286). New York: Academic Press.

JOHNSON, D. W., & JOHNSON, R. (1987). *Creative conflict.* Edina, MN: Interaction.

JOHNSON, D. W., & JOHNSON, R. (1989a). *Leading the cooperative school.* Edina, MN: Interaction.

JOHNSON, D. W., & JOHNSON, R. (1989b). *Cooperation and competiton: Theory and research.* Edina, MN: Interaction.

JOHNSON, D. W., JOHNSON, R., & HOLUBEC, E. (Eds.). (1987). *Structuring cooperative learning: Lesson plans for teachers* Edina, MN: Interaction.

JOHNSON, D. W., JOHNSON, R., & HOLUBEC, E. (1988). *Cooperation in the classroom* (rev. ed.). Edina, MN: Interaction.

JOHNSON, D. W., JOHNSON, R., & HOLUBEC, E. (1990). *Circles of learning: Cooperation in the classroom* (3rd ed.). Edina, MN: Interaction.

JOHNSON, D. W., JOHNSON, R., & MARUYAMA, G. (1983). Interdependence and interpersonal attraction among heterogeneous and homogeneous individuals: A theoretical formulation and a meta-analysis of the research. *Review of Educational Research, 53,* 5–54.

JOHNSON, D. W., JOHNSON, R., & SMITH, K. (1986). Academic conflict among students: Controversy and learning. In R. Feldman (Ed.)., *The social psychology of education.* (pp. 199–231). London: Cambridge University Press.

JOHNSON, D. W., JOHNSON, R., STANNE, M., & GARIBALDI, A. (in press). The impact of leader and member group processing on achievement in cooperative groups. *Journal of Social Psychology.*

JOHNSON, D. W., MARUYAMA, G., JOHNSON, R., NELSON, D., & SKON, L. (1981). Effects of cooperative, competitive, and individualistic goal structures on achievement: A meta-analysis. *Psychological Bulletin, 89,* 47–62.

JOHNSON, D. W., MATROSS, R. (1977). The interpersonal influence of the psychotherapist. In A. Gurman & A. Razin (Eds.). *The effective therapist: A handbook.* Elmsford, NY: Pergamon Press.

KAGAN, J. (1965, Summer). Personality and the learning process. *Daedalus,* 553–563.

KAGAN, S. (1985). *Cooperative learning.* Mission-Viejo, CA: Resources for Teachers.

KAGAN, S., & MADSEN, M. (1972). Experimental analyses of cooperation and competition of Anglo-American and Mexican children. *Developmental Psychology, 6*(1), 49–59.

KERR, N., & BRUUN, S. (1983). The dispensability of member effort and group motivation losses: Free-rider effects. *Journal of Personality and Social Psychology, 44,* 78–94.

KLEIBER, D., & ROBERTS, G. (1981). The effects of experience in the development of social character: An exploratory investigation. *Journal of Sport Psychology, 3,* 114–122.

KOHL, H. (1969). *The open classroom.* New York: Vintage.

KOHN, A. (1986). *No contest.* Boston: Houghton Mifflin.

KOUZES, J., & POSNER, B. (1987). *The leadership challenge.* San Francisco: Jossey-Bass.

KROLL, W., & PETERSON, K. (1965). Study of values test and collegiate football teams. *Research Quarterly, 36,* 441–447.

LAMM, H., & TROMMSDORFF, G. (1973). Group versus individual performance on tasks requiring ideational proficiency (brainstorming): A review. *European Journal of Social Psychology, 3,* 361–388.

LANGER, E., & BENEVENTO, A. (1978). Self-induced dependence. *Journal of Personality and Social Psychology, 36,* 886–893.

LATANE, B., WILLIAMS, K., & HARKINS, S. (1979). Many hands make light the work: The causes and consequences of social loafing. *Journal of Personality and Social Psychology, 37,* 822–832.

LEPLEY, W. (1937). Competitive behavior in the albino rat. *Journal of Experimental Psychology, 21,* 194–201.

LEVINE, J. (1983). Social comparison and education. In J. Levine & M. Wang (Eds.), *Teachers and student perceptions: Implications for learning.* New York: Erlbaum.

LEW, M., MESCH, D., JOHNSON, D. W., & JOHNSON, R. (1986a). Positive interpendence, academic and collaborative-skills group contingencies and isolated students. *American Educational Research Journal, 23,* 476–488.

LEW, M., MESCH, D., JOHNSON, D. W., & JOHNSON, R. (1986b). Components of cooperative learning: Effects of collaborative skills and academic group contingencies on achievement and mainstreaming. *Contemporary Educational Psychology, 11,* 229–239.

LOY, J., BIRRELL, S., & ROSE, P. (1976). Attitudes held toward agnostic activities as a function of selected social identities. *Quest, 26,* 81–95.

MADSEN, M. C. (1967). Cooperative and competitive motivation of children in three Mexican subcultures. *Psychological Reports, 20,* 1307–1320.

MARKUS, H. (1978). The effect of mere presence on social facilitation: An unobtrusive test. *Journal of Experimental Social Psychology, 14,* 389–397.

MASTERS, J. (1972). Effects of social comparison upon the imitation of neutral and altruistic behaviors by young children. *Child Development, 43,* 131–142.

MATTHEWS, B. (1979). Effects of fixed and alternated payoff inequity on dyadic competition. *The Psychological Record, 29,* 329–339.

MAY, M., & DOOB, L. (1937). Competition and cooperation. *Social Science Research Council Bulletin, 25.* New York: Social Science Research Council.

MAYER, A. (1903). Über Einzel- und Gesamtleistung des Schulkindes. *Archiv für die gesamte Psychologie, 1,* 276–416.

MCKEACHIE, W., PINTRICH, P., LIN, Y., & SMITH, D. (1986). *Teaching and learning in the college classroom.* Ann Arbor: University of Michigan.

MEAD, M. (Ed.) (1936). *Cooperation and competition among primitive peoples.* New York: McGraw Hill.

MESCH, D., Lew, M., Johnson, D. W., & Johnson, R. (1986). Isolated teenagers, cooperative learning and the training of social skills. *Journal of Psychology, 120,* 323–334.

MESCH, D., JOHNSON, D. W., & JOHNSON, R. (1988). Impact of positive interdependence and academic group contingencies on achievement. *Journal of Social Psychology, 138,* 345–352.

MILLER, L., & HAMBLIN, R. (1963). Interdependence, differential rewarding, and productivity. *American Sociological Review, 28,* 768–778.

VON MISES, L. (1949). *Human action: A treatise on economics.* New Haven: Yale University Press.

MONTAGU, A. (1965). *The human revolution.* New York: World.

MONTAGU, A. (1966). *On being human.* New York: Hawthorn.

MURRAY, F. (1983). *Cognitive benefits of teaching on the teacher.* Paper presented at American Educational Research Association Annual Meeting, Montreal, Quebec.

NELSON, L., & KAGAN, S. (1972). Competition: The star-spangled scramble. *Psychology Today, 6,* 53.

NESBITT, M. (1967). *A public school for tomorrow.* New York: Delta.

OGILVIE, B., & TUTKO, T. (1971). Sport: If you want to build character, try something else. *Psychology Today, 5,* 60–63.

ORLICK, T. (1981). Positive socialization via cooperative games. *Developmental Psychology, 17*(4), 426–429.

PEPITONE, E. (1980). *Children in cooperation and competition: Toward a developmental social psychology.* Lexington, MA: D. C. Heath.

POSTMAN, N. & WEINGARTNER, C. (1969). *Teaching as a subversive activity.* New York: Delacorte Press.

RATHBONE, C. (1970). *Open education and the teacher.* Unpublished doctoral dissertation, Harvard University.

RENSBERGER, B. (1984, April). What made humans human? *New York Times Magazine,* 80–81, 89–95.

RIPPA, S. (1976). *Education in a free society.* New York: McKay.

ROGERS, V. (1970). *Teaching in the British primary schools.* London: Macmillan.

SALOMON, G. (1981). Communication and education: Social and psychological interactions. *People & Communication, 13,* 9–271.

SANDERS, G., & BARON, R. (1975). The motivating effects of distraction on task performance. *Journal of Personality and Social Psychology, 32,* 956–963.

SELIGMAN, M. (1988). Boomer blues. *Psychology Today, 22,* 50–55.

SHALAWAY, L. (1985). Peer coaching . . . does it work? *R&D Notes, National Institute of Education,* 6–7.

SHARAN, S. (1980). Cooperative learning in teams: Recent methods and effects on achievement, attitudes, and ethnic relations. *Review of Educational Research, 50,* 241–272.

SHARAN, S., & HERTZ-LAZAROWITZ, R. (1980). *A group-investigation method of cooperative learning in the classroom.* Technical Report, University of Tel-Aviv, Tel-Aviv, Israel. (Review article).

SHEINGOLD, K., HAWKINS, J., & CHAR, C. (1984). "I'm the thinkist, you're the typist": The interactions of technology and the social life of classrooms. *Journal of Social Issues, 40*(3), 49–61.

SHERIF, M., & HOVLAND, C. (1961). *Social judgement: Assimilation and contrast effects in communication and attitude change.* New Haven, CT: Yale University Press.

SILBERMAN, C. (1971). *Crisis in the classroom.* New York: Vintage.

SLAVIN, R. (1974). *The effects of teams in Teams-Games-Tournament on the normative climates of classrooms.* Baltimore, MD: Center for Social Organization of Schools, Johns Hopkins University.

SLAVIN, R. (1980). Cooperative learning. *Review of Educational Research, 50,* 315–342.

SLAVIN, R. (1983). *Cooperative learning.* New York: Longman.

SLAVIN, R. (1985). An introduction to cooperative learning research. In R. Slavin, S. Sharan, S. Kagan,

R. Hertz-Lazarowitz, C. Webb, & R. Schumuck (Eds.), *Learning to cooperate, cooperating to learn.* New York: Plenum Press.

SLAVIN, R., LEAVEY, M., & MADDEN, N. (1982). *Team-assisted individualization: Mathematics teacher's manual,* Baltimore, MD: Center for Social Organization of Schools, Johns Hopkins University.

SPILERMAN, S. (1971). Raising academic motivation in lower class adolescents: A convergence of two research traditions. *Sociology of Education, 44,* 103–118.

STAUB, E. (1971). Helping a person in distress: The influence of implicit and explicit "rules" of conduct on children and adults. *Journal of Personality and Social Psychology, 17,* 137–144.

STEVENS, R., MADDEN, N., SLAVIN, R., & FARNISH, A. (1987). Cooperative integrated reading and composition: Two field experiments. *Reading Research Quarterly, 22*(4), 433–454.

TJOSVOLD, D. (1986). *Working together to get things done.* Lexington, MA: D. C. Heath.

TRIPLETT, N. (1898). The dynamogenic factors in peacemaking and competition. *American Journal on Psychology, 9,* 507–533.

TSENG, S. (1969). *An experimental study of the effect of three types of distribution of reward upon work efficiency and group dynamics.* Unpublished doctoral dissertation, Columbia University, New York, NY.

WALBERG, H., & THOMAS, S. (1971). *Characteristics of open education: Toward an operational definition.* Newton, MA: TDR Associates.

WATSON, G., & JOHNSON, D. W. (1972). *Social psychology: Issues and insights.* Philadelphia: Lippincott.

WEBB, H. (1969). Professionalization of attitudes toward play among adolescents. In D. Kenyon (Ed.), *Aspects of contemporary sport sociology.* Chicago: Athletic Institute.

WEBB, N., ENDER, P., & LEWIS, S. (1986). Problem-solving strategies and group processes in small group learning computer programming. *American Educational Research Journal, 23*(2), 243–261.

WILHELMS, F. (1970). Educational conditions essential to growth in individuality. In V. Howes (Ed.), *Individualization of instruction: A teaching strategy.* New York: Macmillan.

YAGER, S., JOHNSON, D. W., & JOHNSON, R. (1985). Oral discussion, group-to-individual transfer, and achievement in cooperative learning groups. *Journal of Educational Psychology, 77*(1), 60–66.

ZAJONC, R. (1965). Social facilitation. *Science, 149,* 269–272.

Glossary

Acceptance: Communication of high regard for another person, for his or her contributions, and for his or her actions.

Additive tasks: Tasks for which group productivity represents the sum of individual member efforts.

Arbitration: The submission of a dispute to a disinterested third person who makes a final judgment as to how the conflict will be resolved. A form of third-party intervention in negotiations in which recommendations of the person intervening are binding on the parties involved.

Base group: A long-term, heterogeneous cooperative learning group with stable membership.

Bumping: A procedure used to ensure that competitors are evenly matched. It involves (a) ranking the competitive triads from the highest (the three highest achievers are members) to the lowest (the three lowest achievers are members), (b) moving the winner in each triad up to the next highest triad, and (c) moving the loser down to the next lowest triad.

Cohesiveness: All the forces (both positive and negative) that cause individuals to maintain their membership in specific groups. These include attraction to other group members and a close match between individuals' needs and the goals and activities of the group. The attractiveness that a group has for its members and that the members have for one another.

Communication: A message sent by a person to a receiver(s) with the conscious intent of affecting the receiver's behavior. The exchange of thoughts and feelings through symbols that represent approximately the same conceptual experience for everyone involved.

Communication networks. Representations of the acceptable paths of communication between persons in a group or organization.

Competition: A social situation in which the goals of the separate participants are so linked that there is a negative correlation among their goal attainments; when one student achieves his or her goal, all others with whom he or she is competitively linked fail to achieve their goals.

Compliance: Behavior in accordance with a direct request. Behavioral change without internal acceptance.

Conceptual conflict: When incompatible ideas exist simultaneously in a person's mind.

Conflict of interest: When the actions of one person attempting to maximize his or her needs and benefits prevent, block, interfere with, injure, or in some way make less effective the actions of another person attempting to maximize his or her needs and benefits.

Conformity: Changes in behavior that result from group influences. Yielding to group pressures when no direct request to comply is made.

Conjunctive tasks: Tasks for which group productivity is determined by the effort or ability of the weakest member.

Consensus: A collective opinion arrived at by a group of individuals working together under conditions that permit communications to be sufficiently open and the group climate to be sufficiently supportive for everyone in the group to feel that he or she has had a fair chance to influence the decision.

Controversy: When one person's ideas, information, conclusions, theories, and opinions are incompatible with those of another, and the two seek to reach an agreement.

Cooperation: Working together to accomplish shared goals and maximize one's own and others' achievement. Individuals perceiving that they can reach their goals only if the other group members also do.

Cooperation imperative: We desire and seek out opportunities to operate jointly with others to achieve mutual goals.

Decision making: Obtaining some agreement among group members as to which of several courses of action is most desirable for achieving the group's goals. The process through which groups identify problems in achieving the group's goals and attain solutions to them.

Delusion of individualism: Believing that (1) one is separate and apart from all other individuals and, therefore, (2) others' frustration, unhappiness, hunger, despair, and misery have no significant bearing on one's own well-being.

Deutsch, Morton: Social psychologist who theorized about cooperative, competitive, and individualistic goal structures.

Developmental conflict: When a recurrent conflict cycles in and out of peak intensity as a child develops socially.

Disjunctive tasks: Tasks for which group performance is determined by the most competent or skilled member.

Distributed-actions theory of leadership: The performance of acts that help the group to complete its task and to maintain effective working relationships among its members.

Divisible task: A task that can be divided into subtasks that can be assigned to different people.

Effective communication: A receiver interpreting the sender's message in the same way the sender intended it.

Egocentrism: Embeddedness in one's own viewpoint to the extent that one is unaware of other points of view and of the limitations of one's perspectives.

Feedback: Information that allows individuals to compare their actual performance with standards of performance.

Formal cooperative group: A learning group that may last for several minutes to several class sessions to complete a specific task or assignment, such as solving a set of problems, completing a unit, writing a theme or report, conducting an experiment, or reading and comprehending a story, play, poem, chapter, or book.

Goal: A desired place toward which people are working, a state of affairs that people value.

Goal structure: The type of social interdependence structured among students as they strive to accomplish their learning goals.

Group: Two or more individuals in face-to-face interaction, each aware of his or her membership in the group, each aware of the others who belong to the group, and each aware of their positive interdependence as they strive to achieve mutual goals.

Group processing: Reflecting on a group session to (a) describe what member actions were helpful and unhelpful and (b) make decisions about what actions to continue or change.

Individual accountability: The measurement of whether or not each group member has achieved the group's goal. Assessing the quality and quantity of each member's contributions and giving the results to all group members.

Individualistic goal structure: No correlation among group members' goal attainments; group members perceive that obtaining their goal is unrelated to the goal achievement of other members. Individuals working by themselves to accomplish goals unrelated to and independent from the goals of others.

Informal cooperation group: A temporary, ad hoc group that lasts for only one discussion or one class period. Its purposes are to focus student attention on the material to be learned, create an expectation set and mood conducive to learning, help organize in advance the material to be covered in a class session, ensure that students cognitively process the material being taught, and provide closure to an instructional session.

Leadership: The process through which leaders exert their impact on other group members.

Learning goal: A desired future state of demonstrating competence or mastery in the subject area being studied, such as conceptual understanding of math processes, facility in the proper use of a language, or mastering the procedures of inquiry.

Lewin, Kurt: Father of group dynamics; social psychologist who originated field theory, experimental group dynamics, and applied group dynamics.

Maximizing task: Success is determined by quantity of performance.

Means interdependence: The actions required on the part of group members to achieve their mutual goals and rewards. There are three types of means interdependence: resource, task, and role.

Mediation: The intervention of a third person to help resolve a conflict between two or more people. A form of third-party intervention in negotiations in which a neutral person recommends a nonbinding agreement.

Motivation: A combination of the perceived likelihood of success and the perceived incentive for success. The greater the likelihood of success and the more important it is to succeed, the higher the motivation.

Negotiation: A process by which persons with shared and opposing interests who want to come to an agreement try to work out a settlement by exchanging proposals and counterproposals.

Norms: The rules or expectations that specify appropriate behavior in the group; the standards by which group members regulate their actions.

Optimizing task: Success is determined by quality of performance; a good performance is one that most closely approximates the optimum performance.

Outcome interdependence: Positive correlation of the goals and rewards directing individuals' actions; that is, if one person accomplishes his or her goal or receives a reward, all others with whom the person is cooperatively linked also achieve their goals or receive a reward. Learning goals may be actual, based on involvement in a fantasy situation, or based on overcoming an outside threat. *Means interdependence* specifies the actions required on the part of group members to achieve their mutual goals and rewards. There are three types of means interdependence: resource, task, and role.

Paraphrasing: Restating the sender's message in one's own words.

Perspective taking: Ability to understand how a situation appears to another person and how that person is reacting cognitively and emotionally to the situation.

Positive environmental interdependence: Group members being bound together by the physical environment in some way.

Positive fantasy interdependence: Students imagining that they are in an emergency situation (such as surviving a shipwreck) or must deal with problems (such as ending air pollution in the world) that are compelling but unreal.

Positive goal interdependence: Students perceiving that they can achieve their learning goals only if all other members of their group also attain their goals.

Positive identity interdependence: The group's establishment of a mutual identity through a name, flag, motto, or song.

Positive interdependence: The perception that you are linked with others in such a way that you cannot succeed unless they do (and vice versa); that is, their work benefits you, and your work benefits them.

Positive outside enemy interdependence: When groups are placed in competition with each other; group members then feel interdependent as they strive to beat the other groups.

Positive resource interdependence: Each member has only a portion of the information, resources, or materials necessary for the task to be completed, and members' resources have to be combined in order for the group to achieve its goal. Thus the resources of each group member are needed if the task is to be completed.

Positive reward interdependence: Each group member receives the same reward for achieving the goal.

Positive role interdependence: Each member is assigned complementary and interconnected roles that specify responsibilities that the group needs in order to complete a joint task.

Positive task interdependence: The creation of a division of labor such that the actions of one group member have to be completed if the next team member is to complete his or her responsibilities. Dividing an overall task into subunits that must be performed *in a set order* is an example of task interdependence.

Promotive interaction: Actions that assist, help, encourage, and support the achievement of each other's goals.

Roadblock: Hurdle that causes temporary difficulties in reaching a goal.

Self-efficacy: The expectation of successfully obtaining valued outcomes through personal effort; expectation that if one exerts sufficient effort, one will be successful.

Social dependence: The outcomes of Person A are affected by Person B's actions, but the reverse is not true.

Social facilitation: The enhancement of well-learned responses in the presence of others. Effects on performance resulting from the presence of others.

Social independence: When individuals' outcomes are unaffected by each other's actions.

Social interaction: Patterns of mutual influence linking two or more persons.

Social interdependence: Each individual's outcomes are affected by the actions of others.

Social loafing: A reduction of individual effort when working with others on an additive group task.

Social skills training: A structured intervention designed to help participants to improve their interpersonal skills.

Socioemotional activity: Behavior that focuses on interpersonal relations in the group.

Superordinate goals: Goals that cannot be easily ignored by members of two antagonistic groups, but whose attainment is beyond the resources and efforts of either group alone; the two groups, therefore, must join in a cooperative effort in order to attain the goals.

Support: Communicating to another person that you recognize his or her strengths and believe he or she has the capabilities needed to productively manage a situation.

Synthesizing: Integrating a number of different positions containing diverse information and conclusions into a new, single, inclusive position that all group members can agree on and commit themselves to.

Team: A set of interpersonal relationships structured to achieve established goals.

TGT (Teams-Games-Tournament): An instructional procedure in which cooperative groups compete with each other by playing instructional games following a tournament format for the purposes of facilitating learning.

Trust: Perception that a choice can lead to gains or losses, that whether you will gain or lose depends on the behavior of the other person, that the loss will be greater than the gain, and that the person will likely behave so that you will gain rather than lose.

Trusting behavior: Openness (sharing of information, ideas, thoughts, feelings, and reactions) and sharing (offering of one's resources to others in order to help them acheive their goals).

Trustworthy behavior: Expressing acceptance (communication of high regard for another person and his or her actions), support (communicating to another person that you recognize his or her strengths and believe he or she has the capabilities needed to productively manage the situation), and cooperative intentions (expectations that you are going to behave cooperatively and that everyone else will do likewise).

Unitary task: A task that cannot be divided into subtasks. One person has to complete the entire task.

Index